christian family
guide explains

The Middle East
Conflict

Series Editor: James S. Bell Jr.

by Stephen P. Adams

ALPHA

A member of Penguin Group (USA) Inc.

Contents

Introduction

You've heard the expression: "I don't even want to *think* about it." That might pretty well sum it up when it comes to this whole Middle East business. Sometimes we'd rather just not have to think about it. Unfortunately, we know that attitude probably isn't going to cut it.

Admittedly, the Middle East is a land of conflicts, contrasts, contradictions, and confusion. Even much of what we think we know often turns out not to be accurate. Many people just give up, assuming the subject is just way too difficult. Maybe eventually it will all just go away, you might think, and nobody will have to worry about it anymore.

Probably not. In fact, it looks as if just the opposite is happening. The Middle East conflict is coming to America. International terrorists and evil dictators aren't going to let us put our heads in the sand and ignore the whole thing. We're going to have to deal with it one way or another. The question is how.

If there was just one place someone could go to find it all explained clearly, simply, and quickly, wouldn't that be great? Well, that's what the *Christian Family Guide Explains the Middle East Conflict* is all about. If you really want to dig even deeper, there are plenty of resources listed in the back of this book. Otherwise, we've put it all together up front in a one-stop-shopping type of format.

In the course of this Middle East shopping expedition, you should come away with enough information and understanding to answer some of the most troubling questions: Why do they hate us so much? Why does the United States always support Israel? Isn't the whole conflict really over oil? Why can't they just settle things and make peace? Isn't the solution a separate Palestinian state? Is it true that Islam is a religion of peace?

The book is divided into seven parts that steadily build a knowledge base for understanding many of the deep and complex issues involved in this troublesome region:

Part 1, "The Players," is an introduction and overview to the conflict in the Middle East. It starts by looking at three major people groups by religion—Jews, Christians, and Muslims.

Part 2, "The History," shows how this conflict originated in ancient times. It also looks at the rise of Islam as a major world power in the Middle Ages and moves into the modern era and the re-establishment of Israel.

Part 3, "The Lands," covers the three major subdivisions of the Middle East and profiles each country within them. It also discusses a handful of countries on the edge of the region that are major players there nonetheless.

Part 4, "The Situation," moves into current-day issues like the Palestinian problem, Arab oil, and international terrorism. We begin to see just how deep-seated and difficult many of these problems really are.

Part 5, "The Challenge," takes up the issue of peace and the long and winding road to get there. We take a lively, comparative look at the differences between Judaism, Islam, and Christianity as well as the argument for Israel's existence. Then we look at the attacks on America and the war on terror, focusing especially on some individuals like Saddam Hussein and Osama bin Laden.

Part 6, "The Future," takes a look at biblical prophecy and the role of the Middle East in the End Times from the perspective of all three major faiths. Finally, Frequently Asked Questions wraps it all up.

That's a lot of ground—from ancient times to the End Times. Much of it is still unfolding right now. With a foundation like this, it will all make a lot more sense.

Extras

This guide to the Middle East conflict is not intended to be a pure information download. It is meant to stimulate thought and reflection as well as to inform. It is directed not just to the gray matter of the brain, but also to the heart and soul and spirit. So, we offer some extra short items called "sidebars" throughout the text in the interest of making the entire experience more interactive. These sidebars are easily recognized by the following icons:

Reality Check

There is an element of the bizarre to much of what goes on in the Middle East. Reality Checks are ironies, surprising facts, unconventional wisdom, and stories behind the story that add some perspective and, well, reality.

Word From the Wise

Here's help for your attitude and spirit as you sort through all this complex information. You'll find such items as Scripture passages, inspirational quotations, family examples, prayers, and more—all related to understanding the times and the Middle East.

MidEast Dictionary

Translation, please. Words like *"jihad"* increasingly are finding their way into our vocabulary. Here are definitions that help you interpret the difficult and sometimes baffling terminology that often complicates understanding the Middle East.

Family Focus

Christian families, like the Old Testament men of Issachar, need to understand the times. These are questions, notes, and suggestions to help get beyond the mere information level and to stimulate discussion and real life application.

The Players

The Middle East is more than just a big confusion. It's also full of trouble and danger. It's a problem that's been developing for a long time, and we ignore it at our own peril. Much of that trouble is now coming to a theater near us, and we need to deal with it. We need to have a basic understanding of the issues, and it's really not that tough. It can be done.

A helpful way to get started is to understand the players. Sure, there are 20-some separate countries in the Middle East, depending how you count them, and that can be confusing. That's why it's easier to start with the three main religious groups—Jews, Christians, and Muslims. You may be surprised by how much you already know. We'll build on this understanding and begin to see how these many things relate to one another as we go.

Chapter
1

Welcome to the Middle East

This chapter addresses some of the challenges facing anyone trying to understand this land of contrasts and contradictions called the Middle East. Keeping a few basic things in mind goes a long way toward avoiding unnecessary confusion.

An Internal Explosion

There was an explosion in Gaza City, killing three people. This time the news media, however, were not getting the normal degree of cooperation. In fact, several cameramen and news photographers were beaten and their equipment seized or smashed while covering this explosion.

In response, the journalists announced a news boycott of Hamas, a group responsible for suicide bombings and other violence since the start of a Palestinian uprising two years earlier, in September 2000.

The journalists also demanded an apology from Hamas and even boycotted the funeral of the three men killed by the bomb, which reportedly had gone off "prematurely." Hamas simply had not wanted this story covered. It was a tragic and embarrassing accident that also injured a number of others in the crowded Palestinian neighborhood, including a 75-year-old man and a 10-year-old girl.

Reality Check

Ironically, two of the injured photojournalists were from Reuters News Service, which had recently banned the use of the word "terrorist" as an emotional term having no place in professional journalism. More acceptable were terms like "militant Islamic group" or "freedom fighters."

Finally, a Hamas leader did call the news service to apologize for the violence against the media. The leader politely explained that the cause of the blast was still under investigation and said "it may have been an *internal explosion*"—meaning a private matter not involving Israel, according to the Associated Press.

Family Focus

Except for the September 11th attack, Americans remain largely unaffected by terrorist violence. What would it be like to live in a country where acts of terrorism occurred all the time? Discuss the frequent criticism that, because of crime, America is considered to be the most dangerous place to live.

So, the Gaza City incident was a private explosion, meaning off-the-record. But in a larger sense, one could almost say that's the exact image to describe this entire tragic and conflict-torn region—an *internal explosion*, a slow-motion disaster.

Welcome to the inside-out world of the Middle East, where things are not always what they seem—nor do they even necessarily make sense. It is the mother of all conflict, the father of too many confusing news stories, and the subject of endless posturing, politicking, and propagandizing. It's even found its way into the pages of military novelist Tom Clancy, who once described it: "Like a bone, an immortal bone fought over by endless packs of hungry dogs."

Word from the Wise

"I will make Jerusalem and Judah like an intoxicating drink to all the nearby nations that send their armies to besiege Jerusalem. ... I will make Jerusalem a heavy stone, a burden for the world. None of the nations who try to lift it will escape unscathed." (Zechariah 12:2–3, NLT) This is certainly true today. None of the nations, including Israel, that try to control or influence Jerusalem and Palestine have been successful or emerged unscathed.

Ancient Empires

The Middle East is the home of vast, ancient empires that have come and gone. Thousands have died in its many conflicts. Statesmen and politicians have seen their careers—or their lives—ended prematurely over this stumbling stone of the Middle East. Still the dramas and tragedies continue to play out to the present day with no end in sight. Today there are three great monotheistic faiths:

- Judaism
- Christianity
- *Islam*

MidEast Dictionary

Islam literally means submission or surrender to God; it is a monotheistic religion worshipping Allah, whose prophet is Muhammad and whose scripture is the Quran (see Chapter 4).

All three faiths were birthed in the Middle East, and all have specific expectations for this cradle of civilization to play the central role in the End Times events of the last days of Planet Earth. Their prophets and holy books say so.

All Over the Map

What is so special about this place? In many ways the Middle East, as the Gaza City incident from the beginning of the chapter illustrates, is a unique state of mind. It's also a region consisting of many peoples, cultures, religions, languages, and nations, though the exact dividing lines are often unclear and vary even among experts. Any map of the Middle East is subject to some dispute. Geographically, it can be defined in terms of a *core* plus *peripheries*.

The core covers a wide swath from Iran on the east to Egypt on the west with the Fertile Crescent and the Arabian peninsula in between.

Comprising the Fertile Crescent are:

- Iraq
- Syria
- Lebanon
- Israel
- Jordan

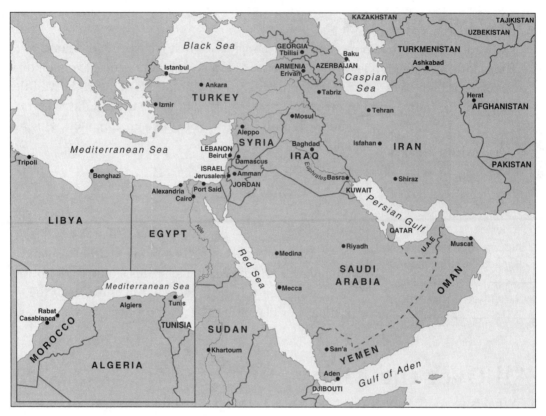

The countries comprising today's Middle East.

Comprising the Arabian peninsula are:

- Bahrain
- Kuwait
- Oman
- Qatar
- Saudi Arabia
- United Arab Emirates
- Yemen

One helpful way of picturing the Middle East is in terms of the lands surrounding the three major river systems:

- Tigris-Euphrates
- Jordan
- Nile

Another helpful frame of reference is the four major cities that have played a major role in the history of the peoples of the Middle East:

- Baghdad, Iraq
- Damascus, Syria
- Jerusalem, Israel
- Cairo, Egypt

The peripheries include Arab North Africa:

- Egypt
- Libya
- Tunisia
- Algeria
- Morocco
- Sudan

The definition of "Middle East" was expanded in more recent years to include the North African states, once they became members of the Arab League. Some would even include Turkey, which is a member of the North Atlantic Treaty Organization (NATO) and a candidate for membership in the European Union. Still others would expand the definition farther east to include Afghanistan and farther south to include other African states such as Ethiopia (a non-Muslim country) and Somalia.

Like many other things in the Middle East, it's a matter of interpretation. It also may be splitting hairs, especially considering the fact that many of these nations are rather recent creations in the first place. For centuries, the Middle East was a land of tribes and clans, kingdoms and city-states. Many of the current nation-states actually go back no further than the collapse of the Ottoman Empire in the early 1900s, and the carving up of the region by the colonial powers at the end of World War I, notably England and France.

MidEast Dictionary

The **Holocaust** was the systematic, genocidal destruction of more than six million Jews by the Nazis before and during World War II. Originally, it was a religious term for a whole burnt offering.

The rebirth of the state of Israel was the biggest change after World War II. It was a people movement already in process, but greatly accelerated in response to the disaster of the *Holocaust*. This new statehood, in turn, has led to the current state of unrest, tension, and conflict in the region between Israel and its neighbors.

What's in a Name?

Even the term "Middle East" is a Western invention, born of colonialism and Euro-centrism. It relates to distance and direction from London and Paris, the principal colonial powers in the first half of the twentieth century who were calling the shots around there. Not that many years ago, the correct term had been "Near East," still a Euro-centric term. From India, China, or any number of other places, this region called the Middle East actually would be west.

The United Nations tried unsuccessfully for years to change the name to West Asia. But in a region where the main constant may be change, the "Middle East" tag seems to have some staying power.

Equally confusing are the terms "Palestine" and "Palestinian" to refer to the "occupied territories" of Israel and their Arab inhabitants. Some of that confusion may be intentional. Most of today's newspaper readers probably would be quite surprised to learn that the term Palestinian originally referred primarily not to Arabs, but to the Jews and other peoples who lived in the Holy Land prior to the rebirth of the state of Israel in 1948.

Word from the Wise

"The land of Judah will be the LORD'S inheritance in the holy land, and he will once again choose Jerusalem to be his own city." (Zechariah 2:12, NLT) Ponder the meaning of the term "holy land" and how a place can be holy. Read the account of Moses and the burning bush. (Exodus 3:5)

Geographically, Palestine was a much broader concept than it implies today—including the land east of the Jordan River, for a while known as Transjordan (present-day Jordan).

The news media have tended to compound the confusion by abandoning older place names in favor of supposedly more neutral terms, unwittingly falling for even more politically loaded verbiage. What Israel knows as Judea and Samaria, for example, have become the West Bank (a "Palestinian" term).

Ironically, one of the most confusing terms of all is "Israel." After the ancient name "Canaan," it was *Eretz Yisrael* (Land of Israel). But then, after King David, the kingdom divided into two nations, a northern kingdom and a southern kingdom. The northern kingdom—including Samaria and Galilee—retained the name Israel, while the southern kingdom—including Jerusalem—became Judah, and later Judea. But when the modern state was reborn in 1948, it reverted to the name Israel.

Then, of course, there are the biblical names that have passed out of current usage but still come up in religious and historical contexts. Those would include names like Chaldea, Sumer, and Shinar (which are really different names from roughly the same region—Babylonia—at different periods of time). Some names equate fairly close to modern-day nation states:

- Elam (Persia, later Iran)
- Mesopotamia (Iraq)
- Assyria (Syria plus Iraq)
- Phoenicia (Lebanon)

The same problem afflicts cities. A visitor to the present-day West Bank city of Nablus may be surprised to learn that this is its fourth name. Originally, it was the biblical city called Shechem, one of the oldest cities of the Middle East. It was where the Bible says God appeared to Abraham to say, "I am going to give this land to your offspring." (Gen. 12:7) Later it became Balata (or else the two grew together to become one). Later still, under the Romans, it became Neapolis, which was later shortened to Nablus.

Contrasts and Contradictions

One thing can safely be said: The Middle East is a land of contrasts and contradictions. Much of what we think we know to be true tends not to be the case at all. This is especially true when it comes to issues involving Arabs and Islam. There's considerable disagreement on what defines an "Arab."

Nor do Islam and the Middle East necessarily equate. Some 80 percent of the world's Muslims actually live somewhere else. The largest Muslim nation in the world—Indonesia—is non-Arab and non-Middle Eastern. Also do not make the mistake of calling Iranians "Arabs." They may belong to the best-known Islamic theocracy in the world, but they are a non-Arab, Indo-European people, as are the Turks.

It doesn't get any easier or simpler in regard to Israel. Only in Israel, it seems, do people not agree on what is a Jew. Israel's congress, the Knesset, has tended to side with the Orthodox view on such issues, leading to vigorous dissent by Conservative and Reform Jews, who claim it tends to disenfranchise the non-Orthodox.

> ### Reality Check
>
> A visit to Israel can get you stopped at the border to a neighboring country if you make the mistake of getting an Israeli stamp in your passport. Other convenient fictions—such as a separate stamped sheet loosely inserted into the passport—are employed to get around this. Not that anybody is actually fooled by all this …. Conversely, security-conscious Israelis have been known to hassle travelers entering from Arab states, too.

It's All Whose Fault?

A number of Israel's neighbors do not even acknowledge Israel's right to exist, and some of them are still technically at war, inasmuch as no peace treaty has been signed since the onset of hostilities in 1948 and 1967.

Yet, at the same time it would be misleading to conclude that all of the turmoil in the region is owing to the presence of Israel, or even its "occupation" of Palestinian territories. The longest war in the Middle East in modern history was the Iran-Iraq war (1980–1988), which had absolutely nothing to do with Israel. Nor did the Gulf War in 1991, in which a U.S.-led coalition of nations drove Iraq out of Kuwait, involve Israel in any way, except when Iraqi leader Saddam Hussein had Scud missiles lobbed into Israel to try to draw the Israelis into the conflict.

The most famous civil war in the region, in Lebanon, was between Muslims and Christians, not Jews. Interestingly, when the Palestine Liberation Organization (PLO) was formed in 1964, it had nothing to do with "occupied territories." Those "occupied territories" are:

- Sinai Peninsula
- Gaza Strip
- Golan Heights
- West Bank

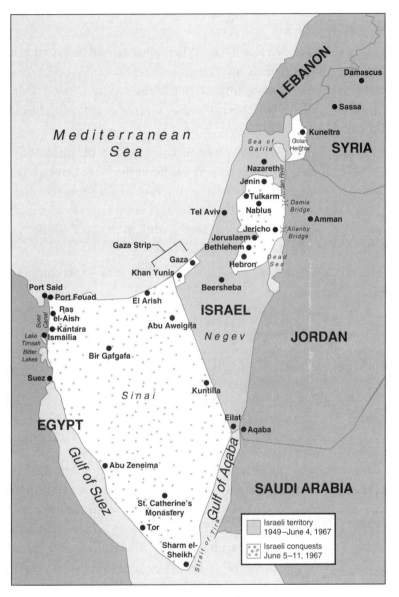

Israel and the so-called "occupied territories."

Israel would not seize those territories until three years later in the 1967 Six Day War. It was actually the Palestinians' objection to the very existence of Israel in the first place that inspired the formation of the PLO.

The Oil Factor

If it's not all about Israel, what is it, then? Is it all about oil? Certainly, nearly two thirds of the world's oil reserves are found in this region. Accordingly, the region has assumed enormous strategic importance in the modern world. Control of the oil fields and the Persian Gulf by a hostile political force could bring industrialized nations to their knees in a fairly short time.

Oil accounts for 95 percent of Arab exports, and it has produced bushels of billionaires. It has changed the modern way of life in the West through industrialization and transportation, and it has been at the root of various recent conflicts, including Iraq's wars with Iran and Kuwait. If it were not for oil, the entire region would have far less significance in modern world affairs and would receive far less attention.

We are still talking recent history—not even 100 years—and conflict has always characterized this region.

Family Focus

> Imagine life without modern modes of transportation fueled by petroleum—automobiles and airplanes. Do you think we'd still be using horses and steam engines? Or would we have devised some other technology? Consider all the ramifications—for example, how shapes of towns and cities changed as downtowns were replaced by quick and easy access to far-flung shopping centers and malls. How has this changed lifestyles?

In some ways geography is to blame. Because of its location, the Middle East—especially Palestine (Israel)—has served for millennia as a land bridge linking Europe, Asia, and Africa. It has been a crossroads between continents and empires in a part of the world where vast deserts are prevalent. Ancient peoples, dependent on the fruitfulness of the land, developed into cultures in these fertile lands surrounding the Tigris-Euphrates, Jordan, and Nile river valleys.

 MidEast Dictionary

Mesopotamia literally means the land "between rivers," meaning the Tigris and Euphrates; modern Iraq.

Civilization's Cradle

Secular historians have called the Tigris-Euphrates valley (then known as *Mesopotamia*) the "cradle of civilization" because of archaeological evidence found there of the most ancient peoples and empires. Mesopotamia was home for the following civilizations: Sumerian, Babylonian, Assyrian, and Chaldean.

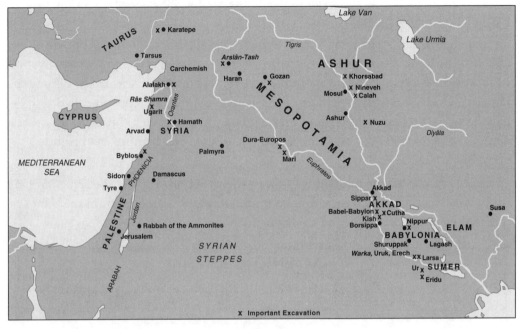

Mesopotamia was home for the earliest known civilizations.

The southernmost part of the land of Sumer was called Shinar, a flat mud plain with rich river sediment conducive to agriculture. It was here that the Bible says the descendants of Noah settled in the generations after the great Flood and built a high tower called a *ziggurat*. It says this self-glorification angered God, who had told Noah and his sons to be fruitful and multiply and fill the earth. So, He confused their universal language—presumably by making them speak in new tongues—and scattered them over the whole earth.

Reality Check

Some modern linguists lend secular credence to the Babel account in their pursuit of theories of *monogenesis*. This is the idea that all language families have a singular common origin, rather than evolving separate languages. It's almost impossible to imagine a time when people spoke all the same language and were essentially one family. Understanding how we got here from there means confronting many contrasts and contradictions.

The Scripture indicates that this ziggurat was made not with stones and mortar but with mud bricks and tar. Tar is a petroleum product, which would indicate the presence of oil in abundance even then, an interesting foreshadowing of the future significance of this region.

In modern times archaeologists have unearthed the hometown of Abraham, father of the Jews. Ur was devoted to the worship of the moon god, whose mystic rituals were observed on the uppermost level of a ziggurat. It was from this pagan idolatry, which eventually spread to pre-Islamic Arabia, that Jehovah called Abraham to go to a new homeland that the LORD would give to him and his descendants. Even this, however, would become one of the core disputes over rightful ownership of the Holy Land.

It's almost impossible to imagine a time when people all spoke the same language and were essentially one family. Understanding how we got here from there means confronting many contrasts and contradictions.

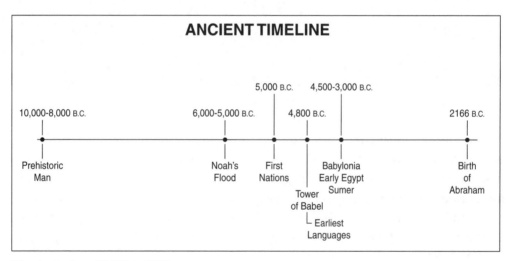

The Ancient era 10,000 to 2166 B.C.

The Jews

To begin to understand the troubled lands of the Middle East, it is important to consider the three main players—the Jews, the Christians, and the Muslims. The entire region, as we suggested in the previous chapter, is a bundle of contrasts and contradictions. The very heart of our understanding, then, may lie with Israel and the Jews.

A Nation Reborn

Israel is simultaneously one of the world's newest countries and most ancient. The Jews, often called God's chosen people, have been arguably the most persecuted people in the world. From the Babylonian captivity, to their attempted extermination by Haman the Persian (found in the Book of Esther in the Old Testament and commemorated in the Jewish feast of *Purim*), they have survived all the way up to modern times through the *pogroms* in Russia and Hitler's Final Solution.

It's been a touch-and-go kind of survival. Fully a third of the Jewish people were eliminated during the Holocaust, and one of the greatest fears among the survivors has been the threat of assimilation (absorption) by the many host cultures with which the itinerant Jews have settled, co-existed, and even inter-married. The nationalistic movement known as *Zionism* was largely a response to these various threats to the Jews' existence as a people.

MidEast Dictionary

Purim is an annual Jewish holiday commemorating the deliverance of the Jews by Queen Esther in Persia from a general massacre plotted by Haman the Persian. **Pogrom** is organized persecution and massacre of a minority group, especially applied to Jews in czarist Russia. **Zionism** is the historic movement to reestablish and support a national Jewish homeland in the land of Israel, named after Mount Zion at Jerusalem. Used as a term of derision by the enemies of Israel.

The Jewish people take great pride in retaining their cultural and religious identity, despite having been so dispersed throughout the world. Whether they hailed from Russia, Morocco, Germany, or Ethiopia, the strength and depth of their common heritage sufficed to bring them together again as a people and a nation. Now this tiny nation has been reborn in the midst of its enemies as a force to be reckoned with. All countries that have attacked it have ended up losers, to the point of forfeiting some of their own territory. Now Israel is a member of the nuclear club with allegedly scores of nuclear missiles in its arsenal.

In Tel Aviv a visitor is likely to see a more secular, cosmopolitan, almost European city with Western-style shopping and entertainment and a spectrum of nationalities and people types, from businessmen in power suits, to artists in grunge, to Africans in native garb, and young girls in more provocative attire than would be accepted in Jerusalem or an Arab town. In the ultra-Orthodox Mea Shearim district of Jerusalem, by contrast, the streets are filled with men wearing long sidelocks and fur-trimmed hats as though they lived in eighteenth-century Poland.

These two cities give Israel the additional distinction of having virtually two capitals—Jerusalem, the self-proclaimed capital, and Tel Aviv, the internationally recognized seat by virtue of where other countries have placed their embassies. This, of course, is owing to the disputed ownership of Jerusalem, which became an international zone, somewhat like Berlin during the Cold War.

Israel claims to be the only democracy in the region. (Other countries may hold elections, but it's typically one-party rule.) It is the only country in the world in which a majority of the population is Jewish. Israel is also the only country in the world whose predominant language is a formerly "dead" tongue, Hebrew. Rabbis and other learned Jews, of course, had continued to read Hebrew for centuries, but it was not until the twentieth century that it once again became a commonly spoken language.

Israel is also a land steeped in biblical history. No matter how much reading up they do, visitors are regularly jarred by the actual experience of these fabled places. It's not just high-profile venues, like the Church of the Holy Sepulcher, the supposed tomb of Christ, or the Via Dolorosa (the route that Jesus walked to the cross).

"If you took to the right," a resident might tell you casually while driving through the desert, "you can see the valley of Elah, the place where the Israelites and the Philistines faced off on opposite sides and David slew Goliath." It's that kind of surprise encounter with history that makes the deep impressions.

Who Is a Jew?

Comparisons with other religions and people groups can be a real eye-opener. While there are approximately 2 billion Christians in the world and about 1.3 billion Muslims, there are merely 15 *million* Jews all together—just more than 1 percent of the Muslim population.

Of course, many different racial and ethnic groups comprise the Christian and Muslim faiths, while Judaism is both a religion *and* a people. With few exceptions—such as the Falasha people of Ethiopia and gentile converts—the Jewish people are the same family of tribes. Biblically, they trace back to Shem, the son of Noah. Hence, the ethnic label *semite* or *semitic.*

The name "Jew" is related to the homeland of Judea, which in turn was derived from Judah, son of Jacob and father of one of the twelve tribes of Israel. Israel— literally, "he struggles with God"—was the new name Jacob received from God after his all-night struggle with the LORD. (Genesis 32) Prophetically, a more appropriate term for this future nation born in turmoil could hardly be imagined.

The term "Hebrew"—besides being the name of the language of the Jews—is sometimes associated with the name of one of Abraham's ancestors, Eber (Genesis 10 and 11).

What defines a Jew today? Any Jewish person has the automatic "right of return"—that is, to immigrate and become a citizen of Israel. It's the definition of Jewishness that's the sticking point. Currently, it's defined by the matrilineal principle—that is, anyone whose mother is Jewish, even if the father is a gentile. If the mother is a gentile, the person desiring citizenship would have to go through an indoctrination process similar to that of gentile conversion. This is the reverse of the patrilineal (father's line) principle found in the Bible.

Reality Check

The matrilineal principle would have been a real problem for some of the ancestors of no less a personage than King David, the founder of the Davidic line from whom the Messiah was to come. Ironically, David himself had a couple of gentile great-grandmothers, Rahab and Ruth. (See Matthew 1:5.)

The whole issue has been politically controversial in Israel, where the religious right has been lobbying for years to restrict it to Orthodox Judaism. Naturally, this is unacceptable to the other branches of Judaism (Conservative and Reform). The Law of Return was adopted in 1950, providing citizenship to all Jews. In practice, non-Orthodox immigrant converts would be accepted for citizenship, while Orthodox and Reform converts among Israeli residents would not. More recent court cases, however, have begun to open the door to citizenship for non-Orthodox Jewish residents as well. The non-Orthodox complained that the more restrictive practice was tantamount to saying Conservative and Reform Jews were not "real" Jews.

Small but Mighty

Relatively speaking, the Jews are not among the world's most populous groups. By comparison there are an estimated 150 million Arabs in the world, about ten times the number of Jews, at 15 million. (The number pales even further in comparison with the total of 1.3 billion Muslims.) There are about as many Jews in the United States—approximately six million—as there are in Israel.

Furthermore, the nation of Israel geographically is only a little bigger than the state of Vermont—and only a fraction of the land size of the original mandate for Palestine.

MidEast Dictionary

Diaspora is the scattering or dispersion of the Jews since the time of the Babylonian captivity and the destruction of Jerusalem.

None of this is to suggest that the Jewish people are a totally homogeneous (uniform) group. Their history of being dispersed about the four corners of the world for centuries—the *Diaspora*—has seen to it that the Jews have become a heterogeneous, or diverse, people in every sense. They have assimilated their adoptive cultures as much as they have been assimilated by them. They have retained their separate identity, yet with a variety of flavors.

Major Divisions

In the Middle Ages two major divisions of the Jewish people emerged that exist to this day—the *Ashkenazi* and the *Sephardic*:

- Ashkenazim—primarily European Jews influenced by Western culture.
- Sephardim—primarily Asian and African Jews.

The name Ashkenaz is associated with Germany, as many of the Ashkenazi in the Diaspora settled there and in other parts of central, northern, and eventually eastern Europe. Their primary language became Yiddish, a Hebrew-German hybrid. The Ashkenazi have comprised the great majority of world Jewry, averaging some 80 to 90 percent of the total Jewish population.

The Sephardic derive from the Hebrew name for Spain *(Sepharad)*, as most of these Jews populated Spain and Portugal, at least until they were expelled in the fifteenth century. Then they settled in many Mediterranean areas, especially North Africa, Italy, Greece, Turkey, and Egypt. They also maintained communities for centuries in and around Palestine. So, the Sephardic, while a minority of the total world Jewish population, have represented a much larger proportion of Israel—somewhere just under 50 percent.

MidEast Dictionary

Torah is the law or the *Pentateuch*, the first five books of the Old Testament containing early Jewish history and God's covenants with the people. **Kosher** is clean or fit to eat according to Jewish dietary laws, originally based on Leviticus 11, such as not eating meat and dairy products together, or blood, or "unclean" animals such as shellfish and pork.

This division, in turn, led to some major religious differentiation in Judaism; Reform, Orthodox, Conservative, and Hasidic.

Those who had been influenced by Western culture tended to adopt more secular, humanistic, and liberal outlooks and worldviews, which came to be known as Reform Judaism. Those who remained largely unaffected by these influences came to be known as the Orthodox Jews. The Orthodox retained more traditional religious practices and rituals, including regular reading of the *Torah*, observance of *Kosher* dietary laws and Sabbath restrictions, and separation of men and women in the congregation.

Seeking a middle way between the Reform and Orthodox have been the Conservative Jews, who strive to preserve many traditional ways in the midst of the modern world. A fourth group, the Hasidic Jews, can be viewed as a subset of the Orthodox with an even stricter legalism and a more mystical view, including fervent anticipation for the imminent coming of a Jewish Messiah.

Chosen People

Perhaps the most distinctive thing about the Jewish people is their sense of being chosen ones. The reasons for this are subject to debate by theologians, but the Bible clearly states: "You have been set apart as holy to the LORD your God, and he has chosen you to be his own special treasure from all the nations of the earth." (Deuteronomy 14:2) The better-known King James Version used somewhat different language in this passage: "chosen … to be a peculiar people unto himself."

And perhaps this concept of "peculiar" captures more of the mystery inherent in the choice of this people—unique and very special.

Abraham: The First Jew

The first Jew, according to the Bible, was Abraham (originally, Abram) of Ur, the pagan city in Mesopotamia devoted to worship of the moon god. Abraham was actually living farther north in Haran—also a center of moon god worship—when God called him. Jehovah told Abraham to leave that place and journey to Canaan.

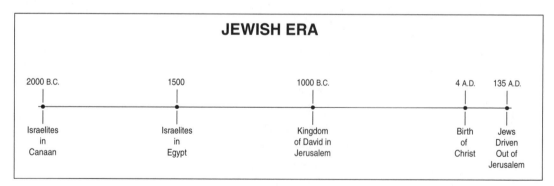

The Jewish era (2000 B.C. – 135 A.D.).

Abraham obeyed God's call and made the 400-mile journey with Sarah, his wife, and Lot, his nephew. Generations of believers have seen this pilgrimage as symbolic of a universal need for all people to leave worldliness and idolatry and to follow God alone. God promised to give "all this land of Canaan to you [Abraham] and to your offspring forever." (Genesis 17:8, NLT) He said the extent of this bequest was "from the border of Egypt to the great Euphrates River." (Genesis 15:18, NLT) The southern border was the river of Egypt *(Wadi el-Arish)*, which is just below Gaza in the Sinai Peninsula.

Family Focus

Discuss God's command to Abraham to "go to the land that I *will* show you." (Genesis 12:1, NLT) What kind of obedience did that require of Abraham? Does this have implications for us? Is God more likely to call us to obey one day at a time or to spell out all the details first?

While these promises might seem abundantly clear, there's a catch: Who exactly are Abraham's offspring and descendants? Certainly, the Jews claim that exclusive position, as well as the title deed to the land now called Israel. The problem is, so do the Palestinian Arabs—and on precisely the same basis. They, too, look to Abraham as their father, through Ishmael, son of Abraham and the maidservant Hagar. Isaac, the father of Jacob, who was the father of the twelve tribes of Israel, was actually the younger half-brother of Ishmael through Abraham and Sarah. So, the Arabs lay claim to the blessings of the Abrahamic covenant as well.

Lest anyone think that any of this is far-fetched or amenable to easy solutions, consider this finding of modern science: Jews and Arabs have been documented to be close blood relatives. The results of their scientific study prompted one researcher to declare flatly that Jews and Arabs are "really children of Abraham." Though the scientists couldn't name him, it appeared certain that there was a common male ancestor of the two peoples.

A 1995 genetic study of Jewish and Arabic men versus non-Semitic groups found that the Jewish men shared a common set of "genetic signatures" with the Arab males—Palestinians, Syrians, Lebanese, Druze, and Saudis. The signatures are unique sequences of chemical bases making up the DNA in the Y male chromosome.

Perhaps it's no wonder that the Arab-Jewish disputes have become so acrimonious down through history. It's a family feud, as science now seems to attest. And those are always the worst kind.

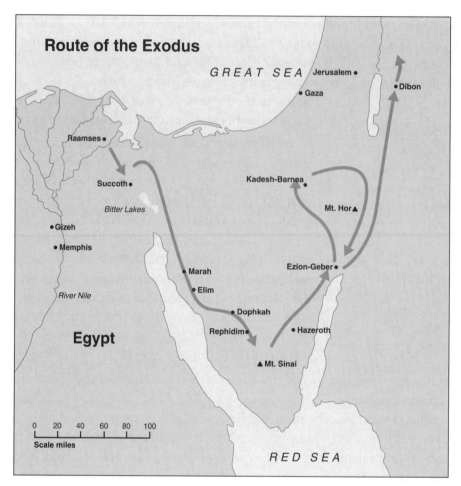

The route of the Exodus.

The Exodus

The twelve tribes of Israel, all sons of Jacob, relocated to Egypt during a great famine in the land of Canaan, according to the Bible. One of those sons, Joseph, became a high-ranking official in Pharaoh's government, and the Hebrew tribes grew into many thousands during their 430-year stay in Egypt. It was a downhill ride that eventually led them into slavery and severe mistreatment under a cruel Pharaoh who was intimidated by the large numbers of Jews in his land.

When Pharaoh rejected Moses' demands to let these Hebrew slaves leave his country, God sent ten devastating plagues upon the Egyptians. It was the tenth plague—the death of all the firstborn sons in Egypt—that did the trick. The people then virtually paid the Hebrews to leave.

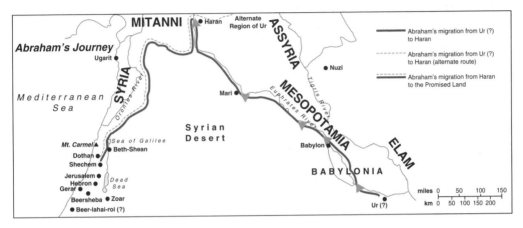

Abraham's journey to the promised land.

Moses at last was able to lead his people out of Egypt in the night, an event forever commemorated by the children of Israel as *Passover* and the Feast of Unleavened Bread. It was one of the seminal events that defined the Jews as a unique people. Their release from captivity and the desert sojourn to reclaim the land of Canaan is known as the *Exodus*.

 MidEast Dictionary

Passover is the incident described in Exodus 12 when all the firstborn males of Egypt died but those of Israel were "passed over" where their doorposts and lintels were smeared with the blood of a lamb. It also made its way into Christian symbology as representative of Christ, the lamb of God whose blood cleanses from sin. **Exodus** is the Latin form of a Greek term for "exit" or "departure," for which the second book of the Old Testament is named.

The Mosaic Covenant

Moses is also remembered as the prophet through whom God transmitted the Ten Commandments on Mount Sinai, a conditional covenant called the Mosaic Covenant. It was conditional in the sense that God told the people: "Now *if* you will obey me and keep my covenant, you will be my own special treasure from among all the nations of the earth …." (Exodus 19:5, NLT)

Why did it take Moses 40 days to speak with God? The rabbinical perspective on these events down through the centuries (in writings and commentaries such as the *Talmud*) has been insightful. The rabbis believed, for example, that Moses' experience with Jehovah on Mount Sinai took so long because it was not just the Ten Commandments he was receiving, but also the entire first five books of the Torah.

Furthermore, some believed that the law was given in the wilderness rather than in the land of Israel, a cause of puzzlement to the Jews, because the teachings of the Torah were not intended just for Israel but for the benefit of all mankind.

Dispossessed: The Birth of "Palestine"

Roughly, the major mile markers would be 2000 B.C. for the time of Abraham, and 1000 B.C. for the establishment of the kingdom under the house of David for the next 400 years. Then began a series of conquests of Jerusalem and Judea by a succession of world empires: Babylonians, Persians, Greeks, and Romans.

The Romans were ruling there at the time of Christ. With the destruction of the temple, the sacrificial system of the Jews came permanently to an end. Solomon's Temple had been destroyed by Nebuchadnezzar and the Babylonians, and now the second Temple ("Herod's" Temple) lay in ruins.

Sporadic revolts against Roman rule continued, the largest one being the rebellion of Bar Kokhba (132 – 135 A.D.), which succeeded in driving Rome out of Jerusalem. Bar Kokhba had presented himself as the Messiah who would deliver the nation of Israel, but it was not to be. When the Romans finally retook Jerusalem, retribution was swift and thorough. The Emperor Hadrian forbade the practice of the Jewish religion, threw the Jews out of Jerusalem, built a temple to Jupiter on the site, and resettled the capital with gentiles.

Furthermore, in order to eradicate its Jewish identity, the Romans abolished the name Judea and renamed the nation "Aelia Capitalina" or "Syria Palestina"—or, simply, Palestine. So it has remained up to the modern era.

The Christians

This chapter is about Christianity, the world's largest religion. It's a story that began in the heart of the Middle East, Palestine, through the birth of a Jewish prophet, Jesus. While its roots—and its holy places—remain in the Middle East, its followers are largely elsewhere in the world today. Through the centuries this religious movement, born under persecution, has grown and changed considerably. But it's a major reason this particular corner of the world has become known as the Holy Land.

The Largest Religion

Christianity is the world's largest religion with some two billion followers, or roughly one out of every three people on earth. You wouldn't necessarily know it from the Middle East. While this is the region of its birth and infancy, Christianity today is a single-digit presence in most countries of the region.

- Lebanon, 38 percent
- Syria, 15 percent
- Jordan, 6 percent
- Egypt, 6 percent

MidEast Dictionary

Nominalism is identification with a faith in name only, as opposed to being a practicing member; such as a *nominal Catholic*, who might check that box on a health form but attends no services and participates in no church activities.

Family Focus

In what sense could Christianity's size work against it? Discuss what kinds of failings and shortcomings on the part of Christians might turn people off or turn them away. What can be done to address those problems?

- Israel, 2 percent
- Iran, 1 percent
- Saudi Arabia, less than 1 percent

Christianity today has outgrown its birthplace, moving from the Middle East to flourish in other parts of the world. Today it is more of a Western and Third World phenomenon. *Nominal* or cultural Christianity is a significant issue. Many countries in Europe, for example, rank high as "Christian," but in truth have become post-Christian (formerly Christian) cultures. Even in the United States, Christians are no longer a majority. Church attendance is about 40 percent, and many of those may be in name only. Many observers believe America is trending toward a post-Christian culture, like Europe.

When a country as large as the United States is perceived as a Christian country, that brings with it a lot of baggage. Plus, the divisions and disaffections within the faith are a stumbling block for many people. If Christianity is the truth, they say, why is there so much disagreement and division?

Disagreements and Divisions

They say a million people a year visit the Church of the Holy Sepulcher in Jerusalem, at least when the periodic turmoil and violence in the area doesn't scare them away. The church's location is the traditional site for the death, burial, and resurrection of Christ, memorialized by a vast stone edifice originally built by Byzantine (Orthodox) Christians.

The Holy Sepulcher became the holiest place in medieval Christianity before it was destroyed by the Muslims and later rebuilt by the Crusaders in the twelfth century. Under the altar in the Greek Orthodox chapel is a favorite photographic subject—a bronze disk with a hole in it, purportedly the exact spot where the cross of Christ stood. The huge complex is said to be capable of holding 17,000 people.

Each morning at dawn, a member of the Nusseibeh family unlocks the front door to the Church of the Holy Sepulcher. Why a Muslim family? Because the competing Christian groups could not agree on who would have the keys after the Crusader invasion centuries earlier. Therefore, they needed a non-Christian to effect a compromise.

Then there's the ladder to nowhere. On a narrow balcony over one of the massive church doors stands a small five-rung ladder, reaching up to the bottom of the second-floor windows. Nobody remembers why it was put there, maybe 200 years ago. There's no question why it hasn't been taken down. Ownership of that area is in dispute, so nothing can be moved.

It's the same reason some paintings, tapestries, and furniture remain blackened and smoke-damaged hundreds of years after a fire: because they are in one of these disputed areas. Ownership of the Holy Sepulcher is shared by the Greek Orthodox, the Latin (Catholic) church, the Armenians, and to a lesser extent, the Copts (Egyptian), Syrians, and Ethiopian Orthodox churches.

Reality Check

The Church of the Holy Sepulcher has a strong rival claimant for authenticity. The Garden Tomb is an ancient crypt just north of the Damascus Gate at the foot of a hill with a remarkable skull-like appearance on the rock face, suggestive of Golgotha ("Skull Hill"). "The place of crucifixion was near a garden, where there was a new tomb, never used before." (John 19:41, NLT)

Such controversies are not exclusive to the Church of the Holy Sepulcher. A few years ago a dispute over who had the right to clean a certain portion of Bethlehem's Church of the Nativity broke out into an actual fistfight between Greek and Armenian clergy.

As one Christian worker in Israel remarked, the example of the Church of the Holy Sepulcher is an unfortunate, but accurate, modern parable. How the world views Christians—and Christianity—is inevitably affected by the internal condition of the church. Sometimes it's not a particularly pretty sight.

From Rome to Reform

Over the centuries Christianity has developed three major divisions:

- Orthodoxy
- Roman Catholicism
- Protestantism

The original church traces its founding to Christ's words to Simon Peter, "… upon this rock I will build my church …." (Matthew 16:18, NLT) Jesus also said he was giving the keys to the kingdom of heaven to Peter the fisherman, who, in effect, became the first pope. This idea, however, became one of the many matters of dispute centuries later among the major divisions of the church.

This new religion was at first tolerated by Rome as a heretical subset of Judaism in the troublesome province of Palestine. However, it soon became violently persecuted as the faith began to grow and spread throughout the empire.

Finally, in the fourth century A.D., it gained acceptance with the conversion of the emperor Constantine and subsequently achieved the ultimate irony of becoming the official state religion. What's more, it even grew to become the only body strong enough to rule after the fall of Rome in 410 A.D., in a sense *replacing* the Roman Empire. The Vatican, in fact, continued to rule much of Italy on into the 1800s.

Meanwhile, Constantine had moved his capital to a more secure location (in present-day Turkey) at Byzantium, which was renamed Constantinople after him and is now called Istanbul. Over the ensuing centuries the church naturally evolved into two very separate and distinct entities—a Western Latin-speaking church headquartered in Rome and an Eastern Greek-speaking church centered in Constantinople.

The two churches had a theological dispute over the nature of the Holy Spirit. Rome said the Holy Spirit proceeded from both the Father and the Son, while the Eastern Church said the Spirit proceeded only from the Father. While this might seem like a fine point, it divided Christianity down the middle. There were other issues, too, including the so-called "iconoclastic dispute," which was a controversy over the appropriateness of holy images (paintings and statues).

In the eleventh century the two finally and irrevocably split after the pope in Rome excommunicated the patriarch in Constantinople, and the Eastern patriarch returned the favor. The break produced a separate Eastern Orthodox Church.

Fierce disagreements over a number of other issues led to a division within the Roman Catholic Church in the sixteenth century called the Protestant Reformation. It was launched by Martin Luther, a German monk who objected to a number of corrupt practices within the church, principally the sale of indulgences. These were papal certificates purporting to shorten one's time in purgatory, a place of temporary punishment until one's sins could be purged away. To Luther and others, these were licenses for the "privilege to sin."

The real issue was the doctrine of "justification by faith," that we are reconciled to God solely by our faith in what Christ has done rather than our own merits. Even our faith is not our own—God chooses to whom he gives the ability to believe. Luther claimed that Rome taught that our own efforts and choice entered into the salvation picture.

> **MidEast Dictionary**
>
> The **Calvinist/ Arminian** split deals with theological differences over such issues as eternal security—"once saved, always saved"— God's sovereignty, and man's responsibility in the process of salvation. Arminians stress human choice while Calvinists stress God's work (election) in a believer's life.

Luther was excommunicated, but his cause generated a huge movement across Europe. Today Protestants outnumber those in the Eastern Orthodox Church and are second only to the Roman Catholic Church.

This turned out to be just the beginning of a proliferation of sects and practices. Today they run the gamut from so-called mainline to evangelical, from traditional to contemporary, from liturgical to charismatic and pentecostal, from *Calvinist* to *Arminian*, and dozens of other emphases in doctrine. One handbook of denominations lists well over 200 different religious bodies just for the United States, alphabetically from Adventists and Baptists to the Worldwide Church of God.

Jesus of Nazareth

It all started in the Middle East in Roman-occupied Palestine …. Jesus was born in Bethlehem, grew up in Nazareth, and lived much of his life in Galilee while traveling widely about the country as an itinerant preacher. He spoke Aramaic, though he could read Hebrew. He was undoubtedly circumcised and studied the Old Testament scriptures, dialoguing with the priests in the Temple at an early age. He had a dramatic impact in Jerusalem, where he was initially hailed as the Messiah, then later condemned and executed as a criminal.

It is in *this* sense, many Christians believe, that the Jews were most clearly God's chosen people. That is, God chose them to be the channel not only for the giving of the law in God's first revelation of himself to man (through Moses) but also for his fuller revelation of himself through the coming of the Word in the flesh (Christ).

His identity and mission were clearly expressed in terms that should have been clear to anyone with an understanding of the Old Testament and the Jewish law. The New Testament writers connected the dots, especially the writer to the Hebrews. Jesus, he wrote, is "the radiance of God's glory and the exact representation of his being." (Hebrews 1:3, NIV) Furthermore, he wrote, Christ was superior to the angels, to Moses, to the priesthood, and to the sacrifice of bulls and goats. These claims, however, earned him the deadly enmity of the religious establishment in Jerusalem.

Word from the Wise

"You will become pregnant and have a son and name him Jesus. He will be very great and will be called the Son of the Most High. And the Lord God will give him the throne of his ancestor David. And he will reign over Israel forever; his Kingdom will never end." (Luke 1: 31–33) Consider the meaning of his name, the significance of his father, whose throne he was to receive, and the extent of his kingdom. What does this say about the continuity of Israel and the Christian church?

Fulfilled Prophecy

Jesus of Nazareth was born of Jewish parents of the line of King David. The circumstances of his appearance on earth, his life, and his death fulfilled dozens of Old Testament prophecies about the coming of Messiah. To name a few:

- Birth at Bethlehem
- Son of a virgin
- From the line of Abraham
- From the tribe of Judah
- From the house of David
- Anointed with power by the Holy Spirit
- Preaching good news to the poor
- Recovery of sight by the blind
- Raising the dead

- Being rejected and forsaken
- Pierced with nails
- His garments divided up
- Numbered with transgressors
- Buried in a rich man's tomb
- Resurrected from the dead

Later, the Jews who did not accept Jesus as Messiah rejected this interpretation of Scripture. Their view called not for a suffering servant, but a victorious deliverer of Israel. Jesus' growing reputation as "King of the Jews" among those who did believe put him at odds with the secular Roman authorities.

Family Focus

Read the Ten Command-ments and discuss their relevance for today. How much attention do Christ-ians need to pay to the Old Testament? Does it dif-fer from Jesus' teachings?

In his public ministry Jesus made clear that while he was establishing a New Covenant, he was neither reject-ing nor totally replacing the Old Covenant. "Don't mis-understand why I have come. I did not come to abolish the law of Moses or the writings of the prophets. No, I came to fulfill them." (Matthew 5:17, NLT)

Jesus' Teaching

This principle was demonstrated in Jesus' teaching that built on Old Testament law but took it a step farther, notably in the Sermon on the Mount. Take Moses' teaching on an "eye for eye, tooth for tooth," the so-called law of retaliation. It was a radical teaching in those days, when blood feuds tended to escalate and people would try to even the score twice over. "But I say," Jesus said, "Don't resist an evil person! If you are slapped on the right cheek, turn the other, too." (Matthew 5:39, NLT)

Similarly, Jesus took his hearers repeatedly beyond the letter of the law in such areas as murder and adultery, saying anger at your brother or lust in your heart is equally sinful. Jesus took them beyond the letter of the law to the spirit of the law, beyond external legalism to a righteousness of the heart. His followers would have the law written on their hearts rather than tablets of stone.

The Sadducees and Pharisees and teachers of the law in Israel thought they could trap him. In response to one of their trick questions Jesus articulated the heart of the gospel. He said there was not one greatest commandment but two—"love the Lord your God" with all your being and "love your neighbor as yourself." "All the Law and Prophets hang on these two commandments," he said. (Matthew 22:37–40, NIV) What he had just done—summarizing two major divisions of their Old Testament in one statement—left them virtually speechless. No one could outwit the Master.

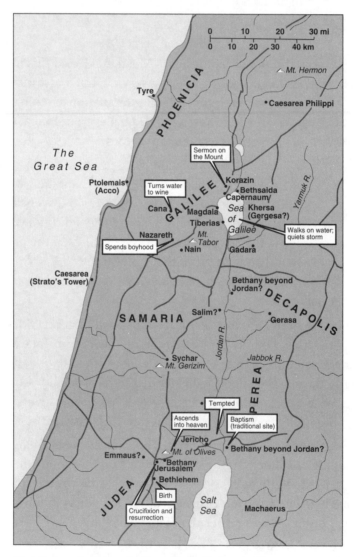

Christ's travels were actually quite limited.

The apostle John captured the heart of Jesus' life and mission on earth:

- a one-time sacrifice for sin for all people (John 1:29)
- the provider of eternal life (John 3:16)
- the only way to the Father (John 14:6)

Reality Check

The great Christian writer C.S. Lewis described the problem of Christianity as the "scandal of particularity." That is, the shocking assertion that God himself invaded the time-space realm of creation in a particular time and place—2000 years ago in *Israel*—and explicitly revealed himself to mankind.

Unlike other religions—notably Islam—that teach that God is essentially unknowable, Jesus personally made God known to the world as "the exact representation of his being."

Paul and the Church

As stated earlier, Martin Luther's motivation to challenge his own religious establishment sprang from a dramatic theological insight from the writings of Paul the apostle. Quoting Habakkuk of the Old Testament, Paul had written: "The righteous will live by faith." (Romans 1:17, Galatians 3:11, NIV) In his great treatise on the Christian faith, the book of Romans, Paul wrote repeatedly of "a righteousness from God." In another epistle he wrote that salvation is by *grace* through *faith* and not by any of man's works. (Ephesians 2:8–9, NLT)

Word from the Wise

In 1 Corinthians 13: 4–7 NLT, Paul says love is patient, kind, not jealous, boastful, or rude. It is always hopeful, never loses faith, and always endures. Relate these qualities to Christ's love. Use them as a benchmark for your own spiritual maturity and growth in grace.

This revolutionary truth—the gospel of grace over and above the dead law and works-righteousness—shook Luther to the core and changed his entire view of salvation. It also inspired a revival in Christianity and a reformation in the church. The true nature of saving faith became apparent as ritual and merit were seen as dead works. It was the heart of Christ's own teaching—love for God and for man, faith in Christ alone as the basis of salvation, putting no confidence in the works of the flesh.

Ironically, it was Paul—himself a Pharisee, a "Hebrew of Hebrews," and a persecutor of the church—who would write the famous "love chapter" of the Bible, 1 Corinthians 13. In it Paul paints a vivid picture of grace and love, the kind of love that "never fails," concluding with the famous statement that the greatest quality is neither faith nor hope, but love. In the Greek it is *agape*, a divine, altruistic love far beyond simple affection or human romance. Some theologians have called it "the characteristic word of Christianity." It is Christ's love.

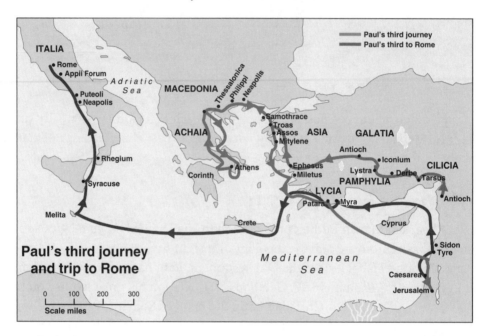

Paul's third missionary journey.

Father of the Church

Paul's untiring work on behalf of the gospel essentially launched the Christian church in the world. Until then, the back-and-forth conflicts across this land bridge of the Middle East would have made such an undertaking impossible amid such a hodgepodge of fractious cultures. Therefore, the gospel was now able to go from Jerusalem to Judea and Samaria and to the ends of the earth.

Reality Check

Since the coming of the Greek empire, the Middle East now had a common language that most people could understand. The gospels, the epistles, and all the other books of the New Testament were written in Greek. Through the coming of the Roman Empire, the region now had relatively safe and serviceable roads for travel with the stability of *Pax Romana* (Roman law and order).

Paul had been an accessory to the stoning of Stephen, the first Christian martyr, in Jerusalem. On that day a great persecution broke out, and the believers were scattered throughout Judea and Samaria. Jews from all over the known world already had heard the gospel preached in Jerusalem by untutored Galileans filled with the Holy Spirit at Pentecost. Now the gentiles were about to hear. Two things happened in neighboring Syria to make that possible:

1. Paul, who became the apostle to the gentiles, was converted in a supernatural encounter with the risen Christ while en route to Damascus to arrest more Christians.

2. The church was established at Antioch, the third largest city in the region.

At Antioch, the believers were first called Christians. The city became a center of teaching in the Christian faith, which was no longer just a Jewish sect. Three of the four gospels probably were written here. Antioch became the launching pad for the first missionary efforts and the mother of the gentile church.

Jewish Roots

The pattern for the church was the Jewish synagogue. With the destruction of the First Temple and the increasing dispersal of Jews farther from Jerusalem, the local synagogue ("assembly") increasingly became the focus of Jewish worship. Study of the law replaced temple sacrifice, and a rabbi who preached homilies replaced the priest. Sunday, resurrection day, became the day of worship, replacing the Jewish Saturday Sabbath. It was in a synagogue in Nazareth that Jesus read from the scroll of Isaiah and informed a startled congregation that the words of good news from the prophet were being fulfilled before their very eyes.

Family Focus

Jesus said, "But the truth is no prophet is accepted in his own hometown. Certainly there were many widows in Israel who needed help in Elijah's time, when there was no rain for three and a half years and hunger stalked the land. Yet Elijah was not sent to any of them. He was sent instead to a widow of Zarephath—a foreigner in the land of Sidon. Or think of the prophet Elisha, who healed Naaman, a Syrian, rather than the many lepers in Israel who needed help." (Luke 4:24-26, NLT) Then the people tried to kill him. What kind of statement was Jesus making about Jews and gentiles?

At Antioch Paul and Barnabas were commissioned to spearhead this missionary movement throughout the region. They started with Cyprus and then moved on to Asia Minor (modern Turkey), establishing churches. On his second missionary journey Paul was dissuaded in a vision from proceeding any farther east into Asia—and instead to turn his sights to the west. Paul's crossing of the Aegean Sea to take his church-planting work into Macedonia (modern Greece) was a monumental event in church history. It was the arrival of the gospel in Europe.

The Gospel in Chains: Success with a Price

Paul was eventually accorded the privilege of preaching the gospel in Rome, but it was mostly to jailers and fellow prisoners while he was in chains. He had been arrested in Jerusalem as a troublemaker and disturber of the peace and had appealed to Caesar as a citizen of the empire. Though Paul eventually was executed in Rome, the new faith of Christianity had taken root and was growing.

Over the next 250 years Rome tried to stifle the movement by exterminating its believers. Christians were:

- beheaded
- fed to lions
- torn apart by dogs in the arena for sport
- tortured

Family Focus

Discuss your feelings about the horrible tortures that first-century Christians faced and how they endured them. Did you know that more Christians have actually died for their faith in the last century than in all others combined? In what ways should Christians respond?

- crucified
- covered with pitch and set on fire as torches in the imperial gardens

When the persecution finally ended, approximately one half of the population of the Roman Empire was Christian. Eventually, that included even the emperor himself. Christianity appealed particularly to the poor with its vision of a kingdom that is "not of this world" to a people who had been ruled by a series of oppressors.

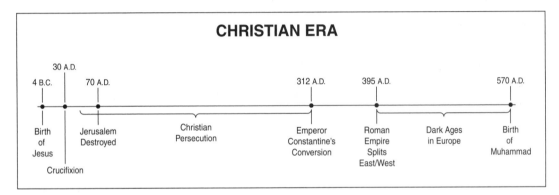

Christian timeline 4 B.C. to 570 A.D.

Christianity, too, is rife with paradoxes. It was a faith founded by a man purported to be a king but who was born in a stable to poor parents. His followers were not the religious or political elite but fishermen, prostitutes, and lepers. He never wrote a book, traveled extensively beyond his immediate region, or won large numbers of followers. Instead of respect and acclaim, he was executed as a common criminal. Yet, he turned the whole world upside down. After his death his followers were willing to be stoned or sawn in two for their faith. They conquered the greatest empire in their weakness and with the power of that faith.

Nevertheless, the paradox doesn't end there. While Christianity became the official religion of the Roman Empire, that success came with a price. Eventually, heresies arose and doctrinal disputes broke out. Much of it centered on the nature of Christ, especially in terms of his humanity versus his divinity. How could he be both human and divine? One heretical faction sprang up, ironically, at Antioch, and the controversies raged particularly intense there and in Alexandria and Constantinople.

Before long, the Eastern Church began persecuting Egyptians and Syrians who espoused these deviant doctrines. In some places there were even brawls and riots—over the true nature of the Prince of Peace. The Christianity that remained in the Middle East was becoming increasingly disenchanted with its European hierarchy in Constantinople.

Ironically, this once-persecuted religion was becoming a persecuting institution. It was a sad legacy that would bear bitter fruit many years later in such forms as the Spanish Inquisition and the Crusades. With growing factionalism, it often became a ladder to nowhere.

The Muslims

This chapter is about Islam, which claims to be the world's fastest-growing religion. It is the story of Muhammad, reputed to be the last great prophet, who founded a religious movement intended to replace Judaism and Christianity. It is also the story of a warrior movement that conquered much of the known world and established a powerful empire. Its legacy can be found not just in violence and conflict, but also in various cultural influences that live on today.

The Islamic Explosion

With an estimated 1.3 billion Muslims in the world, Islam is the second-largest religion in the world, second only to Christianity. Islam accounts for more than 20 percent of the human population.

Some experts predict that at present rates Islam will overtake Christianity in numbers of adherents sometime around 2025. That, too, is vigorously contested by others who claim that Christianity continues to make decent gains as well.

Only 20 percent of Muslims live in the Middle East. While 95 percent of Arabs are Muslim, 80 percent of Muslims are non-Arab. These are peoples scattered all around the world, including some surprising places. Indonesia, for example, is the world's largest Islamic nation with more than 180 million Muslims. In addition, Pakistan, with more than 140 million, is second. Pakistan was formed as a breakaway Islamic republic from a predominantly Hindu India in 1947. India, nevertheless, is the third-largest Muslim nation in the world with more than 120 million Muslims. Other Muslim nations:

- Bangladesh, 110 million
- Turkey, 65 million
- Egypt, 65 million
- Iran, 65 million
- Nigeria, 63 million

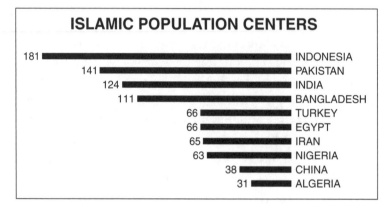

Countries with the largest Muslim populations.

Reality Check

There appears to be a good deal of inflation when it comes to numbers. Others note that Islam is also losing ground in places. They say growth is due more to high birth rates in the Third World than to evangelistic growth—that is, new conversions.

Also not usually thought of as heavily Muslim are nations like China and Russia. Yet, China is home to more than 35 million Muslims, and Russia is said to have some 12 million within its borders, including about a million Chechens who have kept up an underground guerilla war for independence. That's not counting the breakaway Islamic republics on Russia's southern borders, including:

- Uzbekistan, 20 million
- Azerbaijan, 8 million
- Kazakhstan, 7 million
- Tajikistan, 5 million
- Turkmenistan, 5 million

Asia, particularly South and Southeast Asia, accounts for about 40 percent of all Muslims. Another 30 percent come from Africa.

Throughout all of Europe, the Balkans, and the Caucasus region (between Turkey and Russia) are at least 30 million Muslims. This would include the heavily Muslim populations in Bosnia and Kosovo, former Yugoslav provinces where thousands of Muslims died in the "ethnic cleansing" (genocide) persecutions of Slobodan Milosevic. These occurred in Bosnia from 1992 to 1995 and in Kosovo in 1998 and 1999.

Perhaps 12 million Muslims live in Europe proper, including five million in France alone, where they are the second-largest religious group. Much of this population is North African, relating to France's former colonialist days. Great Britain accounts for upwards of two million Muslims, who are second only to Anglicans and Catholics. Germany reportedly has about three million. Combined with the post-Christian slump, Islam is proving to be a mega-influence in twenty-first-century Europe.

Family Focus

Are you aware of the other religious populations in your community or neighborhood? What are they? Are you aware of what they believe? Discuss why population statistics would be politically sensitive and some groups might inflate their own numbers—or attempt to downgrade someone else.

In the United States numbers seem to be somewhere in the three- to five-million range. Canada reportedly accounts for about a half-million. Muslims argue for higher numbers, in the five- to 10-million range for the United States, while some Jewish organizations claim it should be no more than 2.8 million. However, the upward trend is clear. Of the approximately 1,200 mosques in the United States, about 80 percent of them reportedly were built since 1990.

For many Americans, their first impressions of Islam go back to the famous conversion of heavyweight boxing champ Cassius Clay, who changed his name to Muhammad Ali. He was influenced by Malcolm X, a dissident Black Muslim, and then was given his Muslim name by Elijah Muhammad, a founder of the Nation of Islam. That movement is carried on today by Louis Farrakhan, who organized the so-called Million Man March on Washington in 1995.

Muhammad

Islam is the only major world religion to come into existence since the founding of Christianity. This was in the middle of Arabia when the Church in the East was

Family Focus

What lesson can Christians today learn from the squabbles and antiquated institutionalism that overtook the early church? Do these things have an effect on the church's impact on the world? What kind?

MidEast Dictionary

def·i·ni·tion

The **Ka'aba** is a 50-foot cube in Mecca that enshrines a large black stone venerated as holy and believed to have been sent by astral deities; also the object of pilgrimage for every Muslim once in his or her lifetime.

MidEast Dictionary

def·i·ni·tion

Quran literally means "recitation"; collection of revelations in 114 chapters that Muslims believe God delivered to Muhammad through Gabriel, about the size of the Christian New Testament; source of Islamic law, literature, and culture; also known as the Koran.

embroiled in squabbles with Egyptians, Syrians, and others over doctrinal and theological matters. It also had lost much of its spiritual fire and missionary zeal as bureaucracy, complacency, and even decadence settled in.

Muhammad's name means "highly praised." History says he was born in 570 A.D., orphaned early on, raised by a grandfather and then an uncle, and sent off for a time to live with a Bedouin warrior tribe. Muhammad was from a poor branch of the ruling family of Mecca. He married a wealthy merchant widow 15 years his senior and supported himself by managing her caravans.

At that time, the Arabians were polytheists, worshiping some 360 deities, including the local version of the ancient moon god. It was an environment of rampant superstition and belief in sinister supernatural creatures such as the *jinn* (or "genies"). Mecca was the center of this pagan idol worship, which included a mysterious black stone that had fallen from heaven (probably a meteorite) and was venerated in a structure called the *Ka'aba*. The city was a major crossroads for the various trade routes, and young Muhammad probably came into contact with many Christians and Jews there.

Divine Revelations

In 610 A.D. Muhammad began to have a series of visions that lasted for the next 22 years, purportedly from the angel Gabriel. Much of the teaching, later recorded in the Muslim holy book, the *Quran*, was moral instruction on many subjects, such as:

- Caring for widows and orphans
- Honesty in business
- Not killing female babies
- Sexual purity, marriage, family life
- Not drinking alcohol, gambling, eating pork

- Crimes such as fraud, slander, perjury, corruption
- Punishments for stealing, murder, adultery

It also included some skewed representations of Jewish and Christian teachings as well as numerous passages calling for holy war against infidels. It warns of a Day of Judgment for those whose bad deeds outweigh their good but with promises of a paradise of delights for the faithful, including shaded gardens, rivers of wine, and dozens of beautiful virgins for each man to enjoy.

The Last Great Prophet

Muhammad and his followers believed that he himself was the last great prophet from God, whose teachings superseded those of the Jews and Christians. Muhammad was appalled at the pagan idol worship in Mecca and determined to overthrow it. He was appalled, too, at the teachings of Christianity, which also struck him as polytheistic, especially in regard to the doctrine of the three-in-one, the Trinity. Thus, the Quran emphatically teaches the oneness of Allah and that it is wrong to attribute offspring or relatives to him.

 Word from the Wise

"May the grace of our Lord Jesus Christ, the love of God, and the fellowship of the Holy Spirit be with you all." (2 Corinthians 13:14) Some believe Muhammad got the idea from some ill-informed Christians in Arabia that the Trinity meant God, Jesus, and Mary, rather than Father, Son, and Holy Spirit.

Apparently, Muhammad fully expected the Christians and Jews to abandon their flawed and incomplete religions and turn to his newer revelation. When this didn't happen, Muhammad did not take it well. He was especially put out with the Jews. His followers beheaded hundreds of Jewish men, while their wives and children were sold as slaves and their property was confiscated. This occurred in Medina, where Muhammad had been forced to flee after the merchants in Mecca became fed up with his campaign against polytheism, which hurt their idol trade.

Islam Takes Root: The Beginning of Arab History

There is almost no record of Arab history prior to Muhammad other than some oral legends and poetry. Muhammad's departure from Mecca to Medina (the *Hegira* or

Hijrah) in 622 A.D. initiates the Muslim calendar, just as the birth of Christ begins the calendar in the West. After leaving Mecca, Muhammad and his men began raiding the caravans in and out of Mecca. Eventually, Muhammad and his followers became powerful enough to return to Mecca and to overthrow the rulers there.

At first, Muhammad had his followers pray toward Jerusalem, where Muhammad claimed he had been transported in a vision. He had journeyed, he said, on a fantastic winged steed to Jerusalem and then to the seventh heaven, where he viewed a divine Ka'aba and received further revelation from God before meeting Moses and then returning to earth. But after his falling out with the Jews, he had his followers begin praying toward Mecca and the Ka'aba.

When Muhammad and his forces took Mecca, he had the Ka'aba purged of its many idols and made strict rules against graphic depictions of things either heavenly or earthly. That is why to this day Islamic art consists solely of geometric patterns and other non-representational forms.

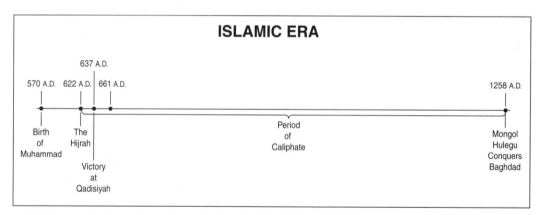

Islamic era (570–1258 A.D.).

Pagan Influences

The one true God, Allah, was not original with Muhammad. He had been around for centuries before the prophet as *al-Illah*, generically "the" god, in addition to three related goddesses. Muhammad's new religion never totally shed all of its pagan trappings of astral deities, especially the moon god. That is why to this day the pilgrimage to Mecca still includes veneration of the black stone, why national flags and other Arab symbols are dominated by the crescent moon and star, and why all of Islam continues to revolve around the lunar calendar.

In the Quranic teaching Jesus is regarded as a prophet but definitely not divine. Islam also challenged the belief that Christ actually died on the cross or served as a sacrifice for sin. Supposedly another man, possibly Judas, was put on the cross in Jesus' place while Jesus was taken up to heaven. The Quran does contain a version of the account of the angel Gabriel informing the virgin Mary that she would be the mother of Jesus. There is no mention of the throne of David or a kingdom that will never end.

Muhammad also taught that Abraham and his son Ishmael visited Mecca and, in fact, built the original Ka'aba. This is one of the central tenets to Islam's claim to be the legitimate successor to the old religion. The time frame, however, conflicts with the Old Testament account.

> **Family Focus**
>
> Christianity, too, has come down through the centuries with some lingering pagan influences. Discuss how such influences are reflected in things like observances of Christmas (winter solstice, Saturnalia, Christmas trees, yule logs) and Easter (spring rites, rabbits, eggs, fertility).

Contradictions

Sometimes the conflict is an outright contradiction. Muslims, for example, interpret a portion of the Quran to mean it was not Isaac but rather Ishmael, the Arab progenitor, whom Abraham was called to sacrifice and who became heir to the Abrahamic covenant with God.

Muhammad himself proved to be flexible when it came to interpreting his own scriptures. In the face of polytheism and polygamy, Muhammad decreed that no man could have more than four wives (at a time). Yet, he himself disregarded this limitation, claiming the privilege of supernatural revelation and special dispensation.

Islam Spreads

Genesis 25 names the 12 sons of Ishmael and the places where they settled, adding: "And they lived in hostility toward all their brothers." (Genesis 25:18, NLT) Similarly, the angel of the Lord had another prophecy about Ishmael for his mother, Hagar, which presages the conflicts of today: "This son of yours will be a wild one— free and untamed as a wild donkey! He will be against everyone, and everyone will be against him. Yes, he will live at odds with the rest of his brothers." (Genesis 16:12, NLT)

Islam spread rapidly by the sword until it conquered virtually every land around, becoming a vast empire over the next several centuries. Muhammad's successors were called *caliphs*. At its height in the eighth and ninth centuries under the caliphs, the Islamic empire encompassed:

- Indians
- Persians
- Chinese
- Mongols
- Turks
- Berbers
- Slavs
- Moors

MidEast Dictionary

Caliph literally means "successor"; title taken by successors to Muhammad as supreme ruler of the Islamic movement, especially mainstream Sunni; equivalent term for Shi'ites is "imam."

MidEast Dictionary

Jihad means struggle, holy war; any form of struggle, including simple personal disciplines of self-improvement, but always the ultimate end of submission to Allah and usually with the connotation of the use of force.

For centuries they controlled much of Spain and probably would have overrun the rest of Europe but for their decisive defeat by Charles "The Hammer" Martel at Tours, France, in 732 A.D. In later centuries the caliphs' empire was overcome by the Turks, also Muslim, who vied for control with the Mongols and Christian Crusaders.

The battle cry of this warrior faith was from the pages of the Quran. It was their holy obligation to bring the whole earth under submission to Islam: "Fight them until there is no more tumult or oppression and there prevail justice [Islamic] and faith in God [Allah]." (Sura 5:48) Nor does the enemy remain nameless: "Christians call Christ the Son of God. That is a saying from their mouth [not God]; they only imitate what the unbelievers of old used to say. God's curse be on them! How they are deluded away from the Truth." (Sura 9:30)

This concept of religious struggle and striving is captured in the Arabic word that has now become so infamous in the West, *jihad.*

The Tree Splits

Like Judaism and Christianity, Islam developed competing divisions. Some of this actually had more to do with politics and power than with religious beliefs. Muhammad had no son to succeed him when he died in 632 A.D., which set off major struggles over the right succession process. This in turn led to many splits in the tree of Islam. Some of the larger branches are:

- *Sunni*
- *Shi'ite*
- *Wahhabi*
- *Sufi*
- *Alawite*
- *Ahmadi*
- *Druze*
- *Nation of Islam*

Sunnis are the majority branch in Islam, basing all their authority on the Quran and the *Hadith* (traditions and oral teachings of Muhammad). Shi'ites were the original breakaway sect, disagreeing over the selection of caliphs. They believe the descendants of Ali—Muhammad's cousin and son-in-law—should be the rightful successors. They confer greater authority on their spiritual leaders—*imams* and *ayatollahs*—for the interpretation of Islam. Shi'ites comprise 10 percent of Islam and tend to be treated as second-class Muslims. They are found in clusters around the Persian Gulf, especially in:

- Syria
- Yemen
- Morocco
- Algeria
- Tunisia
- Southern Lebanon
- Iran
- Iraq
- Bahrain

def·i·ni·tion

MidEast Dictionary

Hadith literally means "tradition"; a collection of many sayings and actions of Muhammad gathered after his death; second holiest book in Islam (after the Quran).

Shi'ites are in the majority in Iraq, Iran, and Bahrain, but only in Iran do they control the political system.

Wahhabism is a puritanical form of Islam that banned music, dancing, and poetry and prohibited the use of silk, gold ornaments, and jewelry. It became the state religion of Saudi Arabia, but also has followers in Central Asia, Afghanistan, Pakistan, and India. Sufis, by contrast, are mystical Muslims who worship through religious music, poetry, and dance. Alawites are a mostly Syrian offshoot of Shi'a who incorporate jihad and reverencing of Muhammad's cousin Ali as their sixth and seventh pillars of faith, as well as a few Christian and Zoroastrian traditions.

Ahmadis are a small but zealous, evangelistic sect whose founder, Ahmad, claimed to be a prophet on the order of Muhammad sent to purify Islam. The Sunnis consider them heretics. Druze are another breakaway sect, whose beliefs are secret, primarily in Syria, Lebanon, and Israel. Members do not really consider themselves Muslims and many even serve in the Israeli armed forces. The Nation of Islam is the U.S. Black Muslim branch. It has taught that the white race is evil and that Armageddon is actually a coming race war between blacks and whites.

The Pillars

Most Muslims are in agreement on the simple fundamentals, which have been defined as the five pillars of Islam:

- *Shahadah*—confession of the creed
- *Salat*—ritual prayer
- *Zakat*—giving of alms
- *Sawm*—fasting
- *Hajj*—pilgrimage

Family Focus

Many Muslims consider themselves spiritually superior because they perform many more acts of piety every day than do Christians. How should this challenge Christians? What kinds of things comprise true spirituality and personal righteousness? Discuss James's assertion that faith without "good deeds" is dead. (James 2:26)

The creed: "There is no God but Allah, and Muhammad is the Apostle (Messenger) of God." Uttering this statement makes a person a Muslim, irrevocably. Renunciation is punishable by death. Prayers in Arabic as prescribed by Muhammad are to be said five set times a day, facing Mecca, accompanied by ritual washings. Alms are given to the poor, generally one fortieth of one's income or property.

The most important fast is the 30-day fast in the month of Ramadan, during which Muslims may not eat from sunup to sundown and are expected to read and study the Quran and pray toward Mecca. Every able-bodied Muslim who can afford it is expected to make a pilgrimage to the holy place in Mecca, where all are expected to participate in a number of rituals, including:

- circling the Ka'aba seven times
- kissing the black stone seven times
- throwing stones at the devil
- making a number of treks in the vicinity
- reciting various written prayers

Many Muslims consider jihad (holy war) to be a sixth pillar of Islam. Since jihad has been declared against the United States, the al-Qaeda terrorist organization has demanded that the United States stop supporting Israel and convert to Islam. This is consistent with Islamic jihad, in which the enemy is to be given a chance to convert. The goal of Holy War is to subject the entire world to Islam.

Islam Today: A Cultural Legacy

Some experts claim that much of what fuels modern Islamic anger is regret over a long-lost golden era, when Islam ruled much of the world and its institutions were bastions of learning and culture. In the modern era, the commercial West has been the dominant economic and cultural force in the world. Clearly Western civilization owes much to the legacy of this bygone Islamic culture. From the seventh to the eleventh century, while Europe was in the Dark Ages, the Islamic empire kept alive the intellectual ideas of Greek culture, along with Persian and Indian influences.

An Islamic astronomer-mathematician perfected the system of calculating by means of nine numbers. Another Islamic mathematician developed the rudiments of *algebra*, itself an Arabic name. Other scientific terms have a similar origin—azimuth, nadir, algorithm. Clearly, the influences on the West have been considerable.

> **Reality Check**
>
> "Guitar" comes from the Arabic (via Spain), as do a number of food terms—tangerine, saffron, coffee, soda, sugar, alcohol. There are clothing items—cotton, muslin, afghan, pajamas, sandals. Then there are more sinister terms, such as "hashish" and "assassin," from Arabic as well.

Part 2

The History

This is the history section. It covers a lot of ground—all the way from ancient Egypt to the modern era—and establishes the roots of the ancient conflict. Without such an understanding, it's much harder to make sense of current events. It also explores some things they don't teach in school—and the possible reasons why.

We meet some characters who may be old friends to some—Abraham, Moses, Pharaoh, David, Solomon, and others. But there also may be some surprises as we move into the Middle Ages and see the powerful Islamic civilization that controlled most of the known world for centuries in an empire that rivaled Rome's in size. Then comes that dark episode in Christendom called the Crusades that heralded the rise of Western power. Finally, setting the stage for the modern conflict is the re-establishment of Israel in our time.

Chapter 5

A Jewish Kingdom

This chapter deals with the establishment of the kingdom of Israel. It is the story of two dynamic kings, David and his son Solomon, and the conflict that drew the people together into a true nation. It's also a story of idolatry and foreign threats that led to the downfall of the united kingdom. But one surviving legacy was the promise of an eternal kingdom without end.

The Davidic Covenant

A thousand years after the establishment of the Israelite nation, the people exulted at Jesus' triumphal entry into Jerusalem—the event now celebrated as Palm Sunday. They strewed palm branches before his donkey and cried, "Praise God *(Hosanna)* for the Son of David! Bless the one who comes in the name of the LORD! Praise God in highest heaven!" (Matthew 21:9, NLT)

What was so significant about being called "Son of David"? It was his Messianic credentials, because of the Davidic Covenant. That's the promise God had made to David upon becoming king of all Israel. Samuel, considered the last of the judges in Israel, anointed David's head with oil to show whom God had chosen.

The first king, Saul, had died in battle, and David was the claimant to the throne. First, he faced formidable tasks to consolidate his rule over the kingdom. He had to win over the former supporters of Saul. He had to finish fortifying Jerusalem as

MidEast Dictionary

Messiah literally means "anointed" one; the promised and expected deliverer of the Jews, who will bring an era of peace and justice; equivalent to the Greek *Christos*, from which the English "Christ" is derived.

his capital and build a palace and perhaps a temple. He had to fight the nation's enemies and complete the expulsion of the troublesome Philistines.

All of these things demanded David's attention, but they would have to wait. David had an even higher priority. His first order of business was to bring the Ark of the Covenant to Jerusalem. In other words, the real king in Israel was to be not a man, but God. Israel, under David, trusted first in God. No doubt this was a chief reason David enjoyed such success as king and was known as a man after God's own heart.

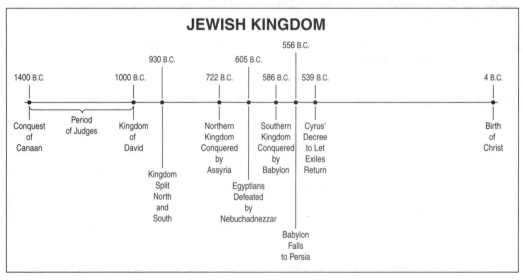

Jewish Kingdom (1400 – 4 B.C.).

The Ark was housed in a tent, and David wanted to build a temple to honor God. That's when God turned the tables on David and said he would build a "house" for him instead—a play on words, meaning a royal dynasty.

This Davidic Covenant was first fulfilled through David's son, Solomon, who did build the magnificent first Temple, which was destroyed generations later by the Babylonians. Nevertheless, its ultimate fulfillment came through Christ, a lineal descendant of David, whose reign would endure far beyond the end of the earthly kingdom. Indeed, it would eventually become the heavenly Jerusalem spoken of in the Book of Revelation.

Word from the Wise

The Bible talks about an eternal line of kings through David. Only Jesus could fulfill this promise. He is spoken of prophetically as the one who would bring the kingdom of David into eternity. "Your dynasty and your kingdom will continue for all time before me, and your throne will be secure forever." (2 Samuel 7:16, NLT)

God's Promises

In the waning days of the kingdom of Judah, it looked like the Davidic dynasty was about to come to an end. The LORD promised that a time would come when he would place "a righteous Branch on King David's throne," referring to the coming Messiah. (Jeremiah 23:5) In the last book of the New Testament, Christ is called "the Lion of the tribe of Judah, the heir to David's throne." (Revelation 5:5, NLT)

Word from the Wise

"What mighty praise, O God, belongs to you in Zion. We will fulfill our vows to you, for you answer our prayers." (Psalm 65:1, NLT) David was a poet and songwriter who wrote some of the greatest devotional literature in history in the Psalms. Since it's fully inspired by God, it's a great tool for your personal praise and prayer time.

The golden era for the united kingdom under David and Solomon lasted less than a hundred years, from about 1010 to 931 B.C. Then the kingdom split in two between north and south, Israel and Judah, under warring factions. By the eighth century B.C. (the 700s), the northern kingdom would be destroyed by invaders, and by the sixth (the 500s) the southern would be overcome as well.

That's why the people of Jerusalem were so excited hundreds of years later to see the Son of David riding into town on a donkey in fulfillment of the words of the prophet: "Rejoice greatly, O people of Zion! Shout in triumph, O people of Jerusalem! Look, your king is coming to you. He is righteous and victorious, yet he is humble, riding on a donkey—even on a donkey's colt." (Zechariah 9:9., NLT)

A Holy Terror

The Book of Exodus said God himself led the Israelites through the desert and into the Promised Land. The visible manifestation was a pillar of cloud by day and a pillar of fire by night, always leading them on or causing them to halt and encamp.

The Lord told the people he would send his "terror"—a true holy terror—upon the people in Canaan to scatter them.

God warned the Israelites to make no treaties and not let these peoples even live among them. (Exodus 23) This was only incompletely obeyed.

God also gave the Israelites a warning: "But if you fail to drive out those people who live in the land, those who remain will be like splinters in your eyes and thorns in your side. They will harass you in the land where you live. And I will do to you what I had planned to do to them." (Numbers 33:55-56) Does this sound like conditions today in the land of Israel?

Israel's Neighbors

Various groups had been migrating from the Aegean and Mediterranean Sea areas to Canaan as well. The Phoenicians were not hostile to Israel, on its northern doorstep. But later, King Ethbaal gave his daughter in marriage to King Ahab of Israel. This was the notorious Jezebel, who was responsible for the spread of Baal worship and fertility cults in the northern kingdom.

A more troublesome people, the Philistines, settled right on the Mediterranean coast south of the Phoenicians. The Philistines had defeated the Hittites in battle, but, unable to defeat the Egyptians, they apparently took this land next to Israel as a consolation prize. When the LORD led the Israelites into Canaan, he took them on a circuitous route away from Philistine territory, an area heavily guarded by Egyptian fortresses.

def·i·ni·tion

MidEast Dictionary

Manna literally means the question "what is it?"; food miraculously provided for the Israelites in the wilderness, appearing on the ground each morning during their stay in the desert; Jesus called himself "the true bread of heaven. (John 6:32)

En route through the desert, according to the Bible, God had fed this horde—upwards of two million people—daily with the divine manna. But even this had been a cause for complaint about how good it had been in Egypt—with all of its fish, cucumbers, melons, leeks, onions, and garlic. No wonder the sojourn took 40 years instead of 40 days. God decreed that this generation of complainers who would choose slavery would have to die off before entering Canaan. Its conquest would require warriors, not slaves.

Word from the Wise

The entire nation that God did so much for all perished because they didn't have the faith of Joshua—the faith to go in and conquer the land of Canaan. "They have seen my glorious presence and the miraculous signs I performed both in Egypt and in the wilderness, but again and again they tested me by refusing to listen.'" (Numbers 14:21–23, NLT)

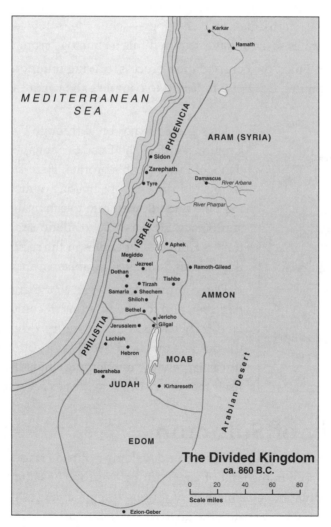

The divided kingdom and its neighbors.

Consolidation

Under Joshua's leadership the Philistines were largely subdued, but they continued to be a threat throughout the following period of the Judges. For a while, they even captured the Ark of the Covenant. What had earlier been a loose collection of Canaanite city-states rather than a true nation became, in effect, a loose collection of Jewish ones during this period.

A major problem was that the Philistines possessed the weapons of mass destruction of their time—iron-smelting technology—while the Israelites were of the Bronze Age. The Philistines seem to have acquired this technology from the Hittites.

Saul had continued the consolidation process, driving out more of the Philistines from the hill country. It was up to David to complete the conquest of the land begun by Joshua.

Reality Check

Archaeological discoveries indicate that in this period of history iron was coveted and hoarded almost like a precious metal. The Israelites under David may not have developed the actual art of iron smelting, but rather imported their smelted iron for weapons from Syria, Cyprus, and Asia Minor.

He scored a major breakthrough by conquering Edom, a region south of the Dead Sea inhabited by the descendants of Esau, Jacob's brother. Here David learned the secrets of iron weapons making, which leveled the playing field and allowed him to establish wider military supremacy. He was able to subdue and eliminate future threats from other peoples in the region, including the Amalekites, Moabites, Arameans, and Ammonites.

David proved to be equal to the great task of kingdom building, and for the first time it could be said that the land truly had become a country, extending roughly to the borders that God had described to Joshua. Ironically, it was largely the unrelenting Philistine military pressure itself that drove the Israelites to become a true nation.

The Folly of Solomon

David's son Solomon had the luxury of developing outside trade relations and building prosperity in the land of Israel during this time of stability. Solomon exploited the situation. One method of forging foreign alliances has been through diplomatic marriages to ensure the goodwill of neighboring kingdoms. Among Solomon's many wives, the first was the daughter of the pharaoh of Egypt.

We can see why God had warned against this kind of polygamy. Centuries before Solomon, God had given warnings through Moses (Deuteronomy 17) about things the king should never do:

- Build up a large stable of horses, especially from Egypt

- Return to Egypt for any reason

- Take many wives

- Accumulate vast amounts of silver and gold

Family Focus

Discuss the moral issues surrounding polygamy and sexual immorality. Is there a spiritual connection? Look into the concept of spiritual adultery in the Old Testament: Exodus 34:15, Judges 2:17, Psalm 106:39. For some strong language, look at the King James Version of these verses.

Taking many wives, God said, would turn the king's heart away from the LORD. Solomon also married Moabites, Ammonites, Edomites, Sidonians, and Hittites. Descendants of some of these peoples may still exist today in Lebanon, Syria, Iraq, and especially Jordan, whose capital—Amman—may be derived from the name "Ammon." These were the same people the LORD had instructed the Israelites not to intermarry with because it would lead them to worship other gods. That's exactly what happened to Solomon. God said he would wrest the kingdom from Solomon's son after his death, though he would leave him a remnant for the sake of David.

Word from the Wise

Solomon sought for wisdom to bless others rather than wealth. When he was later blessed with wealth he fell into sexual immorality, pride, and idolatry. Wealth can be a serious obstacle to a relationship with God if we allow it to be first in our hearts. "Then Jesus said to his disciples, ... it is easier for a camel to go through the eye of a needle than for a rich person to enter the Kingdom of God." (Matthew 19:23, 24, NLT)

The Kingdom Divided

Solomon's son Rehoboam succeeded him on the throne, and God's promise came to pass through a man named Jeroboam, who led a secession movement to create a northern kingdom with ten of the tribes. Rehoboam's kingdom retained the territory of Judah and Benjamin, including Jerusalem, and took the name Judah. Confusion over the similar-sounding names of these two kings has bedeviled students for centuries. In response, someone has come up with a simple memory device:

- Jeroboam jumped
- Rehoboam remained

The people, who had clamored to have a king like other nations, were becoming disenchanted. Among their grievances:

- High taxes
- Forced labor
- Arrogance of the king

Jeroboam was already a known subversive in Solomon's time, and the king had sought to kill him. He returned from hiding in Egypt after Solomon's death to lead the revolt of the northern tribes, which became the kingdom of Israel. Meanwhile, Pharaoh Shishak caused trouble of his own by pursuing a military campaign against Judah. Jeroboam is condemned in the Bible for setting up calf worship in Israel. Rehoboam, son of an Ammonite wife of Solomon, wasn't much better, introducing some idolatrous practices in Judah.

Word from the Wise

"Come, let's get him drunk with wine again tonight, and you go in and sleep with him. That way our family line will be preserved." (Genesis 19:34, NLT) Genesis 19:30–38 tells how two of these pagan nations originated. The two daughters of Lot, Abraham's nephew, got him drunk with wine on two successive nights and lay with him to get pregnant. One offspring was named Moab and the other Ben-ammi—who became the ancestors of the Moabites and Ammonites. Apparently, Lot and his family had stayed in wicked Sodom too long.

Apostasy and Appeasement

For generations there were recurring themes during the reigns of the 38 kings of the divided kingdom:

- The apostasy cycle
- Appeasement of the kingdoms of the East and West

Judah and especially Israel underwent repeated cycles of godly generations giving way to spiritual indifference, then to open apostasy, followed by God's punishment, national repentance, and then another era of godliness. In the process, God used other nations to punish Israel and Judah and bring them to repentance.

The northern and southern kingdoms attempted to play these powers—especially Egypt and Assyria—against each other by making alliances and treaties. It was a dangerous game, and it did not have a happy ending.

Israel or Samaria, the northern kingdom, was conquered by Assyria in 722 B.C. as part of a strategy to annex a strategic forward position from which to engage Egypt. The Assyrians, notorious for their cruelty and iron-fisted policies toward the vanquished, dispersed the people of Israel throughout its empire and forcibly resettled the land of Israel with other peoples. These became the despised Samaritans, named after their capital, Samaria. The Israelites were absorbed and assimilated into Assyrian territories known today as:

- Syria
- Turkey
- Iran
- Iraq

MidEast Dictionary

Samaritans are people from Assyrian territories who were resettled in the former kingdom of Israel, intermarried with the Jews, and assimilated into Judaism, worshipping on Mt. Gerizim; as the Jews of Judea regarded them contemptuously as half-breed aliens, Jesus made the "Good Samaritan" the hero of one of his parables about righteous behavior toward all people. (Luke 10:30–37)

Judah, the southern kingdom, resisted Assyria for a time, only to fall prey to the next world power, Babylon. In 586 B.C., Nebuchadnezzar conquered Judah and Jerusalem and destroyed that symbol of the God-chosen people, the Temple. Many of the people were deported to Babylon, but in this case they were not absorbed or assimilated. They retained their national, cultural, and religious identity.

God's house, however, was in ruins. And so it would seem for David's house, the kingdom that was supposed to have no end.

Daniel's Vision: The Never-Ending Kingdom

In Babylon, King Nebuchadnezzar had a vision of the shape of things to come—in the form of a colossus with head of gold, chest and arms of silver, belly and thighs of bronze, and legs of iron and feet of clay. (Daniel 2) Then it was smashed and obliterated by a rock that grew to be a mountain that covered the whole earth. Nebuchadnezzar had no clue what it meant, and he demanded an answer from his court servants and wise men:

- Magicians

- Enchanters

- Sorcerers

- Astrologers

Not even the threat of a horrible death could evoke the answer from them. However, Daniel, Judah's prophet of the Babylonian captivity, gave the king the meaning of the symbols. They stood for four great kingdoms that were to rule the known world. We know now with the benefit of history that these were:

- Babylon

- Medo-Persia

- Greece

- Rome

 Word from the Wise

"This is what the LORD says: 'I will go before you, Cyrus, and level the mountains.'" (Isaiah 45:2, NLT) God uses evil kings like Pharaoh and Cyrus to fulfill his purposes. How does he use evil for good today?

Sure enough, the Babylonians were conquered by the Medes and Persians. There is good reason to believe that today's Kurds are the direct descendants of the Medes. The Iranians are descendants of the Persians.

This was significant for the Jews because they were gradually allowed to repatriate to their homeland under Cyrus of Persia, who conquered Babylon in 539 B.C. Amazingly, when Cyrus issued a decree the next year to allow the exiles to begin returning to Judah, it was in fulfillment of the words of the prophet Isaiah some 150 years prior, identifying Cyrus by *name*. If God could use other nations to punish the Jewish kingdoms, apparently he could use the same means to bless them.

Some significant historic milestones (B.C. dates):

- 612—fall of the Assyrian capital, Nineveh, to the Medes and Babylonians
- 605—defeat of the Egyptians at Carchemish and Babylonian control of Syria and Palestine; some Jews deported
- 597—Jerusalem under King Jehoiakin surrenders to the Babylonian army; more Jews deported
- 586—final destruction of Jersualem and exile of rebellious remaining people to Babylon
- 562—death of Nebuchadnezzar and beginning of Babylonian decline
- 556—Babylon falls to Cyrus of Persia
- 539—Cyrus's decree to let the exiles begin returning to Judah
- 515—dedication of the rebuilt Temple in Jerusalem

Greek Control

The Persians continued to control the region including Judah and greater Syria (Palestine). Then it was Greece's turn, as Alexander the Great overthrew the Persians and gained control of the region in 330 B.C.

MidEast Dictionary

Palestine refers to the Holy Land; the country west of the Jordan River, so called by the Greeks and Romans from the word "Philistine," referring to the enemies of Israel along the Mediterranean coast; hence, originally intended as a derogatory term.

Alexander, a student of Aristotle, was one of the world's greatest conquerors and spread Hellenistic culture and established Greek as the dominant language throughout the known world, which he ruled for a time. He conquered Egypt, and his kingdom stretched from the Theban capital in the west to the Indus River in India on the east. He established his capital in Babylon, but died there suddenly in 323 B.C from malaria and heavy drinking at the age of 33.

This empire was divided among Alexander's four top generals, and control of Syria after Alexander's death switched off between the Ptolemies and the Seleucids of Syria. There was a brief revolt of the Jews in 165 B.C. after

Antiochus Epiphanes set up an altar to Zeus in the Temple, and the Jews gained independence for several years under the Maccabees until they were reconquered by the Syrians.

Roman Empire

Rome stepped into the vacuum and picked up the pieces of the Greek empire, including Syria. The Roman general Pompey invaded, capturing Syria and Jerusalem in 63 B.C. Roman rule was generally through intermediaries such as the Herods. Herod the Great, an Idumean (Edomite), ruled approximately from 37 to 4 B.C. and was in power at the time of the birth of Christ.

It was later under Hadrian that the country was given the name Palestine as the rebellious Jews were slaughtered and Jerusalem was turned into a Roman colony. Communities of Jews continued to live in different centers in Palestine, and throughout these successive empires there had been a continuous Jewish presence in the land, especially the four "holy cities" of Jerusalem, Hebron, Tiberias, and Safed.

Interestingly, Daniel's vision of the four empires (via Nebuchadnezzar) reached its finale with the birth of the King of the Jews in the midst of the Roman Empire. This was the rock that would destroy empires, the mountain that would cover the earth. World rulers and would-be rulers would still come and go, but this was the Son of David, whose kingdom would have no end.

After Jesus' resurrection the apostle Peter preached boldly in Jerusalem that David had foreseen this in writing Psalm 16, when he stated that God would not leave his "Holy One" to decay in the grave. It wasn't himself David had in mind, Peter said, for David died and was buried. He was referring to the Messiah, the anointed one.

Word from the Wise

The resurrection of Jesus is the core of a Christian's faith. David's tomb was "still here" for all to see, Peter said. "But he was a prophet, and he knew God had promised with an oath that one of David's own descendants would sit on David's throne as the Messiah. David was looking into the future and predicting the Messiah's resurrection." (Acts 2:30–31, NLT) Peter spoke these words to an audience from many nations and thus Christianity spread beyond the Jews to the worldwide religion it is to this day.

Chapter

6

An Islamic Empire

This chapter is about the rise of the Islamic Empire. While Europe was still coming into its own in the Middle Ages, a great civilization under successive dynasties of Islamic caliphs ruled much of the known world for centuries. In the process, the religion itself underwent a painful split. There was definitely a very dark side, too.

"St. John Paul the Baptist"

Pope John Paul II's historic visit to the Umayyad Mosque in Damascus, Syria, in May 2001 was intended to be a healing thing. John Paul would be the first pope to visit an Islamic mosque. The Vatican talked about the need to bring together Christianity and Islam, maybe even hold joint Christian-Islamic prayers at the Umayyad Mosque, described as the oldest existing monumental structure and the fourth holiest site in the Islamic world.

The Muslims were suspicious, suggesting the pope was trying to bring Christianity by stealth to an Islamic holy site or was perhaps trying to reclaim the site for Christianity. They demanded that he remove his cross, calling the crucifix offensive to Islam. They wanted him to apologize for the Crusades. The *mufti* (top Muslim cleric) of Syria tried for a papal statement of solidarity with the Muslims and against the "Zionist Jews."

All the demands were rebuffed. The historic visit to the Umayyad Mosque did go forward, although the Muslims quashed the idea of joint prayers. "Would the pope let us give the Muslim call to prayer at St. Peter's?" one official said.

The Umayyad Mosque was also an important Christian site, which the Vatican felt deserved a papal visit. Inside the structure is the purported tomb of John the Baptist—or, as Arabic News termed it in a moment of confusion, "St. John Paul the Baptist." So the 80-year-old pontiff took off his shoes and padded his way through the mosque, which had been a Byzantine cathedral 1,400 years prior.

Originally, it had been a pagan site, dating back to 1000 B.C. Around the time of Christ, the Romans converted it to a massive temple for the god Jupiter. Later, the Emperor Theodosius banned pagan ceremonies and converted it to the Church of St. John, which it remained until the Islamic conquest of Damascus in 636, when the two faiths shared the site.

Then in 705, the church was razed and replaced with a mosque, retaining a shrine to John the Baptist. Muslims revere John the Baptist as the Prophet Yahia, Jesus' cousin, who was ordered beheaded by King Herod. His shrine at the Umayyad Mosque features a receptacle they claim contains at least the head of John, and possibly more of his remains. Another shrine there is said to contain either the head of Zechariah, the father of John the Baptist, or maybe the head of Hussein, the son of Ali, the fourth caliph.

Muslims believe that in the last days Christ will return to the Umayyad Mosque, proclaim Islam as the world's religion, marry, and later die. He is to be buried next to Muhammad in Medina, Saudi Arabia.

Roots of Terror—The Age of Caliphs

Three of the first four Islamic caliphs (successors) prior to the Umayyad dynasty left office the hard way—by assassination—including Ali, cousin and son-in-law of the prophet. Ali was a son of the uncle who raised Muhammad, and he married Muhammad's daughter Fatima. Many Muslims thought he should have been the first caliph instead of the fourth. As Ali was bypassed several times by the Arab council of elders, powerful political forces waited to overwhelm him. The results would become a permanent stain for Islam.

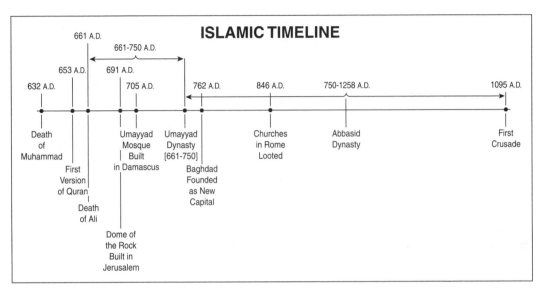

Golden Age of Islam.

An insurrection broke out during Ali's reign. Ali also was accused of not doing enough to round up the culprits who had assassinated his predecessor, Uthman, or perhaps of even having had something to do with his killing. Finally, two armies faced off against each other, one loyal to Ali and the other to the rebels.

Ali eked out a victory, but it was an ominous sign of things to come. It was the first time two Muslim armies faced each other in battle—but it would not be the last.

The First Terror Victim

Among Ali's many enemies was Mu'awiyah, governor of Syria under Uthman. Ali had tried to remove him from office. Mu'awiyah, a cousin of the unfortunate Uthman, began to demand retaliation for his cousin's murder, holding Ali personally responsible.

Uthman, Ali's predecessor, had made his own enemies—especially in Egypt, where he replaced the governor with his own relative. Several hundred irate Egyptian soldiers showed up in Medina, broke into the caliph's house, and killed him while he was reading the Quran.

Mu'awiyah's supporters engaged Ali's forces in battle, resulting in a standoff. Ali's men persuaded him reluctantly to accept arbitration in the dispute. One faction

Reality Check

Uthman is credited as the man who first assembled all the differing versions of Muhammad's teachings into one book. His order to burn all variant versions was unpopular at the time. However, it has allowed Muslims to claim infallibility, as opposed to Jewish and Christian scriptures, which they claim were corrupted over the centuries and are superseded by the Quran.

in particular made real trouble as the dispute dragged on. They were the Kharijites or Seceders, who became essentially the first Islamic extremists. They were outraged, believing Ali had violated God's law by submitting the matter to human counsel.

The Kharijites became radical theocrats, rejecting all human government and believing only in God's law. Their continuing acts of political violence are sometimes viewed as a forerunner of later Islamic terrorism—and the impetus for a tradition of sultanic strongmen who could withstand such challenges.

Finally, some of the Kharijites went on a violent terrorist rampage, attacking a number of people, including Mu'awiyah, who survived, and Ali, who did not. The caliph was stabbed to death as he was entering a mosque.

A Deep Rift

Ali's eldest son, Hasan, was easily intimidated and eventually was bribed by Mu'awi-yah to give up his claims to the caliphate. This was the end of the line of the so-called "rightly guided" caliphs and the true beginning of the first dynasty, the Umayyads, from Muhammad's tribe, the Quraysh.

There were 14 caliphs in Mu'awiyah's line from 661 to 750 A.D. It was also the beginning of the first major split within Islam, as the followers of Ali became known as the Shi'a or Shi'ites (literally, "partisans" of Ali).

After Mu'awiyah died in 680 A.D., the Shi'ites gave it one more go and tried to make Ali's younger son, Hussein, caliph instead of Mu'awiyah's son, Yazid. Hussein was captured by soldiers loyal to Mu'awiyah who killed him and sent his severed head to Yazid in Damascus as a present. This is the head that may or may not be in repose today at the Umayyad Mosque in Damascus.

To Muslims, it is as if these things happened yesterday. In some heavily Shi'ite parts of the Muslim world, Ali's and Hussein's deaths are still remembered as days of mourning and their burial sites in Iraq as objects of pilgrimage. The legacy to this day is a deep rift within the spiritual family of Muhammad.

Warrior Religion

Islam, born in the brutal desert environs of Arabia, has always been to some degree a warrior religion. Its first expansion from Medina to Mecca was a military venture, starting with the raids on the caravan traders. Muham-mad justified this plunder on the grounds of injustices against his people and the inequities of poverty. This naturally led to the notion of holy war (jihad) against the pagan rulers of Mecca who rejected his teaching and then, by extension, to infidels everywhere.

After the prophet's death in 632 B.C., the movement was headed by Muhammad's first convert, best friend, and father-in-law, Abu Bakr. This esteemed leader gathered the greatest military force Arabia had ever seen, and the victories after Mecca came like lightning. Towns and cities fell like dominoes. The Arabs attributed these victories to the power of Muhammad's god, and mass conversions became the norm. Intimidation must have had some part in these conversions, a feature of nations converting to Christianity at times as well.

In the world outside Arabia, the conquering caliphs of Islam found ripe picking. There were two prominent powers in these years:

- Persians
- Byzantines

The Byzantines (eastern remnant of the old Roman Empire) and the Persians were so preoccupied with fighting each other that they missed the greater threat posed by the armies of Islam. Also, the Byzantine church had been persecuting the large *Monophysite* sect, which disagreed with the mainstream over the nature of Christ's divinity. Not surprisingly, the Monophysites began welcoming the Muslim invaders with open arms as liberators.

Family Focus

Discuss how life would be different in a desert environment without modern conveniences and technology. Compare and contrast Christianity and Islam, Christ and Muhammad. For example, John 18:36, NLT, where Jesus says, "I am not an earthly king. If I were, my followers would have fought when I was arrested by the Jewish leaders. But my Kingdom is not of this world."

 MidEast Dictionary

Monophysites literally means "single nature"; these were Christians in the fourth and fifth centuries, particularly Egyptians and Syrians, who opposed the idea that Christ had both a human and a divine nature; their view was condemned by the church in 451 A.D. as heretical.

Desert Fighters

Many of the newly united Arabian tribesmen were seasoned desert fighters and Bedouin warriors, possibly one of the greatest fighting machines in history. They were expert horsemen and knew the desert. Their forces would suddenly materialize out of the distance, falling upon their enemies decisively. Their cavalry would charge with lances extended under a hail of arrows from the infantry, causing the enemy to break ranks and flee.

Armies of the first four caliphs began to conquer the entire Middle East. They overran Jerusalem in 638 A.D., drove out the Byzantine rulers, and completed their conquests of Syria, Palestine, and Mesopotamia in just three years. Within 20 years they had subdued the entire region from Egypt to Persia.

The capital of the new Islamic Empire moved twice, first from Mecca to the ancient city of Damascus, then (under the next dynasty of the Abbasids) from Damascus to the new city of Baghdad (modern Iraq). By the 800s Baghdad had grown to a half-million people, becoming the largest city in the world outside of China.

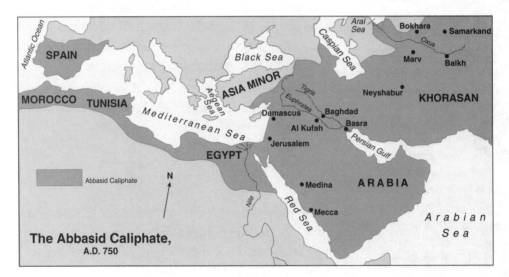

The Islamic Empire eventually stretched from Spain to India.

Life Under Islamic Rule

The Umayyads—especially in the campaigns of the second caliph, Umar—managed to win an empire that eventually extended from Spain to India. The new empire bordered India and China on the east and North Africa and Spain on the west, effectively linking three continents—Asia, Europe, and Africa.

This naturally complicated life for the residents of those lands, who fell largely into two categories: *dhimmi* or *mawali*.

Dhimmi had essentially three choices:

- Conversion to Islam
- Payment of heavy tribute to Damascus or Baghdad
- Death

> **MidEast Dictionary**
>
> **Dhimmi** is a non-Muslim living in Muslim territory and subject to special taxation and some restrictions. **Mawali** is a non-Arab converted to Islam.

When a town was being conquered, the people typically were offered all the benefits of the empire, including the "protection" of the caliph, whether they wanted it or not. Mawali, while technically Muslims, tended to be treated as second-class citizens, and conversions to Islam were not particularly encouraged. Realistically, there was little financial incentive for the Muslim overlords to seek converts when the dhimmi provided greater tax revenue.

Ironically, Islam's success ultimately meant an empire that was increasingly non-Muslim. In fact, the majority were of three groups:

- Jews
- Christians
- *Zoroastrians*

> **MidEast Dictionary**
>
> **Zoroastrians** are a religion of the Persians before their conversion to Islam; belief in the existence of a universal spirit involved in a cosmic struggle between good and evil.

In addition, there were the Islamic dissident Shi'ites and Kharijites. Success required stern measures. Non-Muslims might expect rather constrained lives, including special restrictions:

- Riding only mules or donkeys (no horses or camels)
- Wearing special clothing to identify them as non-Muslim (for example, Christian)
- No building of churches or synagogues without special permission
- No carrying weapons

- No wearing shoes or anything green (Islamic color)
- No retaliation when attacked by a Muslim

Born in Blood

The caliphs were essentially Muhammad's successors at the head of the Islamic Empire. Under the two major dynasties, the caliphate was at the center of centuries of violence.

Early Empire

Caliph Abd al-Malik built the Dome of the Rock atop the Temple Mount in Jerusalem in 691 A.D., in part as a statement about Islam's ascendancy over Judaism and Chris-tianity. A few years later one of the last Umayyad caliphs, al-Walid, built the Great Mosque in Damascus in 705 A.D. right over the top of John the Baptist's tomb and shrine.

The Umayyads were somewhat less successful in challenging the military power of the Byzantine Empire, particularly at sea. The Muslims and the Byzantines began to give each other a wide berth and maintained an uneasy co-existence for many years.

The Umayyad dynasty eventually began to unravel, a process accelerated by various dissident groups within the empire, particularly the Abbasids, descendants from Muhammad's uncle, Abbas. The Abbasids enjoyed great popular support and built a power base through military victories.

Family Focus

What would life be like in a society that discriminated against you on the basis of your religion? Discuss the importance of freedom of religion in America today.

Rise of the Second Dynasty

The forces of Abu al-Abbas overran the Umayyad armies, and Abbas became caliph in 750 A.D. The deposed Umayyad caliph, Marwan, fled to Egypt, where he attempted to hide in a Christian church. He was caught and relieved of his head—which was sent to Abbas as a present. The Abbasids had all the surviving Umayyad men but one put to the sword, and that one only saved himself by fleeing to Spain.

The Abbasids even pursued the Umayyads after death, exhuming their graves and desecrating their bodies. It is not entirely clear what motivated all of this bloodlust. Apparently, some of the Umayyad rulers had some eccentric and shocking tastes—ornate palaces with dancing girls, swimming pools full of wine, and prisoner executions for entertainment. On the other hand, maybe after 120 years, it was just time for a change.

Governing by the Sword

The ascension of the Abbasids signified a bit of a power tilt toward Persia, which had been a center of the Abbasid movement. The zealous Persians initially had been reluctant converts to Islam, considering themselves culturally superior to the Arab camel herders.

Word from the Wise

Jesus had harsh words for the legalists and outwardly religious leaders of his day. He said they were like whitewashed tombs full of dead men's bones—which, ironically, were considered ceremonially unclean. Read Matthew 23:23–28 and consider how this condemnation might specifically apply to Christians, Jews, and Muslims.

The Abbasids, however, apparently feared that some of these second-tier people could become a political threat. Therefore, they simply had them executed. A Persian general who had won major battles against the Umayyads was hacked to death while conversing with the new caliph. He was decapitated and the severed head thrown outside the palace gates.

The Abbasid dynasty reigned for several hundred years. It gradually declined through attrition as it ceased to be a purely Arab dynasty and increasingly became a Persian and Turkish institution. The caliphate itself lingered on into the twentieth century before finally being abolished by the Turks in 1924.

A Culture of Violence

The first significant battle of Muhammad's movement was the Battle of Badr—actually a caravan raid near Mecca in which Muhammad got one fifth of the plunder, which became the standard fare thereafter. This principle was incorporated in writing into the Hadith.

Jihad, according to Muhammad, permitted wholesale looting of the vanquished. If the booty was inadequate, captives could be taken until their families paid sufficient ransom. So there is nothing particularly new today in terms of hostage taking.

The Battle of Badr netted the prisoner Abu Jahl, a longtime archenemy of Muhammad and leader of one of the fiercely pagan tribes of Mecca. The two had fought since childhood, as the stories go, and now Abu Jahl had fallen into Muhammad's hands. He paid with his head, and the prophet declared it a better gift than the best camel in Arabia.

An emboldened Muhammad began dispatching his foes by various means. One prisoner was hacked to death. A Meccan poetess who had been mocking the prophet with satirical verse was tracked down and slain, pinned to her own bed with a dagger. Another poet paid for his literary indiscretions by having his throat cut.

Other examples:

- When several camel thieves were apprehended, the prophet ordered his men to cut off their hands and feet and pull out their eyes.

- The aunt of a notorious robber was caught and, at Muhammad's direction, was pulled in two by a couple of camels while her two young sons were executed by other means.

- A Jewish chieftain, who concealed the whereabouts of a hidden treasure from the prophet, was slowly killed with a fire lit on his chest. Then the holy man took the man's 17-year-old widow to his tent that night and made her one of his wives.

> **Family Focus**
>
> Do we take our freedoms for granted? Imagine what it would be like if you, your friends, and family could not express opinions without fearing for your lives. Discuss how that would affect your life. How important is freedom of speech to you?

In fairness, this kind of violence and brutality was peculiar neither to Muhammad nor to the new religion of Islam. Quite the contrary, it was more the norm of seventh-century Arab culture. The point here is this: The historic Muhammad is not entirely the same figure as the legendary prophet of Allah—the humble friend of widows and orphans—later depicted for religious purposes.

Considering such brutal origins, perhaps no one should be surprised to find some spiritual heirs of this movement today committing acts of violence in the name of religion. To be fair, some Muslims condemn much of this violence as well as saying those who commit it are not good Muslims, though few would repudiate the necessity for violence in any circumstance.

Chapter 7

The West Strikes Back

This chapter deals with the clash of civilizations between the Islamic Empire and the West. Muslim brutality followed by Crusader atrocities created a legacy of poisoned relations that lives on today.

Spain in Chains—Islamic Conquest

The expansionist Islamic Empire managed to control significant parts of Western Europe up until 1492, right to the threshold of the modern era—generally considered 1500 A.D. It was a big year for Ferdinand and Isabella. Not only did they launch Christopher Columbus to the New World, but they also became the first rulers of a united Spain in 1492. That was when they completed the Reconquista (reconquest) of Spain, ending the last Islamic rule in this land the Muslims called Andalusia.

It had been a long occupation, 780 years, which kept the land divided. It had taken centuries to reverse the momentum of this occupation and gradually push the Muslims out. At the pivotal battle of Granada, the advantage was finally on the side of the Europeans, who wielded firearms against Muslim forces with bows and arrows and spears.

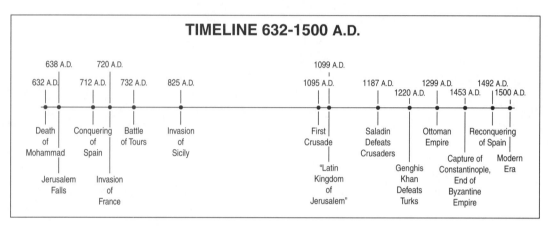

TIMELINE 632-1500 A.D.

| 632 A.D. | 638 A.D. | 712 A.D. | 720 A.D. | 732 A.D. | 825 A.D. | 1095 A.D. | 1099 A.D. | 1187 A.D. | 1220 A.D. | 1299 A.D. | 1453 A.D. | 1492 A.D. | 1500 A.D. |

Death of Mohammad — Jerusalem Falls — Conquering of Spain — Invasion of France — Battle of Tours — Invasion of Sicily — First Crusade — "Latin Kingdom of Jerusalem" — Saladin Defeats Crusaders — Genghis Khan Defeats Turks — Ottoman Empire — Capture of Constantinople, End of Byzantine Empire — Reconquering of Spain — Modern Era

From Muhammad to the modern era.

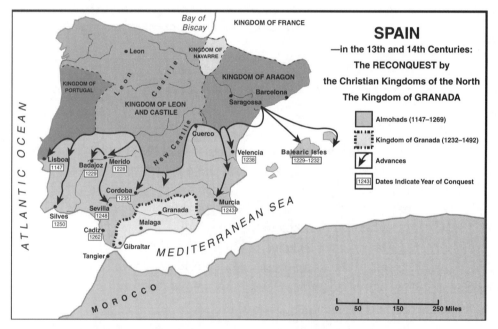

Islam kept Spain divided for hundreds of years.

The Muslims called the Iberian Peninsula (modern Spain and Portugal) "al-Andalus" after the Vandals, one of the Germanic barbarian tribes that had sacked Rome and preyed upon North Africa and Spain as well. In the eighth century the king, Roderic, was from a different Germanic tribe, the Visigoths. By this time the Islamic Empire had entrenched itself firmly in North Africa and began to eye the Iberian Peninsula as its next step toward encircling the Mediterranean Sea.

Caliph al-Walid authorized the invasion of Spain and the ensuing seven-year campaign of conquest, which began in 712 A.D. Al-Walid was the caliph who had the great Umayyad Mosque built in Damascus. The first decisive battle, fought not far inland, resulted in a great Muslim victory. Roderic's head was cut off and sent as a present to the caliph in Damascus.

> **Reality Check**
>
> The Muslim expeditionary force landed at Gibraltar, the rocky peninsula at the southern tip of Spain, which acquired its name from the Moorish commander of these forces, Tarik (*Jabal Tarik*). Moors were Muslims from North Africa of Arab and Berber descent.

The last survivor of the Umayyad dynasty, as you might recall from the previous chapter, fled to Spain during the massacre by the Abbasids. This was Abd al-Rahman. He arrived there in 756 A.D. and promptly drove the Abbasid *emir* (ruler or prince) out of his stronghold in Cordoba. When the Abbasids tried to drive out al-Rahman, he defeated this force, decapitated their officers, and sent the heads to the Abbasid caliph in Baghdad.

One of al-Rahman's successors, distrusting the loyalty of recent Christian converts to Islam, had hundreds of them (some say several thousand) beheaded in the city of Toledo. Elsewhere, other Christians were crucified, some for protesting the high price of food. Here are a couple other examples:

- In the ninth century a dozen or so devout Christians were executed under Abd al-Rahman II in Cordova, where they apparently sought martyrdom by condemning Islam and effectively "insulting the prophet."
- In the tenth century Almanzor (Ibn Abi Amir) conquered the Spanish town of Zamora and executed more than 4,000 Christians.

It was this kind of atrocity that inspired the Reconquista and a reciprocal brutality from the Spaniards. When the legendary El Cid, for example, retook the city of Valencia, he had the Muslim ruler burned alive.

The Battle for Europe

Other Christians in Europe had problems of their own from the Islamic colonizers, particularly the Franks (French). They did send some forces across the Pyrenees to assist their Christian brothers in Spain, including a brief involvement by Charlemagne in 778 A.D. A few years later (801 A.D.) Charlemagne's son, Louis I, led a force into northern Spain to retake Barcelona, a city that continued to seesaw for many years between Spanish and Muslim control.

Charlemagne's grandfather, Charles "The Hammer" Martel, is credited more than anyone else with sparing Europe from total Muslim conquest. The Saracens—as the Muslims were called in Medieval times—had been using Spain as a staging area for raids into the Frankish kingdom, taking city after city, slaughtering the men, and enslaving the women and children.

This led to one of the most decisive battles in world history, the Battle of Tours in 732 A.D., when Charles the Hammer fought off the Saracen cavalry with infantry armed with battle axes, inflicting thousands of Muslim casualties and routing their forces. Exactly 100 years after the death of Muhammad, his empire had been dealt a deadly blow to its expansionist designs—or jihad—upon Europe.

The Battle of Tours may have decided the entire future of Europe.

Family Focus

Discuss how life would be different if Islam had managed to conquer Europe. What would it be like for girls and women? Do you think you would have become a Muslim? Why or why not? Would the New World still have been founded on the principle of religious freedom?

The East Falls

The battle for Europe was far from over. The Muslims already had taken the islands of Cyprus and Crete, and they clearly wanted the continent. In 827 A.D. they took Sicily and drew their sights on Italy. Churches and monasteries were major targets for the rape and pillage of the ecclesiastical treasuries.

The Saracens occupied Sicily for more than 250 years, while their activities in Italy were limited mainly to raids and looting of the churches in Rome, including the churches of St. Peter and St. Paul. That prompted the construction of the Leonine Wall around the city to keep out future marauders.

Constantinople was a much tougher case, but the Muslim forces did realize other major successes in eastern Europe over the next several centuries. By that time the empire had changed hands—to control by the Seljuk and then the Ottoman Turks— but the religion and the worldview remained anti-Christian Muslim, with the intention of overcoming Christian domination in the surrounding regions. This was the period (fourteenth and fifteenth centuries) when Islam made its inroads into what are now the Balkan states:

- Serbia
- Bosnia-Herzegovina
- Kosovo
- Slovenia
- Croatia
- Macedonia
- Albania

In the process, seeds were sown for a bitter conflict centuries later. After the fall of the Iron Curtain and the dissolution of Yugoslavia in the 1990s, there was an eruption of brutality, genocide, and "ethnic cleansing," primarily directed by Christian Serbs against Muslims in Bosnia and Kosovo.

The Fall of Constantinople

In the fourteenth century Ottoman troops crossed the Dardanelles strait from Anatolia (Turkey) into modern Greece and Bulgaria, cutting off the ancient Byzantine capital. By the end of the century, the only thing left to the Byzantines was Constantinople itself. Eventually, even Constantinople fell to the Muslims after many days of heavy cannon bombardment, finally ending the last vestiges of the Byzantine Empire—and, technically, the Roman Empire as well—in 1453.

It was an ignoble chapter as the Turkish sultan, Mehmet II, entered the gates to claim Constantinople as the new capital of his Ottoman Empire. Mehmet ordered the body of the Byzantine emperor, Constantine XI, to be given the customary treatment, with the head sent around the Ottoman Empire for amusement. Hundreds of citizens of Constantinople, including many priests and nuns, who had holed up in the great cathedral of St. Sophia, were slaughtered. Then St. Sophia was converted to a mosque, which it remains to this day.

Muslim conquerors vied for control of the Byzantine Empire.

Word from the Wise

Both Jesus and his disciples taught that Christians should expect persecution in this world. "Dear friends, don't be surprised at the fiery trials you are going through, as if something strange were happening to you. Instead, be very glad—because these trials will make you partners with Christ in his suffering ..." 1 Peter 4:12–13, NLT. Yet, we must not forget that we Christians have done some of the persecuting.

The Rest of the Story: What They Don't Teach in School

Despite all the carnage and unspeakable brutality to this point, it still took something more to provoke a systematic, pan-European response. It took the Muslim occupation of the Holy Land, the birthplace of Christ, to fuel that kind of determination. That was the greatest offense. The response was the Crusades.

In more recent years it has become fashionable to condemn the Crusaders for brutality without telling the rest of the story. The fact that tens of thousands of Christians were murdered and sold into slavery in Europe and the Middle East, including the Holy Land, is not nearly so well known.

There is the story, for example, of the so-called mad caliph, al-Hakim, who ruled from Egypt around 1000 A.D. Because he developed the habit of sleeping during the day and working at night, he decided to put everybody on that schedule and therefore banned working during the day. He also banned the manufacture of women's shoes, in the interest of keeping women subservient and in their place.

Family Focus

Discuss what is being taught in school and promulgated in the media regarding the Crusades and atrocities committed by Christians. What do your own children know and not know? What is being omitted and why?

Some say al-Hakim also came to believe in his own divinity, which was clearly heresy for any follower of Muhammad and Allah. His legend only grew when one day he simply walked off into the sunset, disappearing in the hills outside Cairo, his body never to be found.

A follower of al-Hakim, Sheikh Darazi, managed to convince a number of folks that this caliph was, in fact, divine. These followers in turn became known as Duruz, and that is where the sect of the Druze originated. The specifics of their belief system are secret, but this mystical role was al-Hakim's greatest claim to fame and immortality.

Somewhat lesser known is al-Hakim's intense hatred of Christians. He destroyed hundreds (some say thousands) of churches. He had the original Byzantine Church of the Holy Sepulcher destroyed, even leveling the cave that was believed to be the holy sepulcher itself, the tomb of Christ. As the holiest shrine in Christendom, it had been an object of veneration by European Christians for many years. It was the place where Jesus rose from the dead, and it was the destination of all pilgrims to the Holy Land.

By the eleventh century, however, the Christians of Europe had not only lost the Holy Sepulcher, but they were also being harassed and assaulted on their pilgrimages. In one case, out of a group of 7,000 German pilgrims, only 2,000 made it safely back home. European anger was boiling over, which is the part they do teach in school.

Crusader Jihad—A Phenomenal Response

The year 1095 A.D. is a major milestone in history, the year Pope Urban II called for the European response now known as the *Crusades*. The Muslims had been practicing jihad (holy war) for centuries. Now it was Europe's turn.

The Byzantine patriarch swallowed his pride and called for Western assistance. Pope Urban II agreed to the request, using strong language in his own appeal. He warned that the Turks and Arabs had taken control of territory from the Mediterranean to Byzantium, enslaving, torturing, and killing Christians. He called upon Christian soldiers of Europe to come to their aid and to "destroy that vile race from the lands of our friends."

MidEast Dictionary

The term the **Crusades** is from Latin meaning *crux* for cross; military expeditions European Christians undertook from the eleventh to thirteenth centuries to recover the Holy Land from the Muslims.

The response was phenomenal, proving to be an idea whose time had truly come. The western Europeans' recent successes in initially pushing back the Muslims in Sicily and Spain emboldened their leaders to respond with alacrity. Tens of thousands of volunteers flooded into the Holy Land in what became the First Crusade. From the north they retook Antioch after a nine-month siege, then proceeded to Jerusalem, reaching its hallowed walls in 1099 A.D.

What followed was not one of Christendom's more shining moments. After a six-week siege, the Europeans broke through and commenced an outright slaughter. The Crusaders generally did not distinguish between Jews and Muslims. In their eyes the occupiers were all infidels, and so they were subjected to hideous violence:

- Shot with arrows
- Thrown from towers
- Tortured
- Burned at the stake
- Beheaded

Virtually the entire population, perhaps 70,000 people, was decimated. As these accounts in the same breath generally go on to describe the streets of Jerusalem "knee deep in blood," some exaggeration—or boasting—may have been employed. But there is no denying that it was a bloody, heinous episode.

Family Focus

Discuss the violence that was committed by Christians during the Crusades. How could these men justify their acts? How do we answer the critics of Christianity and the West when they point up such atrocities?

It was a spree of killing and looting. Violence was wrought upon many other hapless individuals outside of Jerusalem, even other Christians, both in Palestine and en route to the Holy Land.

The pope had assured absolution for any Christian killed doing this supposed work of God. It may have been an outrageous assertion, but really little different from the standard Islamic promise of instant paradise for any Muslim martyr who gives his life in jihad—except, of course, for the additional amenity of 72 virgins in the Muslim version. In addition, that tradition is still operative 900 years later.

An Enduring Stain

The Christian Kingdom of Jerusalem lasted less than a century, before the Christians were again driven out in 1187 A.D. They held, for varying periods, four states in all:

- Jerusalem
- Antioch
- Tripoli
- Edessa

In the meantime, the Crusaders did some redecorating. The Church of the Holy Sepulcher was recaptured and rebuilt. The Dome of the Rock was remodeled and converted to a church. The sacred al-Aqsa mosque was turned into a horse stable, profaning one of Islam's most sacred sites.

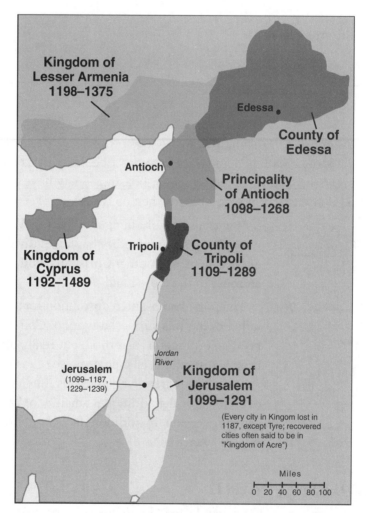

Crusaders controlled the states of Jerusalem, Antioch, Tripoli, and Edessa.

Possession of the Holy Land continued to seesaw between the Christians and the Muslims for many more years, requiring additional campaigns from the West, five major Crusades (depending on how you count them) through the thirteenth century. However, the First Crusade was the only one that could really be called a European success. Some historians believe the Christians prevailed this time only because of divisions between the Sunni and Shi'ite Muslims and competing caliphates in Egypt, Syria, and Turkey that weakened their grip on power.

The Third Crusade, however, may be the best remembered because of its cast of characters—Richard the Lionheart, heroic king of England, and Salah al-Din (Saladin), the complex and noble leader who eventually drove the Christians out of Jerusalem and founded a new Muslim dynasty. These two larger-than-life characters make this episode one of the most fascinating and entertaining historical accounts to read.

Reality Check

The Crusades may have been a long time ago, but when President George Bush once referred to the war on terror as a "crusade," it was a huge gaffe. It gave militants exactly the kind of ammunition they needed to skewer the object of their hatred to the rest of the Muslim world. It was a major "gotcha."

In the last battle of the Third Crusade, for example, Saladin's forces caught Richard the Lionheart and his men asleep in their tents one morning. Though outnumbered four to one, Richard rallied his troops and fought valiantly, personally leading the pitched battle. Saladin, watching from a distance, was horrified when Richard eventually was unhorsed in the heat of battle. Declaring it improper for a noble king like Richard to fight on foot, Saladin dispatched two Arabian horses to his enemy, who survived to fight another day. This was a measure of the respect these two great men had for each other.

The lasting legacy of the Crusades, however, is an enduring stain on relations between Islam and the West up to the present day. When Osama bin Laden hurls invective against the Great Satan, his phraseology nearly always includes the word "Crusader."

Civilization Clash I

While the Christian Crusades did not permanently achieve their stated goals in the Holy Land, it was not all for nothing. They did have some effect in blocking the Muslim drive toward world domination. At its height, the Islamic Empire controlled total territories roughly equivalent to the Roman Empire. Not only did the West strike back, so did the East.

A ruthless Mongol conqueror named Hulegu, grandson of the notorious Genghis Khan, swept down and destroyed the Abbasid caliphate in Baghdad in 1258 A.D. The sheer brutality of these Mongol hordes was terrifying. They didn't stay long before they were off to other adventures, and an Islamic Turkish dynasty called the Mamluks took their place. The Mamluks were the ones who ultimately went on to drive out the Crusaders.

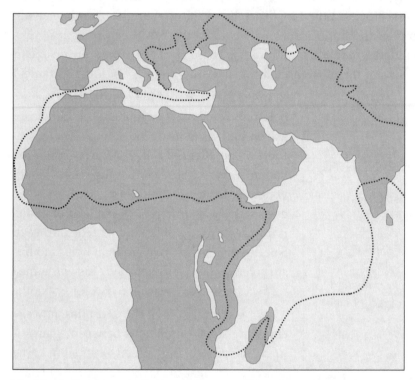

The Islamic Empire controlled vast areas up to the modern era.

By the modern era—1500 A.D.—the hopes of an enduring Muslim empire were definitely fading. It appeared that the Muslim Empire had reached the stage of decline in world power status. Besides Spain, the Muslims met more defeats at Vienna and Malta, clearly signaling a dead end road ahead for them in Europe.

For the West it was just the opposite—a period of conquest and expansion—and, ironically, some of the credit is probably owed to the Muslims. Just as the Philistines challenged Israel to rally and band together in common cause for nation building, so

Reality Check

Historian Paul Kennedy has written that world powers tend to go through three phases— very roughly, periods of conquest and expansion, then consolidation, and finally decay and corruption when all energies go into maintaining status quo rather than advancing.

Word from the Wise

Perhaps this is not just a clash of civilizations, but a clash of how ultimate victory is gained. Jesus' teachings could not be more different from Muhammad's, especially in the area of love and hate. "But I say, love your enemies! Pray for those who persecute you!" (Matthew 5:44, NLT) But even for Christians, that's a hard rule to follow.

the Muslim menace probably forced the nations of Europe, formerly stuck in the Dark Ages, to grow up.

It may be no coincidence that the year 1492 A.D. saw both the birth of a unified Spain and the launching of the first successful voyage to the New World. As a result of the Crusades, Europeans had grown accustomed to exotic goods and luxury items from the Middle East and Asia. This demand did not go away, but rather fueled a desire for increased trade. That, in turn, led to the voyages of discovery and a brand new era in Western life.

Some observers have called today's tensions in the Middle East, international terrorism, and the hostilities of Muslim extremists to Christians and Jews a "clash of civilizations." That may be. Nevertheless, it's nothing particularly new. This clash began in the Middle East many centuries ago and, after a couple of relatively quieter centuries, it is back again with a vengeance. Perhaps these periods should be called Civilization Clash I and Civilization Clash II.

Historically, the clashes have been more the norm than peaceful coexistence. The normal relationship between Christianity and Islam has been one of confrontation, conflict, and clash. For Christians, it may require a shift of perspective to see that what they're experiencing today is in reality just an extension of a centuries-old conflict.

The Return of Islam to Europe?

Across the Middle East the Islamic world has been abuzz with a prophecy of Muhammad that has received scant attention until recently. Based on the interpretation of a well-known Hadith, a number of Muslim clerics have been teaching the faithful to expect the imminent fall of Rome to Islam.

Word from the Wise

Islam has many words of judgment and little of tolerance or compassion for the unbeliever: "When your Lord revealed to the angels: I am with you, therefore make firm those who believe. I will cast terror into the hearts of those who disbelieve. Therefore strike off their heads and strike off every fingertip of them." Quran sura 8.12

There is one little complication: Rome already has a religion. It's called Roman Catholicism. The clerics say this fall will not necessarily be by the sword, but by "preaching and ideology." The West, they say, is suffering spiritually from materialism, and western Europeans are ripe for mass conversion.

A preacher in Sudan declared, "The Muslims conquered Constantinople, where Eastern Christianity is situated, and in the future, a mighty king will arise for the Muslims; through him, Islam will spread and Rome will be conquered."

Constantinople—today known as Istanbul—was conquered in the fifteenth century by the Ottoman Turks, successors to the Islamic caliphs. Representing an entire empire (the Byzantines and the Eastern Church), this was probably the biggest plum ever snatched from the Christian West. Its fall had been predicted by Muhammad in that same Hadith. Rome and Constantinople were really twin imperial capitals—and the second shoe had yet to drop.

The Muslim clerics are absolutely certain that Rome will soon be theirs. They see the signs, and they have the prophet's words. Muhammad had said the city of Heracles (Constantinople) would fall first, then Romiyya (Rome). There is no question about it. It is written.

The Rebirth of Israel

This chapter is about the regathering of the Jews in their own national homeland after centuries of scattering and persecution. The rebirth of Israel following the great Holocaust of World War II created an entirely new set of problems with its Arab neighbors and hundreds of thousands of Palestinian refugees.

A Mufti Ahead of His Time

The mufti of Jerusalem had a firm position regarding the Jews. "Kill the Jews wherever you find them—this pleases Allah, history, and religion," Haj Muhammad Amin al-Husseini declared during a Berlin radio broadcast in March 1944 A.D.

At the time, he was visiting Adolf Hitler and other Nazi leaders regarding the Jewish problem. Al-Husseini worked most closely with SS Chief Heinrich Himmler as the Third Reich considered how it would administer Muslim lands in anticipation of victory over the Allies. He was responsible for developing anti-Semitic, pro-Nazi propaganda for Muslim consumption. Unfortunately, Field Marshall Erwin Rommel's Middle East campaign was not going well, and if things didn't change, they might not get to do any administering in Jerusalem.

Al-Husseini was a man of great stature and influence. As *Mufti*, al-Husseini took charge of the Temple Mount and launched major restoration projects for the Dome of the Rock

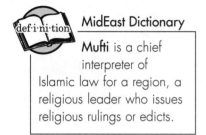

and al-Aqsa mosque, which had fallen into great disrepair. Al-Husseini almost single-handedly pioneered the notion that the Temple Mount was the third holiest site in Islam, after Mecca and Medina. This could have been partly to blunt the claims of the growing Jewish presence in Jerusalem to their ancient Temple site—and the justification for their return as a nation.

Al-Husseini was an Arab nationalist who opposed the British authority and presence in Palestine, called the British Mandate. He became the most significant early leader of Arab Palestinians as alarm grew over the possibility of Israeli statehood. Al-Husseini pressed for restrictions on Jewish immigration to Palestine, which became a real problem for the Jews during World War II. He was a man ahead of his time and was an early advocate for the creation of an independent Arab Palestinian state.

After Israeli statehood in 1948 A.D., al-Husseini tried to form a government in exile for Palestine, but King Abdullah of Jordan annexed the West Bank and secretly negotiated a truce with Israel and then a non-aggression pact in 1950. Ironically, Abdullah bought himself double trouble—larger responsibilities for a fractious population, many of whom considered him a traitor and a British lackey. He also earned the enmity of al-Husseini, which may have been worst of all.

Word from the Wise

For Christians there is no room for racial hatred. In Christ, Paul said, "There is no longer Jew or Gentile, slave or free, male or female." (Galatians 3:28, NLT) And beyond Christians of all stripes, we are called to love our neighbor, meaning all of those created by God in His image.

Many believe it was al-Husseini who ordered Abdullah's assassination the next year, in 1951 A.D. In any case, the king was fatally shot by a young Palestinian man as he entered al-Aqsa mosque in east Jerusalem.

After that, al-Husseini gradually faded into obscurity. He spent a number of uneventful years in Lebanon, where he died in 1974 A.D. He really had become irrelevant after 1964 A.D. with the founding of the Palestinian Liberation Organization, which co-opted al-Husseini's cause.

Ironically, it is commonly believed that al-Husseini's near kin—either uncle or cousin—is none other than PLO chief Yasser Arafat.

A Sleepy Arab Backwater—Shifting Control

A map of the region shows the northern and southern boundaries of Israel and Jordan neatly dovetailing. There is a reason for that. They were originally intended to be one—ever since the modern boundaries of most of the nations of the Middle East were drawn at the end of World War I with the defeat of the Turkish Ottoman Empire.

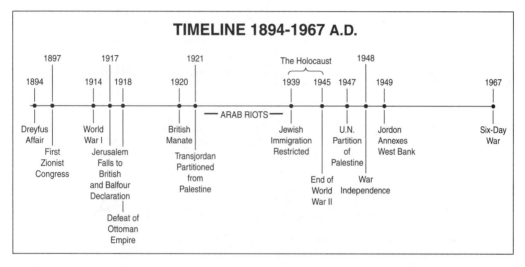

Israel grows from a movement into a nation.

The area called Palestine had been controlled by neither the Arabs nor the Jews for many centuries. (Mamluks and Ottomans were Islamic, but Turkish rather than Arab.) Historically, the sequence looks like this:

- Babylonians, Persians, Greeks 597–563 B.C.
- Romans 63 B.C.–330 A.D.
- Byzantines 330–638 A.D.
- Arabs (Fatimids and Abbasids) and Turks (Seljuks), 638–1099 A.D.
- Crusaders 1099–1291 A.D.
- Mamluks 1291–1516 A.D.
- Ottomans 1516–1917 A.D.
- Great Britain 1917–1948 A.D.

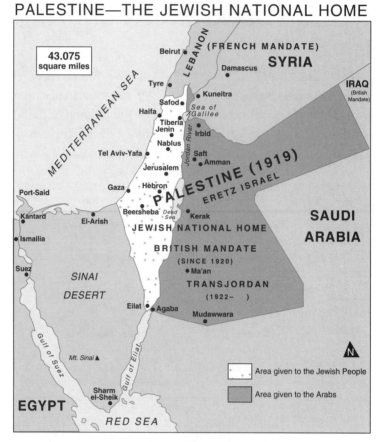

PALESTINE—THE JEWISH NATIONAL HOME

Palestine included both Israel and Transjordan.

Pockets of Jews continued to live in Palestine throughout these periods, but most were scattered throughout other parts of the Middle East, plus North Africa, and Europe. Many eventually made it to the New World as well. Ironically, they fared moderately well in Spain under Islamic rule and even enjoyed a flourishing golden age of Jewish culture.

Unfortunately, things went largely downhill after the Christian Reconquista. Jews were persecuted and even tortured during the thirteenth-century Inquisition, formal tribunals held to purge heretics. Again the year 1492 A.D. is pivotal, as the year the Spaniards gave the Jews an ultimatum—conversion or expulsion. Most fled, many back to their ancient roots in Palestine.

Eastern Europe was developing thriving Jewish communities as Jews were pushed out of many places in western and central Europe. In 1290 A.D., thousands of Jews were expelled from England, and in 1306 A.D. thousands more were expelled from France. Jews were often persecuted by European Christians throughout the Middle Ages and into the twentieth century as "Christ killers" and greedy money-lenders. Major Jewish population centers grew up around the world, especially:

- Damascus, Syria
- Alexandria, Egypt
- Corinth, Greece
- Rome, Italy
- Palestine

The famed British Empire was on the rise. France was also aggressive globally, and in 1869 A.D. French engineers completed the Suez Canal, which connected the Mediterranean Sea to the Red Sea through Egyptian territory. This cut the sailing time from Europe to the Far East in half and opened easier access out to the Arabian Sea and Indian Ocean.

Later, oil was discovered in some of the Arab lands. The effect of all this was to put the Middle East back on the map as strategically important territory to the world's major powers.

Palestine, meanwhile, had been languishing as what countless history books have described as "a sleepy Arab backwater of the Ottoman Empire." For centuries it was little more than a neglected Ottoman province consisting largely of deserts and malaria-infested swamps with little arable land and mostly Arab peasant farmers.

> **Reality Check**
>
> There never had been an actual state called Palestine ruled by people called Palestinians. Up to this time, not even the Palestinians thought of their territory as anything more than a southern region of Greater Syria, as it had been defined under pre-World War I Ottoman rule.

A National Jewish Homeland

Jewish migration to southern Syria (Palestine) accelerated in the late nineteenth century as pogroms began driving them out of Eastern Europe (especially Poland and Ukraine) and Russia. Soon a formal Zionist movement began to take shape, named after the Jerusalem mount upon which the Temple had been built.

Reality Check

There is probably more convenience than mystery to the Zionism name. "Palestine" was an Arab name that connoted Israel's ancient enemies (Philistines). Other names, such as "Israel" or "Judea," were ambiguous, relating to smaller subdivisions over the centuries. But when someone said "Zion," most Jews—whether in Africa, Asia, or Europe—would know instantly what was meant.

Word from the Wise

Was there some wisdom in this opposition view of some Orthodox Jews? "Unless the LORD builds a house, the work of the builders is useless. Unless the LORD protects a city, guarding it with sentries will do no good." (Psalm 127:1) To ponder: Or did God providentially use these political circumstances, created by man, to fulfill his larger prophetic plan?

In the late nineteenth century Palestine's population stood at about a half-million, about five percent Jewish and the rest Arab. By 1914 A.D., the Jewish population had climbed to about 60,000 or 11 percent. More Arabs began arriving, too, attracted by new jobs and commerce.

Zionism became a serious force around the turn of the century, largely through the efforts of Theodor Herzl, a charismatic Austrian journalist and secular Hungarian Jew. He became radicalized while covering the famous trial in Paris of Alfred Dreyfus, a French army officer who was being railroaded in a treason case because he was Jewish. Herzl came to believe that the only solution to Jewish persecution and rampant anti-Semitism was nationalism and statehood, and he began putting together a formal movement to promote it.

The idea caught on slowly. Many Orthodox Jews opposed the idea of a Jewish state, believing only God could restore Israel in his own time plan. To them, the idea of a secular Jewish state was almost anathema. In 1903 A.D., Great Britain offered 6,000 square miles of unsettled land in Uganda, Africa, to the World Zionist Organization as a homeland for the Jews, but the overture was rejected in 1905 A.D. by the Seventh Zionist Congress.

Europeans Carve the Pie

More than anything else, what turned the tide for the Jews was Turkey's entry into World War I on the side of Germany and Austria-Hungary against Britain, France, and Russia in 1914 A.D. Turkish defeat in 1918 A.D. meant the loss of many of its holdings in the old Ottoman Empire. Victorious Britain and France carved up the region between them.

The League of Nations granted the two countries "mandates"—that is, governing authority while the newly created states moved toward self-rule. France received Greater Syria—which eventually split into Syria and Lebanon. To Britain went:

- Palestine
- Transjordan (now Jordan)
- Iraq

Britain had already declared support for a Jewish homeland in Palestine in a famous document known as the Balfour Declaration in 1917 A.D. It also won the support of the United States and other Western powers. The Arabs, at first, were largely indifferent to the proposition. Some were even quite favorably disposed.

Emir Faisal, son of Arab leader Sherif Hussein of Mecca, put his endorsement in writing. "The Arabs," he wrote, "especially the educated among us, look with deepest sympathy on the Zionist movement …. We will wish the Jews a hearty welcome home …. We are working together for a reformed and revised Near East, and our two movements complete one another."

How odd Arab support for Zionism sounds today in retrospect. But this was before Haj Amin al-Husseini began stirring things up in Jerusalem. In addition, it was only later that secret political deals would come to light and severely alienate the Arabs.

British Prime Minister Lloyd George, a conservative Christian, saw this as a chance to recreate the biblical state of Israel "from Dan to Beersheba"—that is, in total, from north to south. Unfortunately, in the execution of the plan, the British government made contradictory and conflicting promises to the Arabs regarding self-governance that it could not keep—if it had ever really intended to do so.

From Disaster to Statehood

Backroom bargaining and secret agreements had been employed from the outset to get the Arabs onboard with Britain and France against the Germans and the Ottomans. Now it was payback time, and the British were caught up short, which only prompted more dealing. They attempted to secure friendly relations by installing members of the pro-Western Hashemite family as rulers.

In 1921 A.D., London agreed to recognize the rule of Abdullah ibn Heussein al Hashem (grandfather of the later well-known King Hussein) in Amman in return for his recognition of the British mandate over Palestine and a new emirate of Trans-jordan. Abdullah agreed, provided the emirate was exempted from provisions regarding the national Jewish homeland. When the Arab League found out about the deal, there was great consternation, but by then it was too late.

This "double dealing" on the part of the British led to much Arab bitterness. It became clear that both the Jews and the Arabs had been promised autonomy and self-governance in Palestine, and they couldn't have it both ways. It was a betrayal that would become part of a long-playing record for generations of Arabs, much like the Crusades.

The double dealings also paved the way for the eventual partitioning of Palestine into two regions—one Jewish, west of the Jordan River, and one Arab, east of the Jordan. Meanwhile, Jewish immigration into Palestine began to accelerate, and the Arabs west of the Jordan, in danger of becoming a minority, revolted against the British and the Jews. It was known as the Arab Rebellion and resembled today's *intifadas*.

> **Family Focus**
>
> What does it mean to "talk out of both sides of your mouth"? What kind of problems can it create? Discuss.

> **MidEast Dictionary**
>
> **Intifada** literally means uprising; insurrection of Palestinian Arabs against Israeli military forces in the Gaza Strip and West Bank. The first intifada began in December 1987 A.D. and the second in September 2000 A.D.

The Holocaust

Spearheaded by Mufti Haj Amin al-Husseini, there were attacks on Jewish settlements and random killings of Jews in the cities. Responding to the mufti's hate-filled preaching, Arabs rioted and attacked a number of Jewish settlements. The Jews abandoned Hebron after more than a hundred were slain and many more injured. Even so, the number of Jews in Palestine tripled in the 1920s to 160,000 and reached upwards of a half-million in the 1930s.

Palestine began to come alive again as Jews drained the swamps, began agricultural communes, built buildings, and started businesses despite violence and persecution. But by the 1930s both the British and the Jews had a bigger problem on their hands—in the person of Germany's Adolf Hitler.

Family Focus

Some historians have called the twentieth century the bloodiest ever. Anne Frank, a young Jewish girl killed in the Holocaust, wrote in her diary, despite everything: "I believe in the good of man." Discuss the Holocaust and your view of human nature and God's view. How much confidence can be placed in man-made—secular—justice and morality?

Now it was the Jews' turn to be betrayed. The British, weary of their burden under the mandate and unable to stop the fighting, succumbed to Arab pressures and began to curb Jewish immigration.

Unfortunately, hundreds of thousands of Jews in Europe were being rounded up and held in concentration camps, where few ever saw the light of day again. When the war ended, the sickening truth was revealed: Six million Jews had been exterminated, largely in death camps like the one at Treblinka, Poland. A third of the world's entire Jewish population was dead. The Nazis called it the Final Solution. The Jews called it the Holocaust—from the Hebrew word for a whole burnt offering.

Birth of the Nation

Thousands more Jews arrived in Palestine, many illegally. Many more refugees from displaced persons camps were refused entry at port, arousing sympathetic world opinion. Arabs bombed Ben Yehuda Street, a major Jewish thoroughfare in Jerusalem, killing many people.

The Jews began forming paramilitary organizations and fighting back. Jewish guerrillas massacred Arabs at Deir Yassin, a village west of Jerusalem. In 1946 A.D., the paramilitary group Irgun blew up a wing of the King David Hotel in Jerusalem, killing many in the British administration.

In 1947 A.D., the United Nations agreed to the partition of Palestine into separate Jewish and Arab states, triggering even more Arab violence. The British announced an end to their mandate in Palestine. On May 14, 1948, as British troops were withdrawing, Jewish leader David Ben-Gurion announced the Declaration of Independence of the State of Israel. That night the Egyptian air force bombed Tel Aviv. The Arab invasion of Israel began the next day.

War of Independence

The new country's Arab neighbors refused to recognize Israel's right to exist. Armies from five Arab states—Lebanon, Syria, Iraq, Jordan, and Egypt—launched attacks.

These became known as the Arab Legion, with Abdullah of Jordan as commander-in-chief.

Israel as it existed from 1949 to 1967 A.D.

Israel had an army of not quite 40,000 soldiers to face a similar number of Arabs armed with heavy artillery, tanks, and modern airplanes. For the Israeli side:

- A few thousand rifles
- A few light machine guns
- Several mortars
- No heavy artillery
- A half-dozen biplanes

Consequently, the Arab Legion captured substantial territory within Arab Palestine now known as the West Bank, but it failed to take some major strategic areas, including Jerusalem, which remained a mixed bag. The war was largely a draw, but Israel had its independence.

More Jews had become refugees overnight as several hundred thousand were expelled from angry Arab countries, including 260,000 from Morocco alone. Upwards of 750,000 Palestinian Arabs also became refugees as they fled from Israel into neighboring Arab countries, especially Jordan. Israel continued to grow by leaps and bounds. In the first three years of statehood, 700,000 immigrants arrived, doubling the population.

Amazing Discovery

Israel was founded as a secular state in 1948 A.D., but that same year the fledgling nation amazed the world with one of history's most significant archaeological discoveries, the Dead Sea Scrolls. They were discovered accidentally in some caves near the ruins of an old ultra-orthodox community called the Essenes from around the time of Christ.

The 2,000-year-old texts were 1,000 years older than the world's oldest biblical texts to that point, but were nearly identical in every respect. It was a major confirmation of the reliability of the Old Testament as the word of God—and a major setback for some modern secular critics.

Reality Check

Biblical scholars had long puzzled over Jesus' instruction in Luke 7 to tell John the Baptist that the blind, the lame, the lepers, and the deaf were being healed—and *the dead were being raised*. The last phrase was not in our modern text of Isaiah. But, lo and behold, it was in the Dead Sea Scrolls' version—the older version from which Jesus must have quoted!

The Six Day War

Under the fiery nationalist leader Gamal Abdel Nasser and with the support of the Soviet Union, Egypt continued to harass Israel. Egyptians trained young raiders called *fedayin* (sacrificers) in the Gaza and Sinai refugee camps, sending them into Israel on commando missions of terrorist violence. Finally, Egypt began blocking

Israeli shipping at the Suez Canal and the Gulf of Aqaba and moved troops across the Sinai to Israel's southern border in 1956 A.D. Egypt nationalized the Suez Canal, which got the unfavorable attention of the West.

Aided by Britain and France, Israel invaded the Sinai, pushed the Egyptians back across the Suez, and held on to the Sinai peninsula. In the face of international criticism—especially from U.S. President Dwight Eisenhower—all forces withdrew from the Sinai and were replaced by United Nations peacekeepers. However, Israel's Arab neighbors continued to threaten holy war against the Jewish state.

In 1967 A.D., Nasser ordered the UN troops out and moved his forces right back to the border. Jordan and Iraq agreed to place their troops under Egyptian command, threatening Israel from all sides with help from Syria. Israel, now much better armed and prepared for battle, struck first, conducting a successful lightning campaign from June 5 to June 10 that became known as the Six Day War.

Reality Check

Indicative of the degree of hostilities was a 1961 headline from a Saudi newspaper following the apprehension of a major German war criminal: "Capture of [Adolf] Eichmann, who had the honor of killing 5 million Jews."

This time Israel prevailed, destroying much of the Egyptian air force and pushing back enemy forces from her borders. Israel recaptured the Sinai peninsula and also took the Gaza Strip from Egypt. They also took the Golan Heights from Syria and the West Bank from King Hussein—including the Old City of Jerusalem, which had remained under Arab control and off limits for Jews.

Many Jews wept as they flocked to Zion and beheld with their own eyes the Temple Mount and prayed at the Western Wall, the last remnant of Herod's Second Temple wall that became known as the Wailing Wall.

Also a result of the war, Israel more than quadrupled its territory—from 8,000 to 34,000 square miles. Israel finally had some peace, security, and breathing room. In the process, however, a new problem was created—hundreds of thousands of Palestinian refugees.

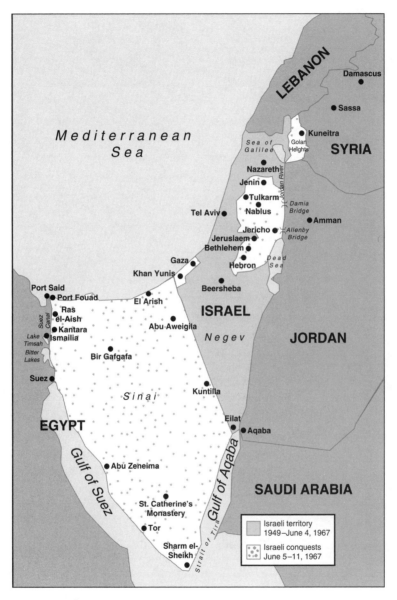

Israel after the Six Day War in 1967 A.D.

The Lands

We have explored the people, the religion, and the history. We have seen the three major subdivisions of the region—the Crescent, the Arabian Peninsula, and the Peripheries. Now it is time to drill down to a deeper level of detail and look at the individual nation states comprising the Middle East. We will profile each one by region plus a handful that are just outside the normal definition of the Middle East—such as Afghanistan— but are major players nonetheless. We'll even look at one that's not even a real nation, yet.

This is where it all starts to come together. Americans are accused of being among the most ignorant people when it comes to world geography. These profiles will not make anyone an expert, but they will serve as a basic introduction and fill out the foundation of our Middle East knowledge base. Some of these countries will get further attention later. Note at the end of each section are several vital statistics, including population, land size, and capital.

Chapter 9

Profiles: The Crescent

In this chapter, we will take a look at the countries comprising the "core" of the Middle East lands, sometimes called the Crescent (as in Fertile Crescent). At the heart of this story are the nations that are most synonymous with the Middle East—Iraq, Syria, Lebanon, Israel, and Jordan.

Iraq: A Fractious Mosaic

If the Arab National Congress in Damascus had had its way in 1920, there might have been something very much like a *pan-Arab* state in the world today. This congress voted to make Faisal ibn Hussein al-Hashem king of Greater Syria. Faisal was one of the Hashemite nobility, a direct descendant of Muhammad (37th-generation) and friendly to the British. He had been a key player in the Arab revolt against the Ottomans during World War I and a commander of forces opposing Turkish troops in a major operation.

Greater Syria, as envisioned, would have been sizeable, including:

- Syria
- Lebanon
- Israel
- Palestine
- Jordan

MidEast Dictionary

Pan-Arabism is the belief that Arabs everywhere belong to one community; some adherents have literally sought to create a single Arab state, reminiscent of the caliphate that ruled during the old Islamic Empire.

MidEast Dictionary

The **Sykes-Picot Pact** was a secret agreement between British and French diplomats to carve up the old Ottoman Empire among Britain, France, and Russia after their victory in World War I. Britain was to govern an area roughly equivalent to Iraq. France would rule the area of Syria. Russia would control Constantinople (now Istanbul) and parts of Turkey.

Faisal actually took the throne in Damascus briefly. The plan, however, ran into a little snag. Faisal was the British client in what had become a French spoil of war, Syria, as part of the post-World War I deal-making (especially the Sykes-Picot Agreement, 1916). The finishing touches were applied at a European conference in Cairo in 1921 as the parties literally spread out a map on the table and drew the new national boundaries. This is where the old land of Mesopotamia got its new name, Iraq.

As a result, Faisal was in a bit of a spot. The British had promised him a throne, but the French didn't see it that way, and now it was gone. Not to be blown off, he took his case to London and got a throne for his efforts, after all. The British installed him in Baghdad as Faisal I, king of Iraq, in August 1921. The state became a sovereign kingdom in 1932, the first Arab territory in this new world order to achieve independence. It would be nice to say everybody lived happily ever after, but that was just not the case.

The Wise Uncle

When the British deported Haj Amin al-Husseini from Palestine for his part in stirring up anti-British and anti-Jewish violence, the mufti of Jerusalem ended up for a time in Baghdad, Iraq. That was 1939. By 1941, Nazi sympathizer and propagandist al-Husseini was again stirring up trouble, this time against the pro-British monarchy in Iraq.

The mufti set up a political organization in Baghdad and cultivated relationships with pan-Arab nationalist officers in the military, including some who also had Nazi sympathies. A group of them attempted an abortive coup, prompting intervention by British forces to save the government. Al-Husseini, again just one step ahead of the British, fled to Iran, never to return to Iraq.

One of the ringleaders of the attempted coup was a man named Khayrallah Tulfah, who had been deeply affected by al-Husseini's fiery brand of politics and nationalism. His role in the abortive uprising had cost him his army career. It did not stop his political career, though, as Tulfah eventually became the mayor of Baghdad. None of that probably would have happened, however, except for his sister.

Tulfah's sister, a widow named Subha, was very poor and eventually remarried, wedding an illiterate peasant named Ibrahim. Ibrahim apparently had a mean streak and used to drag Subha's young son out of bed each morning, yelling, "Get up, you son of a whore, and look after the sheep!" The young boy became a child of the streets, selling watermelons in the village and dreaming of a better life.

At the age of ten, he moved to Baghdad to live with his Uncle Khayrallah, who treated him much better than his stepfather had back in the village. The uncle also infused him with liberal doses of radical pan-Arabism. Much later, the boy even ended up marrying Khayrallah's daughter, Sajida Tulfah, his cousin. Khayrallah invested well. It was through the boy that Khayrallah Tulfah was to see his political career resurrected.

The boy, you see, was a future national leader who would make history—Saddam Hussein.

One Fractious Country

Anger and resentment against the British and the Iraqi monarchy seethed for years until the country became a republic in 1958. Unfortunately, it came by way of the assassination of the 23-year-old grandson, Faisal II, in an army revolt. That led to martial law and a succession of repressive military governments replete with all kinds of thuggery.

This fractious country that had been united, at least, in its hatred of the British and the *Hashemites*, now lacked a central focus. It was—and still is—a very fragmented society, an artificial creation lacking major unifying features. In fact, it had many antagonistic elements:

- Sunnis and Shi'ites
- Christians and Jews
- Arabs and Kurds

In some ways, this was a situation virtually crying out for strongman rule.

MidEast Dictionary

Baath Party literally means "renaissance" in Arabic; an international Arab movement that advocated public ownership of major industries and natural resources and constitutional, representative government with guaranteed civil rights for citizens, such as freedom of speech, at least on paper. **Hashemites** are descendants of the prophet Muhammad's clan (named after his great-grandfather Hashem ibn Abdul Manaf) and a royal line that was displaced by the Ottoman sultans.

Into this mix came the Iraqi *Baath* Socialist Party, clandestinely at first. It was a branch of the larger, international Baath Socialists that had been growing in the region. Baathists were pan-Arabists, believing in one Arab nation, no matter how it was divided into individual states.

In Iraq, the Baaths fought their way into power. In 1959, Iraqi strongman Abdul Karim Qasim barely escaped an assassination attempt with injuries. Young Saddam Hussein, admitted triggerman in the machine-gun attack, also was injured. He nevertheless made a daring escape, managing to dig a bullet out of his leg in the process, according to his own claims. Qasim was overthrown by a coalition of opposition forces five years later, and then in 1968 the Baath Party seized sole control in a purge of its rivals.

Reality Check

Another major development under Saddam Hussein was the rebuilding of the ancient city of Babylon in the middle of the desert in the 1980s, mostly as a tourist attraction. There was also a political motive in drawing a connection to their most famous ancient conqueror. Every six feet is a brick stamped: "The Babylon of Nebuchadnezzar reconstructed in the era of Saddam Hussein."

Saddam Hussein became vice president and eventually deposed President Ahmad Hassan al-Bakr in 1979. Fighting an alleged coup threat, Hussein had 22 government officials executed, though accounts vary as to whether it was by hanging or firing squad. In more than 20 years of strong-man rule under Saddam Hussein, Iraq has had a colorful career. Some major events are as follows:

- 1981—Israeli jet bombers attack and destroy a nuclear reactor at Al Tuwaitha, just outside Baghdad, that would have been capable of producing weapons-grade nuclear material.

- 1980–1988—Iraq attacks Iran over territorial disputes, leading to an inconclusive and costly eight-year war.

- 1988—Iraq drops chemical bombs on Kurds at Halabjah, killing 5,000, as part of a weapons "test."

- 1990—Iraq invades Kuwait and attempts to annex the country.

- 1991—A U.S.-led coalition drives Iraq from Kuwait in Operation Desert Storm. The United Nations imposes trade sanctions until Iraq complies with required destruction of weapons of mass destruction and long-range missiles.

- 2002—UN weapons inspectors, barred for several years, return to search for evidence of chemical, biological, and nuclear weapons under threat of renewed military action from the United States and allies.

- 2003—United States and Coalition forces invade Iraq to disarm the country of weapons of mass destruction and to remove Saddam Hussein from power.

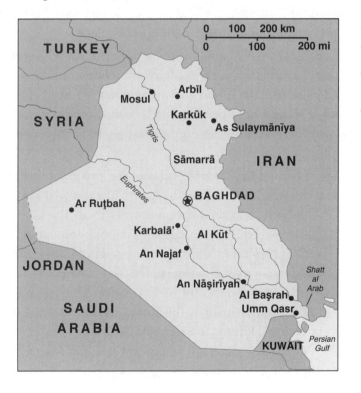

Iraq has about 24 million people in a country slightly more than twice the size of Idaho; its capital is Baghdad. It is a major oil-producing nation.

Iraq is one story that just won't quit. It will come up again as a central player in several later chapters dealing with oil and several Persian Gulf wars.

Syria: A Wiley Political Player

Syria, awarded to France after World War I, was administered by the French until it gained independence right after World War II. In the interest of the pan-Arab movement, Syria accepted an invitation in 1958 to merge with Egypt in a short-lived creation called the United Arab Republic (UAR). The union never progressed much beyond paper, partly because Egypt's Nasser and the rising Baath Party in Syria came into conflict.

The UAR came to an end in 1961 with a Syrian military coup that changed the government. Two years later the Baath Party took over. An air force commander, Gen. Hafez al-Assad, became defense minister in the new regime. Then in 1970, he led a bloodless coup that put him in the driver's seat for the next 30 years. He was long known as one of the wiliest leaders in the Middle East. When Assad died in 2000 from heart disease, his son, Bashir, stepped right into his place.

Assad and many of his associates have come from the minority Alawite sect of Islam. Like Saddam Hussein, Assad stacked the top government and military positions with his relatives and close friends. Assad and many other Syrians believed that Lebanon and Syria never should have been divided. Assad sent troops into Lebanon during the civil war there in the 1980s, and there they have stayed, ostensibly as peace-keepers.

Syria under Hafez al-Assad tended to play both sides of the street politically, especially when it came to terrorism. It was home to players like terrorist kingpin Abu Nidal and the Muslim Brotherhood. The United States placed Syria on its list of nations sponsoring terrorism. Britain broke off diplomatic relations after Nizar Hindawi, a man attached to the Syrian embassy, placed a bomb on an Israeli airliner in London. During an uprising of Sunni Muslims, the Syrian military leveled the city of Hamah, killing an estimated 20,000 people.

Syria lost the Golan Heights to Israel in the 1967 war, which has been a constant source of friction ever since. Israel has built new settlements there, and many Druze also live there.

> ### Word from the Wise
>
> Consider God's possible purposes in the rise and fall of nations and leaders. "He determines the course of world events; he removes kings and sets others on the throne." (Daniel 2:21, NLT) How might you see that being played out in the Middle East today?

Syria has been a vocal and vehement critic of United States policy in the Middle East for years. Nevertheless, Syria allied itself with the United States coalition in the 1991 Gulf War after Syrian negotiations with Iraq failed to roll back the Kuwait invasion. Syria even contributed some troops to the defense of Saudi Arabia.

All of that, however, may have had more to do with chilly relations it has had with Iraq for years. Syria also has testy relations with its neighbor to the north, Turkey, especially over water.

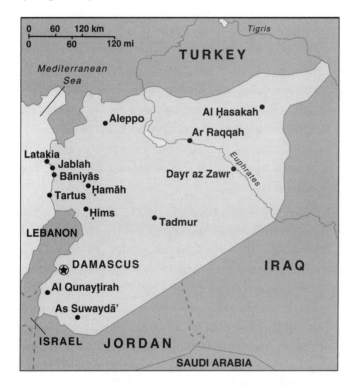

Syria has 17.2 million people and is slightly larger than North Dakota; its capital is Damascus.

Lebanon: Uneasy Home of Christians and Muslims

Lebanon is the land of the ancient Phoenicians, a seafaring people who migrated to that part of the Mediterranean just north of the land of Israel during Bible times. Modern Lebanon was part of the Syrian mandate to France following World War I and gained its independence from France at the end of World War II.

It is unique in its religious composition for an Arab nation, being evenly split for generations between Christian and Muslim. That has changed in recent years with a drop in the Christian portion to more like 30 percent as many Christians have fled the civil strife plaguing the nation. The legacy continues to echo in Lebanon's institutions. By law, half the representatives to the national assembly are Muslim and half Christian, and the same principle applies in the executive branch.

MidEast Dictionary

Hezbollah ("party of God") is an Iranian-backed Palestinian terrorist organization headquartered in the Bekaa Valley of southern Lebanon.

Family Focus

Discuss the idea of "Christian" militias involved in ethnic and religious fighting. The Bible clearly gives nations the right to defend themselves and execute criminals, but what about religious groups? What kind of testimony is it to the world when Christians commit violence?

Lebanon endured a long, exhausting civil war from 1975 to 1990 A.D., largely between Muslim and Christian militias. During those years, it also became a hotbed for terrorism with the Palestinian Liberation Organization opening a headquarters in Beirut, and *Hezbollah* following closely behind. Beirut, once known as the Paris of the Middle East, turned into a war zone as militias traded fire from East Beirut to West and back. It ceased to be safe for Americans, as journalist Terry Anderson and several others were held captive for months and years by hostage-taking terrorists.

In 1978, Israel, tired of terrorist incursions across its border, invaded south Lebanon to destroy PLO bases there only to return four years later. This time they set up a more permanent security zone and occupied major portions of the south for some time. Military peacekeepers from several nations also entered Lebanon in an ill-fated attempt to put a lid on. In 1983, tragedy struck in the form of a terrorist truck bomb, killing 241 U.S. Marines in their barracks in Beirut. That same night 50 more French troops were killed in a separate attack at a command post.

Finally, Syria intervened in 1987, sending in its troops. An estimated 20,000 troops are still there in what has become a de facto occupation. Initially, the forces came at the request of the Lebanese president, concerned about prospects for an imminent slaughter of Christian forces.

Nevertheless, Jeanne Kirkpatrick, former U.S. ambassador to the United Nations, has denounced the Syrian occupation of Lebanon, calling it a "death grip" by a repressive regime. Considering the unceasing controversy over Israel's "occupied territories," it does seem ironic that the international community has remained silent by comparison regarding Syria's military intervention. Perhaps it's just collective relief that the fighting finally had stopped.

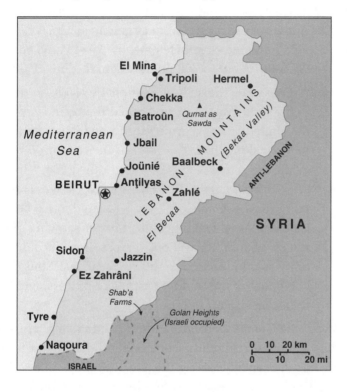

Lebanon has a population of 3.6 million and is about three fourths the size of Connecticut; its capital is Beirut.

Israel: Surrounded by Adversaries

If you count from the Jews' expulsion from Jerusalem in 135 A.D. by the Romans after the Bar Kochba revolt, it was all of 1,800 years between ancient and modern statehood for the Jews when Israel was reborn in 1948. However, the Jews in small numbers maintained a continuous presence in the Holy Land throughout those centuries, though in scattered pockets and in a definite minority status.

Actually, it wasn't until 1967 that the Jews were back in the Old City of their ancient capital, Jerusalem. That was the year of the war that won back major portions of real estate in Palestine—and the event that the Arabs call *An Naqba*, the catastrophe, when they not only failed to push Israel out, but they themselves suffered major setbacks. No doubt about it—there was going to be a rematch.

Israel was caught largely by surprise in 1973 when its Arab neighbors, particularly Egypt and Syria, struck again, in an attempt to win back what they'd lost in 1967. This time the conflict lasted 19 days and resulted in heavy casualties on both sides, but the results were largely inconclusive. Israel held on to the Golan Heights, the West Bank, and the Gaza Strip, but took a pounding in the Sinai Peninsula.

Word from the Wise

The ancient nation of Israel had a very effective secret weapon: "Some nations boast of their armies and weapons, but we boast in the Lord our God." (Psalm 20:7, NLT) The original language speaks of trusting in horses and chariots. What was the modern state of Israel trusting in—God or its armies and weapons?

The conflict raised international tensions in the midst of the Cold War. Moscow backed Egypt and Syria, and the United States, alarmed that a huge disaster might be in the making, had its forces on nuclear alert for a time. While the actual results of the so-called Yom Kippur War of 1973 were far short of earthshaking, it was a definite point for the Arab side. They had fared much better this time militarily, making a much better showing of themselves. That, in turn, shook Israel's illusions of invincibility as it looked to the future. Some mark this as the beginning of the Middle East peace process, which continues on and off today.

Three years after this war, the Israelis were sitting down and talking terms. The world was surprised when Egyptian President Anwar Sadat did an about-face and established relations with Israel, even addressing the Israeli Knesset. In a series of historic meetings at Camp David, Maryland, President Jimmy Carter brokered a peace treaty between Sadat and Israel's Menachem Begin. Israel agreed to return the Sinai Peninsula, and Egypt agreed to formal recognition of Israel, which for an Arab nation was a radical step.

It was so radical, in fact, that Sadat was assassinated two years later by Islamic militants. The PLO and others felt that Sadat had betrayed them. Pan-Arabists especially believed individual states should not be making separate peace deals with Israel.

Others claimed major progress, noting that most Arab states were now moving away from absolute opposition to Israel's existence and toward more specific issues in their adversarial relationship. The PLO, in this view, had shifted its focus and energies from the destruction of Israel to the creation of a Palestinian state. At least, that's the claim.

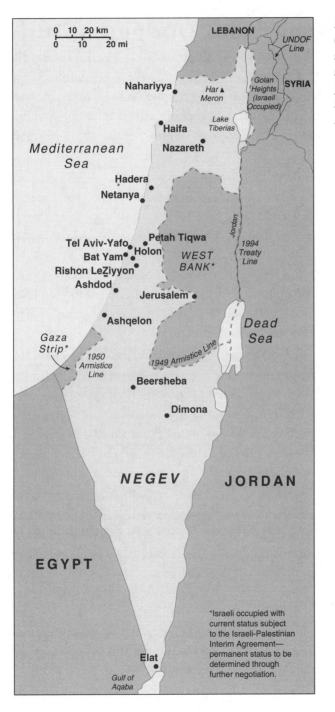

Israel has a population of about 6 million and is slightly smaller than New Jersey. Its self-proclaimed capital is Jerusalem, but most nations have their embassies in Tel Aviv.

Jordan: The King Who Dodged a Bullet

Jordan was the land of Ammon, Moab, and Edom in Bible times and later the land of various *Bedouin* tribes. After World War I, Hashemite leader Abdullah ibn Hussein al Hashem entered Transjordan with his troops and set up rule in Amman. The British colonial secretary for the region (Winston Churchill) agreed to an independent emirate of Transjordan in 1923 A.D. upon Abdullah's agreement to abide by the British mandate.

Jordan became an independent kingdom in 1946 A.D. under Abdullah I, who was the grandfather of longtime Jordanian leader King Hussein and great-grandfather of the current king, Abdullah II. (Abdullah's son, Talal, served very briefly on the throne due to mental illness.) Young Prince Hussein was standing right next to King Abdullah when assassins' bullets felled his grandfather, killing him outside the al-Aqsa mosque in Jerusalem. The way Hussein told it, one bullet glanced off a medal on his own chest, narrowly averting serious injury.

MidEast Dictionary

Bedouin is an Arab of any of the nomadic desert peoples of Arabia, Syria, or North Africa.

Reality Check

The new King Abdullah also has some Western tastes, including science fiction. Before becoming king, he visited the television set of "Star Trek: Voyager" in 1995 in Los Angeles. Moreover, he was given a walk-on (non-speaking) role as a medical technician in the episode "Investigations." That's definitely one for the Trekkie record books.

King Hussein grew quickly into his position. He responded to the merger of Egypt and Syria in the United Arab Republic by proposing a merger of his own—Jordan with Iraq. Those plans were derailed by a military coup in Iraq. While Egypt and Syria plotted to depose him, Hussein pursued close ties with the United States and maintained an intelligence-sharing relationship.

Jordan had a more troubled relationship with the quarter of a million Palestinian refugees it absorbed from Israel. The king's patience with the Palestinians was exhausted during the 10-day Black September civil war in 1970 A.D. A terrorist group, the Popular Front for the Liberation of Palestine, blew up several Western airliners near Amman when Israel refused to buckle to demands to release its Palestinian prisoners. The government eventually subdued the insurgents and expelled a number of the Palestinian commandos.

Trying a political approach to the Palestinian problem, Hussein proposed creating a United Arab Kingdom—essentially a merger of Jordan and Palestine (West Bank) with East Jerusalem as its capital. This presumably would have forced the Israelis to withdraw from those occupied territories. The idea was rejected, however, by the Palestine National Council in 1972. The Council also rejected a similar proposal 15 years later involving Yasser Arafat that would have created a Palestinian state in tandem with Jordan.

Hussein defied stereotyping. He refused to join Egypt and Syria in the 1973 war against Israel, but he also refused to join in the Camp David peace process in 1979. Jordan sided with Iraq in both the Iran-Iraq war and the later Gulf War, costing him some points in the West. In 1994, Hussein signed a peace treaty with Israeli Premier Yitzhak Rabin, becoming the second Arab nation to make peace with Israel. Western-educated Abdullah bin Hussein (Abdullah II) took the throne in 1999 upon his father's death.

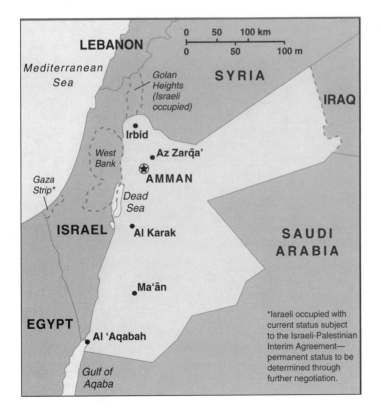

Jordan has a population of 5.3 million and is slightly smaller than Indiana; its capital is Amman.

Chapter 10

Profiles: The Arabian Peninsula

In this chapter we will focus on the birthplace of Islam and the home of the world's largest oil reserves, the Arabian Peninsula. Here we find some of the most conservative Arab states and even some strong United States allies among the seven—Saudi Arabia, Bahrain, Kuwait, Oman, Qatar, United Arab Emirates, and Yemen.

Fundamentalist Fervor

It may have been the world's record for total number of hostages taken at one time—50,000. However, the fact that it happened at Mecca's holiest place was even more shocking.

It was November 1979, and a great multitude of pilgrims had gathered for prayers at dawn in the courtyard of the Grand Mosque when shots rang out. Then a bearded man came forward, identified over the public address system as the long-awaited *Mahdi*. Thousands of panicked worshipers tried to escape, but hundreds of armed followers of the "Mahdi" were inside, locking the gates and shooting those who resisted.

The rebels, led by this extremist named Juhaiman, denounced the Saudi regime as illegitimate for corruption, Westernization, and plain old bad habits, like drinking and gambling. King Khalid ordered in the Saudi Army and National Guard, but the rebels had managed to hole themselves up in a labyrinth of underground passages beneath the mosque complex. Also, according to Islamic law, it was forbidden to pollute a holy place, especially by the shedding of blood.

The standoff lasted for several weeks. The government obtained special dispensation from the *ulama* for bearing arms in a holy place since it had already been desecrated by bloodshed. Finally, the troops managed to overpower the rebels, with tactical advice from France, but not before more than 200 rebels and troops had been killed in the fighting. In the aftermath, 63 rebels were publicly beheaded, including Juhaiman.

This was also the year that the Ayatollah Khomeini came to power in Iran, setting up the first Islamic theocracy. Khomeini-style fundamentalist fervor had inspired the uprising against the Saudi royal family. Khomeini, a harsh critic of the Saudis, lashed out at the United States and Israel, suggesting that the Americans and the Zionists were behind the desecration of Mecca's Grand Mosque.

Just the suggestion was enough to trigger anti-American riots in a dozen countries, including Pakistan, where the U.S. Embassy in Islamabad was burned down. Twenty-two years later a Saudi expatriate named Osama bin Laden was railing against the royal family and the infidel U.S. troops desecrating the land of the Holy Places. Except in this case, bin Laden had the wherewithal to bring down the World Trade Center, symbol of U.S. world power. When the smoke had cleared, America learned that 15 of the 19 hijackers, too, were Saudis.

Saudi Arabia: Islam and Oil

Saudi Arabia is most famous for two things—the birthplace of Islam and the world's largest oil reserves. The kingdom developed in just half a century from a poor desert tribal society into one of the world's wealthiest nations.

In the seventh century A.D. Muhammad received his revelations here, establishing the new religion first in Medina, then Mecca, before Islamic armies carried it to the rest of the Middle East. Arabia declined in importance a few years after Muhammad's death as the Islamic capital moved to Damascus and eventually to Baghdad.

In the sixteenth century Ottoman Turks gained control of most of Arabia. In the eighteenth century the Wahhabism movement, a strict, puritanical form of Islam, swept the peninsula. The Wahhabis hated appearances of idolatry, especially veneration of Muslim saints, and they even destroyed tombs of these saints. They believed in the strictest adherence to the doctrines of *Sharia*, and desired to purify Islam from diluting and corrupting influences.

MidEast Dictionary

Sharia is Islamic law and detailed code of Islamic behavior; Sharia calls for murderers to be beheaded by the sword, thieves to have their right hands cut off, adulterers to be stoned to death, and drunkards to be flogged.

A religious-political alliance of its founder, Muhammad bin Abdul al-Wahhab, and Muhammad ibn Saud, the founder of the Saud family dynasty, made Wahhabism into a powerhouse. Though the Ottomans tried to suppress it, the sect spread all the way down to present-day Yemen and the Arabian Sea. It is the dominant form of Islam in Saudi Arabia today, and it is even a strong influence on the growth of Islam in North America, as the Saudis have made development funds available for schools and mosques.

The Saudi Kingdom

The Saud family had been driven out of Arabia, partly because of religious differences, into Kuwait, where they lived for many years. Then clan leader Abdul Aziz ibn Abdul Rahman al-Saud returned to the homeland at the end of the nineteenth century. His forces captured Riyadh, today's capital, in 1902 and defeated the Arab clan allied with the Ottoman Empire. Abdul Aziz spent years consolidating new territories, finally proclaiming a unified kingdom of Saudi Arabia in 1932 A.D.

Abdul Aziz (also called Ibn Saud) ruled for the next 21 years until his death in 1953, but they were very busy years. Like King Solomon, Abdul Aziz believed in political marriages. First he married a princess from the defeated Rashid clan, then proceeded to wed a daughter from virtually every tribe in his kingdom.

Abdul Aziz eventually fathered some 45 sons. From these princes came the next four kings, half-brothers Saud, Faisal, Khalid, and Fahd—each with his own unique style of leadership and outlook.

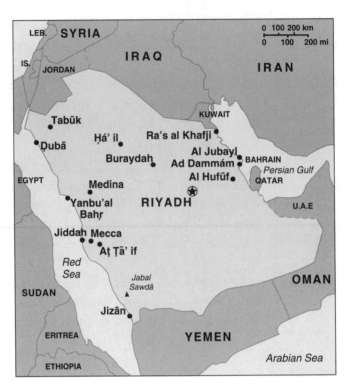

Saudi Arabia has a population of 23.5 million and is slightly more than one fifth the size of the United States; its capital is Riyadh.

 Word from the Wise

According to Deuteronomy 8:18, where do we get the ability to produce wealth? What does 1 Timothy 6:17 say about where we are to place our hope? "Tell those who are rich in this world not to be proud and not to trust in their money, which will soon be gone. But their trust should be in the living God, who richly gives us all we need for our enjoyment." Can we trust God to provide for us, even in our own desert?

Oil was discovered in the kingdom in 1938, which would bring incredible change to the desert kingdom. However, World War II broke out before oil production could get into high gear. These hostilities prompted the United States to recognize the strategic importance of Saudi oil reserves and to begin cultivating a close relationship with the kingdom, pledging U.S. protection.

In 1951, the two countries entered into a mutual defense pact. The United States established a permanent training mission for Saudi forces and helped build a number of military facilities. America has been a major arms supplier to the kingdom, and both sides continue to have much invested in this relationship.

Saud, the family leader after Abdul Aziz, was not a particularly savvy king. Worse, he caused the family embarrassment with wild living and extravagant spending. Slowly and secretively, Saud finally was deposed in 1964 through family maneuverings behind closed doors.

He was succeeded by Faisal, who was in power when the Arab-Israeli war broke out in 1973. Faisal led the Arab oil producers in an oil embargo of the United States for its support of Israel and especially its resupply of military hardware. The price of oil eventually grew fourfold.

Culture Shock

Oil-producing Arab nations were experiencing unprecedented prosperity and a rapid rise in the standard of living. Many of their best and brightest young people were being sent overseas to get their education in the West precisely at a time when counter-cultural forces—especially drugs and the sexual revolution—were at their height. For Middle Eastern families, this produced a great deal of culture shock.

The pendulum was bound to swing the other way in time. The trigger was the 1975 assassination of King Faisal by a mentally troubled nephew. After police questioning to establish he'd been acting alone, the nephew was publicly executed.

> **Family Focus**
>
> Discuss the deterioration of family values here in the United States. How are unwholesome values—such as drug use, sexual promiscuity, obscenity, and violence—expressed in the entertainment media? How is this different from a generation or two ago? Discuss how to deal with these influences.

Faisal, a devout Muslim, nevertheless had been pushing a modernization effort, including the introduction of Western technology. The first television broadcasts began in 1965 A.D., offending some Muslims, including another of the king's nephews, who was killed in a police shoot-out during an assault on one of the television stations.

Faisal's killer, the younger brother of that other nephew, may have been acting out a political vendetta. It was well known that this young man had come under Western influence as a frequent visitor to the United States and Western Europe. He had attended several American colleges and reportedly had dabbled in hallucinogenic drugs.

The Faisal assassination sent shock waves through an Arab world already inclined to believe that the West and Westernization were the root of all evil. Moreover, it seemed to confirm that only an unconditional return to the ways of traditional Islam could avert the same fate for the Arab nations as had already befallen the wicked West. A real backlash was beginning.

Modernization

Khalid, who succeeded Faisal, also was a modernizer. He invested petrodollars into major public construction projects, infrastructure, and improvements in social services, particularly education and health care. He also funded the numerous *madrassas* in Saudi Arabia and elsewhere that may have been used to train militants to fight in Afghanistan against the Soviets in the 1980s.

MidEast Dictionary

Madrassa is a Muslim school, especially for the study of the Quran and Islamic law.

Word from the Wise

Can we pray expectantly for a turning of Arab peoples to Christ? Isaiah 60 is filled with references to various Arab peoples in the eternal kingdom established at Christ's return. "The flocks of Kedar will be given to you ..." (Isaiah 60:7, NLT). How might God bring that to pass? Read Isaiah 60:1–7 prayerfully.

Khalid suffered from heart problems and died of a heart attack in 1982. He was succeeded by Fahd, who was on the throne when Iraq invaded Kuwait in 1990. He alienated some in the Arab world by calling for help from the United States to protect Saudi Arabia from the aggression next door. Ultimately other Arab nations agreed and actually joined the Desert Storm coalition.

Since then, about 5,000 U.S. troops have remained in the kingdom. Violently disagreeing was Osama bin Laden, son of a very wealthy Saudi construction magnate. Bin Laden and his followers claimed that even having U.S. troops on Saudi soil was a desecration of the land of the Holy Places.

More recently, Crown Prince Abdullah, Fahd's half-brother, has been running the day-to-day business of the kingdom since Fahd suffered a heart attack in 1995. Abdullah is less friendly to America and more sympathetic to Islamic causes, especially the Palestinian issue.

In 1996, 19 U.S. servicemen were killed in a truck bomb attack on the Khobar Towers, a U.S. military residence in Dharan. A United States federal grand jury indicted 13 Saudis for the attack, but Saudi Arabia was uncooperative in the investigation to the point of refusing extradition.

In 1997, the Saudis were one of only three countries to recognize the Taliban government of Afghanistan. The Taliban were followers of Deobandi Islam, a radical form of the faith closely resembling Wahhabism. After the September 11th attack on America, the Saudis broke off relations, blaming the Taliban for evil influences on the Saudis involved in the attack.

A "Faustian Bargain"

The United States and Saudi Arabia continue to have an uneasy relationship. The kingdom may have bankrolled the Pakistan nuclear weapons program. Human rights groups say the Saudis perform some 200 beheading executions a year, including adulterers and drinkers convicted for the third time. (Otherwise, drinkers only get 100 lashes.) It is a special worry for Christians—spreading the gospel is a capital offense.

Reality Check

Faust was a philosopher in legends from medieval times and later literature who bargained with the devil to obtain special knowledge and power, in exchange for his soul. It has come to mean any agreement that costs too much in the end.

Some Americans have come to wonder whether the Saudis are friends or foes. Senator John McCain and others have been particularly critical of the Saudis' financial support for radical causes. The Saudis, said McCain, have been "engaged in a Faustian bargain with the radical Islamic fundamentalists for many, many years in order to stay on the throne."

Bahrain: A Little Pioneer

Tiny Bahrain, a 33-island archipelago in the Persian Gulf, is the smallest of the Arabian peninsula states.

As a gulf island nation, its inhabitants have had greater exposure to foreign people and outside ideas than the Arab tribes of the interior. So Bahrainis lead a somewhat less strait-laced and more laid-back lifestyle. Other Arabs tend to come here to kick back and relax. There are also many foreign workers living here.

Bahrain was the first Arab state to discover oil and has been a pioneer in other things. It was the first to build an airport, to install satellite-based telecommunications, and to provide free public education. Bahrain produces some oil, but does more processing and refining. The country also serves as a major international banking center.

It is a kingdom, ruled for years by the Khalifa dynasty. Bahrain is one of three nations in the world with a Shi'ite Muslim majority, but the royal family, as in Iraq, are actually Sunni.

Bahrain has a population of 650,000 and is 3.5 times the size of Washington, D.C.; its capital is Manama.

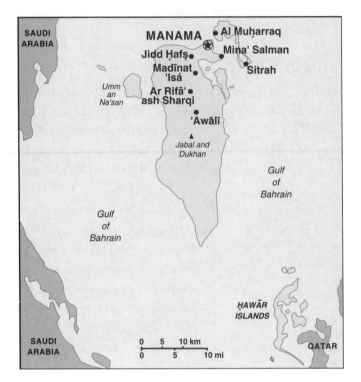

Kuwait: A Vulnerable Oil Kingdom

Kuwait means "little fort" in Arabic, which reflects its defensive position sandwiched between two giants, Iraq and Saudi Arabia. Oil has been Kuwait's blessing as well as its curse.

It has 10 percent of the world's oil reserves, which has made it one of the world's richest nations. It is a land of millionaires, and there is virtually no poverty. Kuwait provides free health care and even free higher education for all, even for studying overseas.

This oil wealth also has made it a target for aggression. It angered Iraq in 1990 by flooding the market with oil, depressing oil prices and harming Iraq's economy just

Family Focus

Are you aware that there are a few countries in the world that have a higher average standard of living than the United States? Would you prefer to live in a country like Kuwait that provides even greater material benefits to its citizens? Why or why not?

when it was struggling to recover from the long Iran–Iraq war. Iraq invaded and attempted to annex Kuwait, which led to the 1991 Gulf War with the United States and its allies.

Coalition forces expelled the Iraqis in four days, but much damage was done. Iraq's seven-month occupation was marked by brutality, including summary execution, rape, and confiscation of Kuwaiti property.

Kuwait was a British protectorate in the early 1900s. It is a monarchy, ruled by a hereditary emirate. Fully half of Kuwait's residents are foreign laborers.

Kuwait has a population of 2.1 million and is slightly smaller than New Jersey; its capital is Kuwait City.

Oman: The Land of Frankincense

Oman, the land of *frankincense*, is strategically located on the southeastern edge of the Arabian peninsula by the Strait of Hormuz, the narrow passage from the Persian

Gulf to the Arabian Sea. It was once a virtual colony of Great Britain and is now a staunch ally of the United States.

Under a joint military cooperation agreement, the United States provides aid and enjoys use of Omani air and naval facilities. Oman was the only Arab state to endorse the Camp David peace accord in 1979 and one of the few not to sever relations with Egypt for making peace with Israel. Oman also joined the U.S.-led coalition against Iraq in Operation Desert Storm.

Oman fought a lengthy civil war with leftists beginning in 1963, finally quelling the rebellion in 1976 with help from Britain, Iran, Jordan, and Saudi Arabia. Britain helped engineer a coup in 1970 to replace the tyrannical sultan with his son, Qaboos, a more progressive leader.

Oman has become a significant oil producer. Three fourths of the population are Ibadhis, followers of another reformist sect of Islam.

MidEast Dictionary

Frankincense is a costly, fragrant gum resin obtained from Arabian and African trees, among the royal gifts to the Christ child; some see this as evidence that the magi might have come from Arabia rather than Persia or Babylon.

Oman has a population of 2.7 million and is slightly smaller than Kansas; its capital is Muscat.

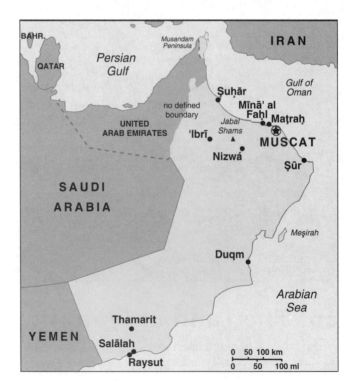

Qatar: Progressive U.S. Ally

Qatar, a thumb of land projecting from Arabia into the Persian Gulf, is perhaps an even stronger United States ally in the Gulf region and is firmly committed to rapid modernization.

It is a significant producer of natural gas and is a home for many foreign workers, particularly Asians. Qatar already has made major strides toward a high standard of living, and it has a per capita GDP (gross domestic product) similar to that of many Western nations.

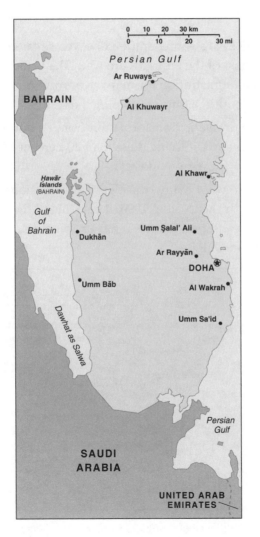

Qatar has a population of 793,000 and is slightly smaller than Connecticut; its capital is Doha.

Qatar has provided the United States with a very strategic base for launching an attack on Iraq, which became more crucial with Saudi Arabia's refusal to allow its territory to be used for that purpose. Qatar also was a coalition partner in the U.S. Desert Storm operation.

The country, a former British protectorate, is a monarchy ruled by the al-Thani family. It is largely Sunni Muslim of the Wahhabi sect, like the Saudis.

United Arab Emirates: A High Standard of Living

The United Arab Emirates (UAE) is a confederation of seven separate emirates that merged in 1971–1972. The largest of the emirates are Abu Dhabi and Dubai. The emirates had been under British administration for many years and are now ruled by a president and seven emirs who form a Supreme Council of Emirs.

The UAE has experienced a dramatic transformation from a poor desert region to a modern state with a high standard of living. Less than 20 percent of the population are UAE citizens, the rest mostly foreign workers.

The country joined Kuwait in what many considered an intentional plot to harm Iraq by flooding the market with cheap oil in 1990. It also joined the U.S. coalition in the war against Iraq in 1991. In addition, the UAE has ongoing disputes with Iran over some islands in the Persian Gulf.

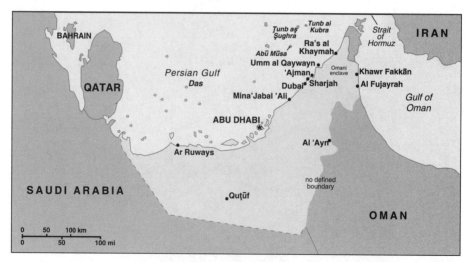

The UAE has a population of 2.4 million and is slightly smaller than Maine; its capital is Abu Dhabi.

Yemen: Strife-Torn Land

Yemen, separated from the rest of the Arabian peninsula by a mountain range, has traditionally been one of the poorest countries in the Arab world. Even today, it may still be the best place to go to observe Arab lifestyles as they existed centuries ago.

Reality Check

In relation to the Arabian peninsula, the former South Yemen is actually east of North Yemen. In fact, South Yemen actually extends farther north than North Yemen.

It also has been a land of great strife with long civil wars, coups, and presidential assassinations. Now it is a republic, formed from the merger of North Yemen and South Yemen in 1990. The British withdrew in 1967 from South Yemen, which became a Marxist state. This is unusual for Islamic countries, which have been antagonistic to the atheistic worldview of communism.

South Yemen became known as the People's Democratic Republic of Yemen. Hundreds of thousands of residents fled into North Yemen as a result of the political turmoil. Nevertheless, the Marxist regime lost steam as Soviet aid dried up at the end of the Cold War.

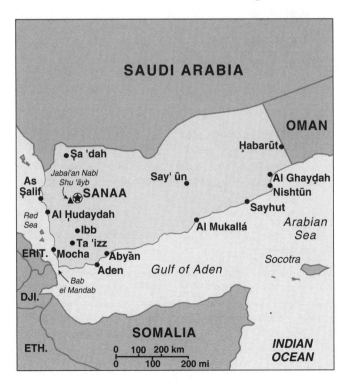

Yemen has a population of 18.7 million and is slightly more than twice the size of Wyoming; its capital is Sanaa.

Yemen continues to march to a different beat. Unlike most of its neighbors, it opposed the Gulf War and even voted against it on the United Nations Security Council. This action did nothing to endear them to the Saudis. Yemen has continued to struggle economically, but increased oil production has helped to ease some of its debt.

Profiles: The Peripheries

This chapter deals with the nations at the southern and western extremes of the Middle East. Technically, Egypt—the largest country in the region—is sometimes considered part of the Middle East core. It certainly has been one of the major central players. Yet, Egypt has one big thing in common with the others—Libya, Tunisia, Algeria, Morocco, Sudan, Ethiopia, and Somalia: They are all part of northern Africa.

The Egyptian Who Changed History

October 6, 1981, was the eighth anniversary of the Yom Kippur War and Egypt's crossing of the Suez Canal to push back Israeli occupation forces in the Sinai Peninsula. That was when Egypt finally restored its national pride following its humiliation in the Six Day War of 1967. The occasion was marked in Cairo by a festive military parade.

President Anwar Sadat rose to face four soldiers as they approached the reviewing stand, thinking they had come to salute him. They hadn't. They had come to empty their guns into him. In the tradition of Arabic assassins, they had taken hashish and then successfully hit their target. Two hours later the president was dead from gunshot wounds.

Reality Check

The name "assassin" is actually from the Arabic *(hashshashin)* for a secret terrorist sect of Muslims of the eleventh to thirteenth centuries who killed their political enemies as a religious duty while under the influence of hashish, a concentrated form of hemp (marijuana).

The men involved in the attack were connected with a Libyan-backed terrorist group. Vice President Hosni Mubarak, who had been injured in the attack, succeeded the very complicated and unpredictable Anwar Sadat, the man who changed history in the Middle East.

Few Egyptian tears were shed for Sadat, compared with the massive outpouring of grief following the death of his predecessor, Gamal Abdel Nasser—who made history himself by championing Arab nationalism against the West. Even Nasser's death made history with the world's largest-ever funeral, according to the *Guinness Book of World Records.*

After five wars with Israel, Egypt was weary of continually providing the cannon fodder for the Arab cause while it had problems enough at home. Still, many Arabs viewed this treaty as a sellout of the Palestinians. Consequently, Egypt was thrown out of the Arab League, and a number of Arab states broke off diplomatic relations.

Not that the peace treaty was the sole reason for Sadat's demise. There were plenty of other reasons that could have cost his life:

- The high and rising misery index—including inflation, cost of housing and food, and unemployment.
- Unpopular crackdowns on religious extremists and banning of strikes and demonstrations.
- Increasingly cavalier and autocratic behavior, such as exempting himself from the six-year, one-term limit on the presidency.
- Providing a haven for the dying Shah of Iran at the very height of Islamic revolutionary furor in the region.

Egypt: Major Middle East Player

Egypt is the largest country in the Middle East and also the largest recipient of U.S. foreign aid, about $2 billion a year. Some claim this was the price tag for Egypt's peace agreement with Israel.

Egypt is also one of the oldest civilizations in the world, extending back to the time of the first pharaohs several thousand years before Christ. Supported by the fertile Nile valley, the nation flourished for many centuries, except for brief periods of domination by Assyria and Persia, until the time of the Greek empire. Alexander the Great extended his rule to Egypt and built the great city of Alexandria, named after himself, which held a famous library of ancient learning. The region was then ruled by the Ptolemies, a dynasty founded by one of Alexander's generals.

Reality Check

The three sons of Noah were Ham, Shem, and Japheth. Descendants of Shem—Jews and Arabs—are known as semites. Descendants of Ham—including most North African peoples—are hamites. Nevertheless, Egyptians and others consider themselves just as much a part of the larger Arab culture of the Middle East.

MidEast Dictionary

Coptic is the name for the ancient Christian church of Egypt, which still uses the Coptic language, derived from ancient Egyptian and written with the Greek script; in the fifth century the Roman church condemned the Coptics as heretical because of their belief that Christ had only one nature, not two, human and divine, which was monophysite doctrine.

Later, Egypt was controlled by the Arab Fatimid dynasty—part of a Shi'ite sect. Then the Islamic hero Saladin drove out both the marauding Crusaders and the Fatimids, reestablishing Sunni rule. Egypt also had a strong Christian presence in the form of the *Coptic* church.

Egypt came under control of the Ottoman Empire and then the British. The World War II Battle of El Alamein was fought on Egyptian soil. This is where the Allies in 1942 stopped the Afrika Korps under German Field Marshall Erwin Rommel, the Desert Fox, in a drive to the Suez Canal from Libya. More than 80,000 soldiers were killed or wounded in this long series of battles with some 1,500 tanks.

King Farouk was overthrown by a military coupled by Nasser in 1952. This represented the first true Egyptian rule in many years, as the Farouk family was Albanian. Nasser became the symbol of pan-Arab nationalism and inspired a generation of Arab leaders. He nationalized the Suez Canal, tilted politically toward the Soviet Union, implemented socialist policies, and engineered a short-lived merger with Syria (the United Arab Republic) as a hopeful prelude to a larger Arab consolidation.

Nasser's Waterloo was the 1967 Six Day War, in which Israel humiliated Egypt by destroying most of its air force while it was still on the ground. He lost much prestige among the other Arab states, which ironically had egged him into provoking the conflict in the first place. Three years later, Nasser died of a heart attack, as he tried to mediate a conflict between the PLO and the Jordanian army.

Just as Sadat alienated the rest of the Arab nations, Mubarak brought Egypt back into the fold, including reinstatement in the Arab League. It became a strong United States ally and participated in the U.S.-led coalition to drive Iraq out of Kuwait. Islamic fundamentalism meanwhile continued to foment, and Egypt's economy, heavily dependent on tourism, was hurt by killings of tourists by terrorists in the 1990s.

Egypt has a population of 70.7 million people and is slightly more than three times the size of New Mexico; its capital is Cairo.

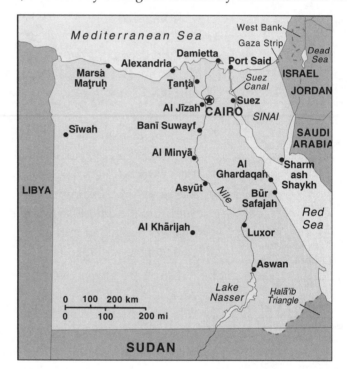

Libya: Major Mischief Maker

Libya, in ancient times, was the name for all of North Africa west of Egypt. Cyrene, built by the Greeks, was one of three major cities of this region during the Greek and Roman empires. It had a major Jewish community, so it is more likely that Simon, the man from Cyrene who carried Jesus' cross, was a Jew who happened to be in Jerusalem for the Passover than a hamitic African, as is sometimes supposed.

After Libya became its own separate kingdom, the rest of the Mediterranean states of North Africa—mainly Tunisia, Algeria, and Morocco—became known by the Arabic name, *Maghreb*.

Word from the Wise

What a picture of Christ's humanity: After his night-long ordeal with the Jews and Romans—especially the flogging—he may not have been physically capable of carrying his own cross, as was customary. "A man named Simon, who was from Cyrene, was coming in from the country just then, and they forced him to carry Jesus' cross." (Mark 15:21, NLT)

MidEast Dictionary

Berbers are the earliest known inhabitants of North Africa, hamitic peoples with their own separate languages, many living as desert nomads, herdsmen, and traders.

The country was controlled by Turkey for several centuries prior to World War I, and then occupied by Italy under oppressive rule. During World War II it was placed under British and French military rule. One of the bloodiest battles of World War II was fought in Libya, at the port city of Tubruq.

Libya received foreign aid for many years in exchange for military bases for the British, Americans, and NATO. It became an independent kingdom under United Nations provisions in 1951. It had one monarch, King Idris, before he was unseated by a military coup in 1969.

The leader of the revolt was an army officer who hated Westerners, whose grandfather had been killed by the Italians, and whose father and uncle had been imprisoned by them. Muammar Gadhafi, an ardent admirer of Nasser, became military dictator of Libya at the age of 27.

Gadhafi, from a family of *Berber* nomads, shared the same aspirations as Nasser for uniting the Arab nations and eliminating Israel. One of his first acts was to promote himself to colonel. Thereafter, he encouraged his countrymen to refer to him simply as "Brother Colonel."

Libya took the longer name Great Socialist People's Libyan Arab Jamahiriya (state of the masses). Gadhafi has dedicated himself to the overthrow of both communism and capitalism under a system he calls the Third Universal Theory, essentially a combination of socialism and Islam.

Under Gadhafi, Libya became a major sponsor of terrorism and foreign adventurism. It has supported many insurgent groups, including the Irish Republican Army (IRA), the Palestine Liberation Organization (PLO), the Basque separatist movement in Spain, South African rebels, American extremists, Black Muslims in the United States, and former cutthroat dictator Idi Amin in Uganda. Gadhafi also called for Muslim reconquest of Spain and Sicily.

Libya tried for a time to annex a mountainous area of its neighbor Chad that is rich in uranium—allegedly for the development of a nuclear weapon—until French troops intervened. Evidence also showed that Libya was behind the 1988 explosion of a United States passenger airliner (Pan Am Flight 103) over Lockerbie, Scotland, resulting in the deaths of many innocent people (including 259 Americans onboard). The United Nations imposed sanctions on Libya in 1992 for its support of terrorism.

Many nations have cut diplomatic relations with this dangerous and unpredictable nation. Libya still has much poverty despite significant oil production. Spurned by the Arab League, Gadhafi has turned his attention to military adventures in seven African countries, especially those rich in gold, diamonds, and uranium.

Libya has a population of 5.4 million and is slightly larger than Alaska; its capital is Tripoli.

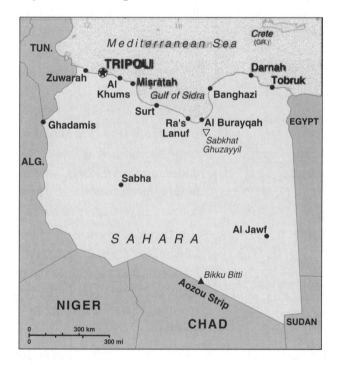

Tunisia: Ancient Power

In the land now called Tunisia was a powerful ancient empire called Carthage. It was a city-state of the sea-faring Phoenicians that became the main power in the Mediterranean. It had colonies in France, Spain, and Sicily in the fifth century B.C., long after Phoenicia itself had been conquered by the Assyrians. Carthage fought a devastating series of wars (the Punic Wars) with Rome, which finally conquered it in 146 B.C.

Carthage is now a ruin in the northern suburbs of Tunis. Tunisia's earliest inhabitants were the Berbers. After the Romans came a succession of other conquerors—Vandals, Byzantines, Arabs, Ottomans, and the French.

The Vandals, run out of Andalusia (Spain) by the Visigoths, seized this part of North Africa under Genseric in the fifth century. After capturing Carthage, the Vandals attacked Rome itself, at that time on its last leg. In 455 A.D., Genseric's forces sacked Rome and purportedly even seized the sacred vessels from Solomon's Temple that had been brought there by Titus. What might have happened to these treasures after that is not known.

The Vandals had become followers of a deviant Christian sect called *Arianism*. They were fanatically hostile to the Church, which was strong in North Africa at the time, and so weakened it through persecution that it was unable to withstand the later Islamic invasion.

After the fall of Rome, the Byzantines (the Eastern Empire) captured North Africa from the Vandals. The expanding Islamic empire, in turn, defeated the Byzantines. Tunisia today is home to one of the holiest places in Islam (after Mecca, Medina, and Jerusalem)—the holy city of Kairouan and the Great Mosque, built in the ninth century. It is also where Islam first gained its foothold in the Maghreb (the Arabic name for the Mediterranean states of North Africa—mainly Tunisia, Algeria, and Morocco).

Tunisia was a French protectorate after 1883, gaining independence in 1956. It became a republic in 1957, and President Habib Borguiba dominated the country for the next 31 years with strict one-part rule. Borguiba was a modernist, suppressing Islamic fundamentalism and establishing more extensive rights for women than other Islamic nations. Today it has entered a special free trade association with the European Union.

Tunisia has a population of 9.8 million and is slightly larger than Georgia; its capital is Tunis.

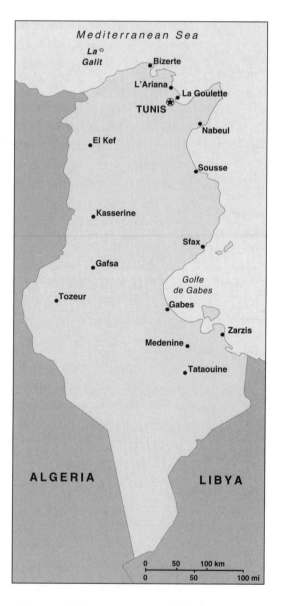

Algeria: Decades of Unrest

Algeria is the second largest country in Africa. It was here that St. Augustine, bishop of Hippo and noted theologian, made an enormous impact on the early church in the fourth and fifth centuries with his teachings on the role of the church in a pagan world.

The nation was a great producer and exporter of wheat. In 1830 A.D., France attacked Algeria with 37,000 men and 600 ships in a dispute over France's payments for grain. It forcibly annexed Algeria four years later. Later famines in the land killed thousands of Algerians.

Algerians frequently revolted against French rule, which tightened during the presidency of Charles DeGaulle. In 1945, a peaceful demonstration at Setif turned into deadly riots when French troops opened fire. Villages were shelled, and 45,000 Algerians were killed. The resulting seven-year war became an independence struggle in which a million Algerians died, plus many Europeans in retaliatory killings.

More than a century of French rule ended in 1962 when Algeria became a republic. Houari Boumedienne seized power in a bloodless coup in 1965, and in 1976 Algeria became a socialist state with Islam as the official religion.

In 1990, Arabic was declared the official language, and French and the Berber languages were banned in public. The country was plagued by long periods of unrest in the 1990s from Islamic fundamentalists, and during one state of emergency, the United Nations considered intervention.

The country has large oil reserves and is the world's second largest exporter of natural gas. It also is entering a special association relationship with the European Union.

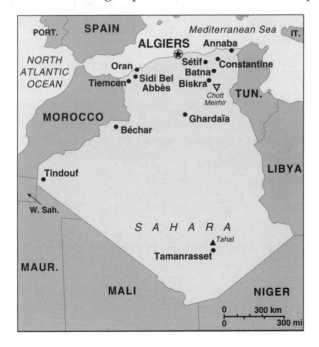

Algeria has a population of 32.2 million and is slightly less than 3.5 times the size of Texas; its capital is Algiers.

Word from the Wise

There may come a time when peace cannot be found on the earth. "And another horse appeared, a red one. Its rider was given a mighty sword and the authority to remove peace from the earth. And there was war and slaughter everywhere." (Revelation 6:4, NLT) Even Jesus said he came not to bring peace to the earth, but a sword. Can we give thanks for the uncounted blessing of peace?

Morocco: Exotic Place of Intrigue

Just across the Strait of Gibraltar from Spain, Morocco has been romanticized by Hollywood as an exotic place of intrigue with picturesque Arab towns and cities, including Marrakesh and Casablanca. Like Syria, Morocco claims to have the tomb of John the Baptist. Also like Syria, it is dominated by Alawite Muslims who came and conquered in the seventeenth century.

Reality Check

The movie *Black-hawk Down*, with its tragic loss of American commandos, was filmed in Morocco rather than Somalia, where the actual fighting took place, because Morocco, while similar in many other ways, is a more stable country.

Morocco had experienced the normal North African progression—shifting control by Berbers, Phoenicians, Romans, and Christians. France occupied the country in 1912. During World War II, Allied forces used Morocco as a base from which to drive the Germans out of North Africa.

Morocco won independence from France in 1956, and in 1957 King Hassan II seized major portions of Western Sahara, which are still in dispute. The country for years has had uneasy relations with its neighbor Algeria. Under King Mohammed VI, there have been some democratic reforms.

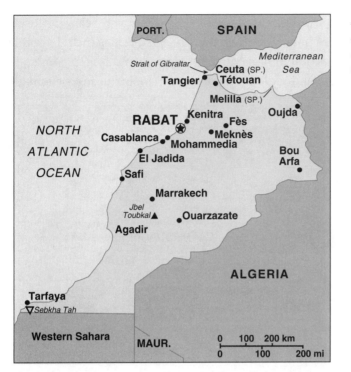

Morocco has a population of 31 million and is slightly larger than California; its capital is Rabat.

Sudan: Land of Human Tragedy

Sudan is the largest country in Africa—and one full of human tragedy of all kinds, ruled by an authoritarian regime. The country was ruled by joint British-French and British-Egyptian administrations during the first half of the twentieth century before gaining independence in 1956. A coup in 1989 brought in an Islamic regime and strict Sharia law.

Sudan has been engaged in the world's longest modern civil war since 1983, between the Arab Muslim forces in the north and the non-Muslim African rebels in the south. Ethnically, Sudan is 52 percent black and 39 percent Arab. War and famine have killed 2 million and displaced another 4 million.

Family Focus

Discuss the U.S. Civil War. Did you know that until the pivotal Battle of Antietam, European powers were prepared to recognize the Confederacy as the sole legitimate government of America? How would that have changed history? What would it be like if the country were permanently divided by ongoing hostilities yet today?

Human rights groups say 300 Sudanese die daily from war-related causes and there are a half-million refugees in neighboring countries. Atrocities include bombing of civilians, religious persecution of non-Muslims, slavery and forced conversions, conscription of child soldiers, and violence against women, including systematic rape.

Sudan has a population of 37 million and is slightly more than one fourth the size of the United States; its capital is Khartoum. It is an oil-producing nation burdened with heavy international debt.

Troubled Ethiopia and Somalia

Now we venture just a bit south of what's usually meant by "Middle East" to two countries that can't be totally ignored, either.

Ethiopia and Somalia have been very troubled countries at the strategic Horn of Africa. This is the prominent northeast corner of the African continent across the Red Sea and Gulf of Aden from Yemen and Saudi Arabia. Along with Eritrea and Djibouti, these countries converge at a narrow strait for a major international shipping route.

Ethiopia is the ancient land of Cush and was part of the old Nubian empire. It was also known in biblical times by the name Abyssinia. It is nearly half Muslim but also has a substantial Christian presence through the Ethiopian Orthodox church. Ethiopia was ruled for more than 40 years by Emperor Haile Selassie until he was overthrown by a Soviet-inspired military coup in 1974. The resulting socialist state in turn was overthrown by rebels.

This nation of 67 million people has been plagued by coups, uprisings, droughts, famines, and massive refugee problems. By 1995, Ethiopia had a constitution and multiparty elections. There has been considerable border fighting involving Eritrea, a breakaway province that became independent in 1993.

Family Focus

Discuss what it means to serve your country and possibly to give your life. Some people believe it is not appropriate to send young Americans in harm's way except for situations directly affecting our national security. The Somalia involvement would not have qualified in this view. Do you agree? Why or why not?

Somalia, a nation of 7.7 million people, has been an ongoing basket case of anarchy and violence for years as various warlords and factions struggle for control. It was the subject of the major movie and book of the same title, *Blackhawk Down*, based on a real incident. In October 1993, U.S. Special Forces attempted to capture one of the warlords, General Aidid, who had been confiscating international food shipments and interfering with the establishment of a stable government.

The action was undertaken in conjunction with the United Nations. However, U.S. forces sustained many casualties as two Blackhawk helicopters were downed, and the bodies of dead American servicemen were dragged through the streets of Mogadishu, the capital.

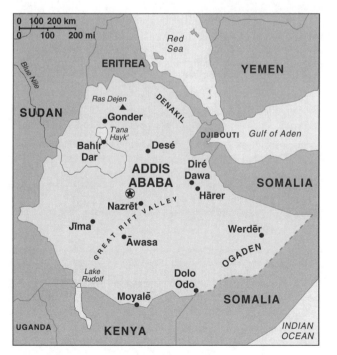

Ethiopia and Somalia. Ethiopia's capital is Addis Ababa. Somalia's capital is Mogadishu.

Profiles: Other Players

This chapter deals with some countries that are sometimes not even included in the Middle East proper. One is a nuclear power. One is a member of NATO. One is perhaps the greatest purveyor of Muslim extremism in the world today. One is not even a real country—yet. There is no question, however, that these six—Iran, Afghanistan, Pakistan, Turkey, Cyprus, and Kurdistan—have been key players in the region.

Keys to Paradise

One of the ironies of the Middle East is that while Iran is almost synonymous in most people's minds with Muslim extremism, it has been at swords points with the Arab world for centuries, all the way from ancient to modern times.

Iranians are not Arab, but a non-Semitic, Persian people. The very name "Iran" was chosen to convey the idea of *Aryan* ancestry. The Persians were proud people with a highly developed culture, who looked down on the Arab invaders centuries ago as "lizard eaters." Their ancient empire (Sassanian) was so preoccupied with endless wars with the Byzantine Empire that it failed to see the serious threat posed by Islamic conquerors in the 7th century A.D.

Therefore, 80,000 Persian cavalry troops with elephants and heavy armor were shocked to find themselves being routed by a band of some 10,000 Arabs with sandals, head scarves, leather

MidEast Dictionary

Aryan means of Indo-European or Indo-Iranian descent, from a root meaning noble or superior; term popularized by the Nazis in the 1930s to mean a Caucasian of non-Jewish or non-Semitic descent.

MidEast Dictionary

Basiji are members of Iranian Basij or volunteer corps; generally old men and young boys inducted during the Iran-Iraq war to serve as cannon fodder, enticed by the promise that death in the war would mean automatic acceptance in heaven.

shields, and crude swords. Apparently, swift horses and a convenient dust storm helped make the difference for the Arabs.

This was in 637 A.D. on the field of Qadisiyah, a pivotal battle that eventually led to Persian withdrawal from what is today Iraq. It was an Arab victory that Saddam Hussein has recycled many times for his own propaganda purposes.

In a few short years, Persia was entirely overrun and converted from the religion of Zoroaster to the faith of Muhammad. However, the form they adopted was not the majority Sunni Islam, but the minority Shi'ite version.

Fast forward 1,300 years plus. Old Persian-Arab hostilities were replayed in the long Iran-Iraq war of the 1980s. More than 400,000 Iranians were killed and close to a million wounded. Many of these casualties occurred in human wave attacks in 1983 and 1984. Iranian teenage and even pre-teen martyrs, known as *basiji*, charged across Iraqi minefields to clear the way for the next troop assault.

Around their necks they wore plastic keys, supposedly to unlock the doors to paradise.

Iran: An Ancient Empire

Persia ruled a vast empire in Bible times, defeating the Babylonians and in turn being conquered by the Greeks. In modern times it was ruled by a succession of shahs after freeing itself from foreign overlords, notably Mongols, Turks, and Afghans. It has been an independent country for some 2,500 years.

The Persians ruled Palestine during the last century of Old Testament history, the period of the books of Esther, Daniel, Ezra, and Nehemiah. Jews had been taken captive by Nebuchadnezzar and the Babylonians and then allowed to return and rebuild the Temple and Jerusalem's walls under the Persians.

Iran is just to the east of the usual definition of the Middle East, between Iraq to the west and Afghanistan and Pakistan to the east. Nevertheless, it's a big player in

Middle East affairs. Geographically, it's a strategic land bridge between the Middle East and Central Asia, where the influences and interests of India and Arabia intersect.

It became a British protectorate after World War I and adopted the name Iran in 1935. A key to understanding Iran is in the degree of foreign interference it has endured. Displeased with Iran's neutrality in World War II, Britain and Russia occupied Iran in 1941 and forced its leader, Reza Shah Pahlavi, a Nazi sympathizer, to abdicate. They then installed his son, Muhammad Reza Pahlavi, as Shah.

Iran has a population of 66.6 million and is slightly larger than Alaska. It is a major oil-producing nation; its capital is Tehran.

Fall of the Shah

This Shah—who turned out to be the last—was overthrown in a coup, but the U.S. Central Intelligence Agency helped a counter-coup reinstall him. The Shah launched a campaign to modernize Iranian society, which to Islamic conservatives smacked of hated Westernization. Meanwhile, Ayatollah Ruhollah Khomeini, leader of the fundamentalist Shi'ite Muslims, was expelled to Iraq, where he lived in exile until Saddam Hussein had him deported. Khomeini then moved to France, while his following continued to grow.

The Shah adopted repressive measures, attempting to crush all dissent, often through the brutal secret police, Savak. Finally, internal dissension became so

Reality Check

Western culture has been so globally pervasive in recent decades that some Middle Easterners, especially conservative Muslims, often feel inundated. In reaction they have invented terms like "Westoxification" and complained of the "Coca Colanization" of their values.

MidEast Dictionary

The **Twelver Shi'as** are the majority faction of Shi'ites who believe in the line of twelve imams through Ali and expect the twelfth and last imam (the Madhi) to return some day; Iran's Khomeini asserted that the faithful meanwhile should be led by a supreme religious figure.

Reality Check

Iranian law, reflecting Muslim beliefs, sets the minimum age of marriage for women at nine. This was the age of Muhammad's favorite wife, Aisha, when he consummated marriage with her.

intense that the Shah fled the country and eventually died in exile in Egypt. Khomeini returned victorious to Iran and set up an Islamic republic in 1979.

"Death to America"

In late 1979, militant students seized the U.S. Embassy and held American hostages for 444 days until January 1981, when Ronald Reagan became President. For more than a year, Americans had watched "America Held Hostage" on their television news programs as young Iranians marched, chanting "Death to America!"

Some attribute Iranian fanaticism to their Shi'ite faith—as *Twelver Shi'as* and "partisans of Ali." Ali was murdered, and his son, Hussein, defied the caliph's military forces, though it meant certain death. Iranians, then, are sometimes viewed as emulating Hussein's model of protest and self-sacrifice—even to the point of fighting their enemies with human waves.

The Shi'a tragedies of Ali and Hussein are re-enacted annually in a religious observance called Ashura. Shi'ite men march and wail, beating their breasts, and even beating themselves with whips until the blood flows freely, weeping over the unjust death of Hussein centuries ago.

Under Iran's current constitution there is both a secular president and a Supreme Religious Leader. Many positions are filled by election, but the clergy have veto over positions, legislation, and executive actions. Another unique feature is that the constitution virtually requires Iran to work to overthrow non-Islamic governments.

Enormous Impact

It would be difficult to overstate the impact of the 1979 Iranian Islamic revolution to the region and the world. Secular Arab nationalism had proven a big disappointment, especially since the military humiliation of the

1967 Six Day War with Israel. The Marxist dream, never all that attractive to most Muslims, was also starting to wear thin.

A return to Islamic fundamentalism and even theocratic rule was an idea whose time had come. It did cause a number of other precarious regimes in the region, however, to begin to worry.

It took several years to consolidate the Khomeini revolution in Iran. Meanwhile, leftists continued to wield some political power. A socialist Islamic group based in Iraq carried out a number of bombings and assassinations. In 1981, Iran's new president and prime minister, 27 members of Parliament, and 10 cabinet officials were assassinated.

Eventually, Khomeini's regime took firm hold and dissidents were suppressed. Soon Khomeini-inspired radicals were causing all sorts of mischief in various places. The U.S. Embassy and Marine barracks in Beirut were bombed, apparently by pro-Iranian militias. The despised secular regime next door in Baghdad was harassed by Kurdish insurgents supported by Iran.

In 1980, Iraq invaded Iran and started an exhausting eight-year war. Part of the dispute was territorial, involving possession of the Shatt al-Arab, the confluence of the Tigris and Euphrates rivers that divides the two countries. Neither Khomeini nor Hussein was willing to stop fighting so long as the other remained in power.

Finally, though, Khomeini agreed to a cease-fire in 1988. He died less than a year later. As bad as it was, however, the war may have solidified the Iranian Islamic regime similar to the way the Philistine threat solidified the kingdom of Israel.

"Axis of Evil"

Iran was also a player in the U.S. Iran-Contra scandal, when the Reagan administration was found to have sold arms secretly to them to secure the release of hostages held by Iranian-backed terrorists and using the proceeds to circumvent Congress in funding anti-Communist activities in Central America.

Iran deployed its Revolutionary Guard in Lebanon's Bekaa Valley and created Hezbollah, the terrorist organization that practically invented suicide car bombing. Pro-Iranian groups were also kidnapping Americans. Iranian dissidents abroad have been assassination targets, including attacks in France, Austria, Germany, and Switzerland.

The United States implemented a total economic embargo against Iran in 1995 for supporting international terrorism. The sanctions, however, were not observed by most European and Asian nations. More recently President George W. Bush branded Iran as part of the "Axis of Evil" (along with Iraq and North Korea) and the most active state sponsor of terror.

The U.S. State Department lists Iran as a major abuser of human rights. Intelligence sources have warned of Iran's intense attempts to obtain weapons of mass destruction (nuclear, biological, and chemical). They say Iran is on the verge of becoming a nuclear power. Specifically, Iran is said to support:

- Hezbollah
- Hamas
- Palestinian Islamic Jihad
- Popular Front for the Liberation of Palestine

> **Word from the Wise**
>
> There are those who call themselves good Christians, Muslims, and Jews who are unwitting tools of evil: "For we are not fighting against people made of flesh and blood, but against the evil rulers and authorities of the unseen world ..." Ephesians 6:12, NLT.

Seeds of Change

Iran today is in flux. During the bloody Iran-Iraq war the Khomeini regime encouraged Iranians to replenish the population, and the population nearly doubled. By 2000, half of the country's population was under 21 years of age. Now only a minority of the population can even remember the old days of repressive rule by the Shah.

Now, after more than 20 years of Islamic fundamentalist rule, there are great pressures, especially from the young, for liberalization and reform. It no longer sits so well that this regime is still issuing death sentences to intellectuals who criticize the theocracy.

Afghanistan: Rise of the Taliban

While Khomeini was taking over in Iran, the Soviets were rolling into neighboring Afghanistan in 1979 to install their own Communist puppet government. The 10-year military occupation was fiercely resisted by rebel Afghan Mujaheddin fighters, supported by the United States, Saudi Arabia, Pakistan, China, and other Arab states. It cost the United States billions in arms and ammunition but cost the Afghans 1.5 million lives plus several million more refugees to neighboring countries.

Finally, the Soviets were forced to withdraw in 1989, and the United States lost interest, allowing allies Pakistan and Saudi Arabia to sort things out. Afghans considered the disengagement a betrayal, and in retrospect, it was probably a big mistake. Infighting among various ethnic Afghan factions led to civil war among rival warlords and the rise of a new group called the Taliban.

The Taliban (meaning "students of Islam") were a kind of second-generation Mujaheddin. Their fighters began conquering in the early 1990s and by 1996 had captured Kabul. Washington at first welcomed this development, as the Taliban were anti-Iranian. However, the warning signs were there: One of the Taliban's first acts was the torture and execution of former President Najibullah. A soccer stadium that had been rebuilt at great expense by the United Nations aid agencies was converted to a site for public executions.

The Taliban were devotees of Deobandi Islam, an ultra-conservative sect named after the town in India where it originated. They received financial assistance from the Saudis, whose own Wahhabism is similar. The Taliban banned virtually all forms of entertainment—music, television, movies, sports, and games. They closed all girls' schools, and required women to be totally covered in *burkhas* and all men to wear beards.

The Taliban were considered the most secretive political movement in the world, after the Khmer Rouge of Cambodia. They alienated most of their neighbors, but did maintain diplomatic relations with Pakistan and Saudi Arabia. Their most controversial decision was to provide a safe haven for multimillionaire terrorist kingpin Osama bin Laden, who moved to Afghanistan with the promise of building roads and other infrastructure in the impoverished nation.

By that time bin Laden and his *al-Qaeda* terrorist organization were already implicated in several deadly attacks against United States overseas facilities, and America demanded he be handed over. The Taliban danced around

> **Family Focus**
>
> Discuss how you would view the policies of the United States in the Middle East if you lived in a country like Iran or Afghanistan. Would your perspective be different? How? Would you regard America as a reliable friend?

> **def·i·ni·tion** **MidEast Dictionary**
>
> A **burkha** is an all-enveloping head-to-toe veil worn by Afghan women under the Taliban allowing only the eyes to be seen.

> **def·i·ni·tion** **MidEast Dictionary**
>
> **Al-Qaeda** literally means "the base" in Arabic; terrorist group founded by Osama bin Laden to destroy Israel and the United States and establish a global caliphate (theocratic state under Islamic law) through jihad.

the issue, saying it was against Islamic tradition to evict a guest. When al-Qaeda suicide terrorists began crashing planes into the World Trade Center and the Pentagon, the Taliban's days were numbered.

The United States and allies invaded Afghanistan in late 2001 and after several weeks of aerial bombardment, and with help on the ground from rebel groups like the Northern Alliance, managed to oust the Taliban. At a December 2001 conference in Bonn, Germany, a transitional government for Afghanistan was created with Hamid Karzai as chairman of the Afghan Interim Authority.

Culturally, Afghanistan is a fusion of Persian and Central Asian influences. It continues to be wracked by extreme poverty, violence, crumbling infrastructure, widespread land mines, and severe social problems, including lack of basic food, clothing, housing, and medical care.

Afghanistan has a population of 27.7 million and is slightly smaller than Texas; its capital is Kabul.

Pakistan: Major Influencer

Pakistan to the east would be the largest nation on the basis of population if it were part of the Middle East proper. Instead, it is in the category of a major influencer of regional affairs. It has a huge Muslim population and on that basis was separated from predominantly Hindu India in 1947 after years of civil war.

Its president is General Pervez Musharaf, former Chairman of the Joint Chiefs of Staff, who seized power in a military coup in 1999. Under Musharaf, Pakistan has been a staunch ally of the United States, despite frequent riots and protests against U.S. Middle East policy by its large segment of Islamic fundamentalists. Many are strong supporters of bin Laden.

Ironically, Pakistan was also a strong ally of the Taliban—at least, until things got totally out of hand. Large numbers of ethnic Pashtun people live in both Afghanistan and Pakistan. However, more than kinship or common religious ideologies, the real reason for this connection may have been appreciation for the Taliban's willingness to harbor Muslims waging guerrilla war against India in the disputed state of Kashmir.

India and Pakistan have fought several times over disputed Kashmir. These confrontations are particularly worrisome now that both countries are nuclear powers. Pakistan, however, continues to be an impoverished and underdeveloped country.

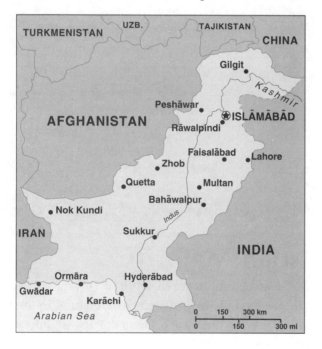

Pakistan has a population of 147 million and is slightly twice the size of California; its capital is Islamabad.

Turkey: Large Muslim Ally

Turkey, formerly known as Anatolia, was also known as Asia (or Asia Minor) in Bible times. The apostle Paul planted churches here, and it was where the seven churches were located to which Christ dictated letters of warning and encouragement in John's Revelation.

Reality Check

The highest point in Turkey is Mt. Ararat, the legendary landing place of Noah's Ark from the book of Genesis. That doesn't necessarily mean, however, that was the actual place—the name came about in much later times because of the legends.

Turkey was the seat of the Ottoman Empire, which controlled most of the Middle East for some six centuries, up to the early 1900s when it was defeated in World War I. Then a powerful leader, Kemal Ataturk, almost single-handedly transformed Turkey into a Western-style democracy. Ataturk abolished the sultanate and the caliphate, banned the traditional fez cap, and adopted the Western calendar and the Roman alphabet.

Turkey, a United States ally and a member of NATO, is attempting to become the sole Islamic member of the European Union. In 2002, the country elected a president from an Islamic party for the first time. Still, Turkey continues to be a strategic military partner for the United States.

Turkey has a population of 67 million and is slightly larger than Texas; its capital is Ankara.

Cyprus: Christian Majority

Cyprus, a large island in the Mediterranean Sea south of Turkey, gained independence from Britain in 1960. It is the only majority Christian nation in the region with 78 percent of the population Eastern Orthodox. There are also significant Maronite Christian and Muslim populations.

Greeks and Turks have vied for control of Cyprus for years, coming to actual blows in 1974 as Greeks attempted to seize power. Since then the country has been divided about 60/40 respectively between the Greek Cypriot state in the south and an autonomous Turkish Cypriot state in the north, separated by a United Nations buffer zone. Because of its offshore proximity to the Core countries, Cyprus has been a convenient site for various Middle East peace conferences.

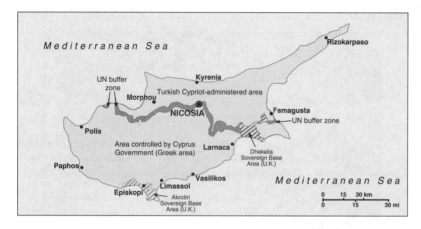

Cyprus has a population of 767,000 and is slightly more than half the size of Connecticut; its capital is Nicosia.

Kurdistan: The Country That Never Was

The Kurds today are believed to be the descendants of the Medes, who formed half of the ancient Medo-Persian Empire that conquered Babylon in Bible times. The Kurds are Muslims but are ethnically distinct from Arabs, Turks, and Persians. They are the world's largest people group without a country, inhabiting large, mountainous portions of Iran, Iraq, Syria, Turkey, and parts of Azerbaijan and Armenia. Fully half of them live in southeastern Turkey, while there are entire regions in Iran and Iraq with the name "Kurdistan."

In carving up the Ottoman Empire at the end of World War I, the Western powers omitted any homeland for the Kurds, almost as an oversight. Therefore, for decades the Kurds have had hostile relations with their host countries, where they are often treated as second-class citizens or subversives. The Kurds themselves have a saying: "We have no friends but the mountains."

Human rights groups have complained that Turkey has persecuted and even tortured Kurds. On the other hand, armed struggle by the largest Kurdish insurgency group, the Kurdistan Freedom and Democracy Congress (formerly PKK), has resulted in the deaths of an estimated

Word from the Wise

"A man of many companions may come to ruin, but there is a friend who sticks closer than a brother." (Proverbs 18:24, NIV) If the Kurds are friendless, they haven't met the friend who sticks closer than a brother. "What a friend we have in Jesus, all our sins and griefs to bear!"

30,000 people in Turkey and elsewhere. As part of its efforts to gain admittance to the European Union, Turkey commuted the death sentence of leader Abdullah Ocalan to life in prison.

Kurdistan, if it existed, would have a population of upwards of 25 million and would cover an area larger than California.

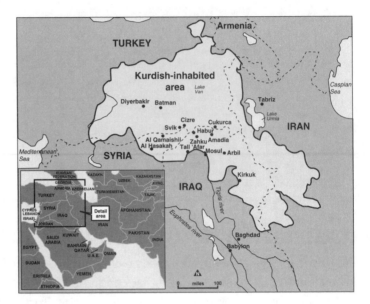

Kurds profess gratitude to the United States for protecting them from persecution by Saddam Hussein by enforcing "no-fly" zones in northern Iraq. However, they are apprehensive about their future in a post-Saddam Iraq. It is a big political question mark for the United States in any war with Iraq. The Kurds, like the Northern Alliance in Afghanistan, could be invaluable allies in the fight, but at the cost of alienating other important allies, like Turkey, whose support is also vitally important.

Family Focus

Discuss what it would be like to live in another country as an alien, without a country of your own to go to. Should the United States try to create a Kurdistan homeland for the Kurds? What problems would there be?

Certainly, if the Kurds were to fight on the side of a U.S. coalition, they would expect to be rewarded with their long-awaited prize—the statehood that they missed out on 80 years ago. Moreover, in Iraq, the Kurds are just one ethnic minority among many. A post-Saddam era could be truly dicey—a Pandora's box of inter-ethnic conflicts just waiting for the lid to come off.

That may be just one more indication of the wisdom in the saying that it's often harder to win the peace than to win the war.

Part 4

The Situation

Finally, we're ready to grapple with some real current issues. Here we begin to deal with the Palestinian problem, Middle East oil, other major forces in the Arab world today, and terrorism. A word of warning: The more you know, the harder it is to be optimistic about simple solutions. The Palestinian refugee problem, for example, didn't develop overnight, and it probably won't be solved quickly, either. We'll look at some of the reasons for this.

Almost overnight, however, was just how dramatically the face of the Middle East was transformed by the discovery of oil and the growth of the petroleum industry. Oil also played a major role in many of the subsequent conflicts. It certainly elevated the entire region from obscurity to a place of vital strategic importance to the industrialized world. However, casting a dark cloud over it all was the rise of hostile forces frighteningly expressed in the form of international terrorism. We look at the major groups and major incidents.

The Palestinian Problem

This chapter looks at the problem of the Palestinians—who they are, the nature of their grievances, and how they came to lose control of the land through political deals, land purchases, and conflicts between Arabs and Israelis. It is a problem that affects hundreds of thousands of people and is Israel's number-one domestic problem.

Loss of Palestinian Control

In the late 1800s and early 1900s, thousands of acres of old Palestine, including some of the best agricultural land, were bought by overseas investors. Much of it was owned by various Ottoman interests. Jewish immigration by that time was picking up, and deals were being made.

By one estimate, 90 percent of all land purchased by Zionists was sold by absentee Turkish landlords. Much of the rest, then, was purchased from local Palestinian Arabs. Zionists created a large financial mechanism, the Jewish National Fund, to purchase land in Israel for Jewish settlement. Moreover, some Arabs were directly profiting.

By 1935, the Grand Mufti of Jerusalem, the colorful Haj Amin al-Husseini, called on Arab religious leaders and issued a fatwa condemning land sales to the Jews as treason. The penalty for violators would be disgrace and denial of Muslim burial. By then, most of the damage had been done.

The net effect was that the Palestinians were losing control. The idea that the Jews "stole" the land of Palestine, however, was simply not true. They may have been smart businessmen, however, which is not a crime.

The occupied territories were a different story. These were areas that the Jews had not managed to acquire—or, as in the case of Hebron, had been driven from by violence. Their occupation came as the result of war with the prior owners—Jordan in the case of the West Bank and Egypt in the case of the Gaza Strip. To the victor, as they say, go the spoils.

Jewish Colonialists?

The Palestinians assert longtime residence and ownership claims dating back to the seventh century A.D., when Arab invaders captured Palestine from the Byzantine Empire during the Islamic conquests. The Jews, then, would be twentieth-century Johnny-come-latelies acting in the same arrogant, high-handed manner as the hated European colonialists.

Occupied territories of the West Bank and Gaza Strip.

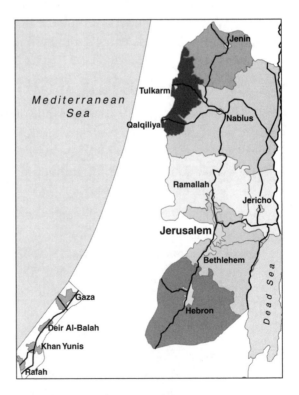

The Palestinians naturally reject the argument of the Jews, whose claims to the land are about 2,000 years older. Then, some Arabs argue, the same principle ought to apply everywhere else as well. Mexico, then, would have rights to parts of the United States, Spain could claim Mexico, and the Arabs could claim Spain—Andalusia, when it was under their control. In effect, they're laying the charge of *ethnocentrism* on pro-Israel Westerners.

MidEast Dictionary

Ethnocentrism means a built-in bias according to one's ethnic group, nation, or culture that colors one's perceptions, often resulting in judgmental attitudes, racial and ethnic stereotypes, and double standards.

There is also a religious issue. Once a place has been conquered by Allah, according to Islamic law, it must remain Allah's property forever. It would be unlawful to give it back to the infidel. Similarly, it is not technically possible for the PLO to make peace with Israel, for its charter requires no cessation of hostilities until Palestine and Jerusalem are again under their control.

To the Jews, it was all a matter of simply recovering what originally had been theirs. They believed God had given them the land through Abraham and a permanent kingdom through David (the Davidic Covenant). The Arabs, of course, saw it differently. One argument was that the promises rightfully came (or should have come) down through Isaac's elder brother Ishmael, Abraham's firstborn and the father of the Arab peoples.

Twice-Promised Land

As with so many other things regarding the nations of the Middle East, the seeds of the Palestinian problem were sown in World War I and the Europeans' dismantling of the old Ottoman Empire. In issuing the Balfour Declaration in 1917, British Foreign Secretary Arthur Balfour hoped to encourage Jews in America and Russia to support the cause of the Allies in the war against Germany.

It said in part: "His Majesty's Government view with favour the establishment in Palestine of a national home for the Jewish people, and will use their best endeavors to facilitate the achievement of this object …."

This was the green light for which Zionists had been waiting, and England was able to make it stick under authority of the League of Nations, called the British mandate, which gave it oversight of Iraq and Palestine. At the same time the Arab nations had been promised something, too, in exchange for their allegiance during the war against Germany and the Ottomans—independence.

That was all well and good for countries like Egypt, Iraq, Syria, and Lebanon. But it ran into a big problem in Palestine—that is, independence for whom, the Jews or the Arabs? The British could have it both ways only so long before it caught up with them. The situation prompted some wags to refer to Palestine as the "twice-promised land."

TIMELINE 1450 B.C. – 2002 A.D.

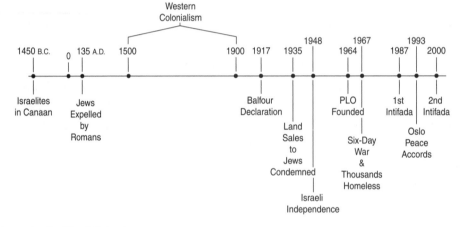

Stages in the life of Palestine.

The solution was to create *two* states out of Palestine. Theoretically, an Arab Palestinian state east of the Jordan River and a Jewish one (Israel) west of the river. Never mind whether England had any real authority to do this; they were making it up as they went along.

Word from the Wise

It is tempting to be upset by the tangled political webs woven by men on earth. But lasting peace will never come to this world; it will be destroyed and a new heaven and new earth will appear. Paul said, "But we are citizens of heaven, where the Lord Jesus Christ lives. And we are eagerly awaiting for him to return as our Savior." (Philippians 4:20, NLT)

Unfortunately, Transjordan, which was 75 percent of the original Palestine mandate, came into the ensuing political events as just another Arab kingdom, rather than a Palestinian state. So, the problem was simply concentrated in the remaining 25 percent of the territory, the part west of the Jordan that became Israel. For the Israelis and the Palestinians, it was the worst of both worlds—one nation with two peoples claiming ownership.

Israel did not attain statehood until after the conclusion of World War II. During the war, the United States assured the Saudis that nothing would be done in regard to Palestine without consulting the Arabs. Yet, when the war was over, the United States pulled the strings at the United Nations to get the controversial approval rammed through—by one vote. President Truman reportedly commented later that his Jewish constituency at home was a lot bigger than the Arab voting bloc.

MidEast Dictionary

Colonialism is the political control by one power over a dependent area or people for economic exploitation, natural resources, new markets, or influence; the most active colonialists were countries of Western Europe from 1500 to 1900 A.D.

The other problem in all this was actual real estate. Why should Palestinians, any more than anyone else, have to forfeit their own homes and properties? Why should other Arab nations be obliged to absorb them? Wouldn't that be like the United States expecting Canada and Mexico to take in the Native Americans so the United States could appropriate their land?

The only real explanation was the *colonialist* mindset. Under colonialism it was not that unusual to evict and relocate large numbers of people if necessary. That was simply the way things were done. Even though this was the twentieth century, old habits and attitudes died hard.

Who Are the Palestinians?

This in turn raises the question of who *are* the Palestinians. Golda Meier, Israeli prime minister in the 1970s, used to make the provocative statement, "There is no such thing as a Palestinian people."

What did she mean by that? There are three aspects to that assertion:

- Nationally
- Ethnically
- Politically

First, there was never a state called Palestine with Jerusalem or any other city as its capital. Ever since the Romans destroyed Jerusalem in 70 A.D. and expelled the Jews in 135 A.D., it existed largely as a possession of one regional power after another until it once again attained independence as a Jewish state in 1948 A.D. Prior to that it was just a southern subset of Greater Syria under the Ottomans, who had acquired it from the succession of Byzantine, Arab, and Turkish powers who colonized the region.

Second, there has never been a distinct Palestinian ethnic group. At times, they assert Arab heritage in order to establish their claim to the land back to the seventh century A.D. However, in order to overcome Israel's much more ancient claim, some have advanced the argument of Canaanite descent, since the Canaanites preceded even the Israelites.

That argument, however, has even worse problems. According to the Old Testament, the Canaanites were wicked people whom God told the Israelites to exterminate and expel. Apparently most of them were eliminated. Moreover, the Canaanites were non-Semitic Hamites, meaning they were not descended from Abraham and could make none of those claims. A similar argument has been made for descent from the Philistines, another non-Semitic people, but they only arrived on the scene about the same time as the Israelites or even later.

Third, when it comes to Palestinian refugees, the picture is equally confused as to statehood and citizenship. Those who were uprooted at the outset of the 1948 war of independence were actually subjects of a British territory at the time. Those who became refugees from the West Bank during the 1967 Six Day War were actually Jordanian.

So, whose citizenship would they claim now? That confusion, at least, presumably should be settled with the creation of a proposed Palestinian state that would include all those refugees.

Terrible Conditions

The Palestinian world population, according to Palestinian sources, is more than seven million. More than half actually live in other countries in the region. About 1.9 million live in the West Bank and another million in the Gaza Strip. The birth rate is very high, and half of the population of these two areas is under 15 years of age. Some Israelis have expressed concern that the Jews could become a minority in their own country as early as 2020 A.D.

Most of the Palestinians in the occupied territories live in small villages. The most significant towns of the Gaza Strip and their population:

- Gaza City, 283,000
- Khan Yunis, 86,000

Reality Check

"We're not just leaving the city," the cab driver says over his shoulder as you exit Jerusalem. "We're leaving the country." What he means is Jerusalem is wholly controlled by Israel, but it's like an island in the middle of a Palestinian sea. The moment you leave, you're no longer in Israel but in the West Bank, an occupied territory.

Family Focus

Have you ever been in a slum or ghetto with serious social problems? On top of that imagine raw sewage in the streets and widespread health problems, as in refugee camps. How would it affect you to be forced to live in those conditions?

The most significant towns of the West Bank:

- East Jerusalem, 180,000
- Hebron, 120,000
- Nablus, 103,000
- Bethlehem, 22,000
- Jericho, 15,000

More than half of the total population of the Palestinian areas are refugees displaced from the 1948 war. More than 400,000 of those refugees still live in 28 overcrowded camps established by the United Nations Relief and Work Agency (UNRWA) in the Gaza Strip and West Bank. Two dozen other camps are scattered in Jordan, Lebanon, and Syria. UNRWA provides assistance through food, clothing, schools, job training, and health clinics.

Living conditions in the Palestinian camps, however, are terrible. Sanitary conditions are poor, resulting in disease. The population density is close to 100,000 per square kilometer, and Palestinians claim that makes them the most densely populated areas on earth.

More than 160 Israeli settlements have been established in the West Bank and Gaza with some 170,000 Jewish settlers, who are generally regarded by fellow Israelis as pioneers and heroes. However, they are bitterly resented by the Palestinians, who refer to them more often as thugs and criminals.

All of the Above

The actual truth to the question of who are the Palestinians is probably "all of the above." That is, they appear to be a composite through intermarriage of Arabs with local Canaanite, Philistine, and Bedouin peoples along with a myriad others, including Turks, Greeks, Syrians, Egyptians, Sudanese, Druze, Armenians. These and many others were recorded in the census of 1931.

Ironically, the real identity that has eluded the Palestinians in the past is only now coming to reality. It is through the decades of scare tactics, deportations and expulsions, blowing up of homes, confinement to refugee camps, curfews, rubber bullets, taunts, broken arms, and insults that they are finding this identity. Tragically, it may be only the Palestinians' common experiences as enemies of Israel that have defined them.

The Palestinian Refugees

Israel's biggest problem today is the same one it had the day it became independent: the Palestinian refugee problem. Upwards of 750,000 refugees were created at the outset—Palestinian Arabs who either could not get back into the country after the war of independence or who found no home to return to if they did. The issue has dogged Israel ever since, providing continued ammunition for Arab enmity.

Eventually, many of these Palestinians ended up in refugee camps in the West Bank and Gaza Strip. Not only were they not assimilated into the neighboring Arab states, but these countries appeared to resist all attempts to resettle them.

Jordan, as the original Arab half of "Palestine," might have been the obvious choice, but it wasn't working. There were increasing battles between Palestinian guerrillas and the Jordanian army, and their host (King Hussein) finally expelled many of them, especially their leaders. This was the beginning of the ongoing Palestinian refugee problem, as it is still known today.

Eventually, the problem was taken out of Jordan's hands entirely. The Palestine Liberation Organization,

 Word from the Wise

What should be our behavior toward refugees? What would Jesus do? "'For I was hungry, and you fed me. I was thirsty, and you gave me a drink. I was a stranger, and you invited me into your home … I assure you, when you did it to one of the least of these my brothers and sisters, you were doing it to me!'" (Matthew 25:35, 40, NLT)

founded in 1964, finally became the acknowledged sole representative of the Palestinian Arabs and the refugees in 1974. At that point Jordan's involvement ceased, and King Hussein was able to wash his hands of the entire matter.

Nevertheless, serious questions remain. Israel obviously deserves criticism for refusing to repatriate these refugees. Indeed, there is evidence that during the war of independence Israel actively encouraged Palestinians to leave the country, even to the point of scare tactics and psychological warfare. Israel may have been exercising some obvious self-interest in terms of maintaining a Jewish majority.

Other rulers in the Middle East had no such qualms governing a majority population of a different ethnic or religious persuasion. Israel had no intention of being a monarchy or dictatorship. It was a democracy, but also a national Jewish homeland. They were not about to commit demographic suicide.

Ironically, there was no similar outcry in the international community demanding that Morocco or any other Arab state take back its Jewish refugees when they were homeless and excluded from Palestine because of immigration restrictions. Yet, Israel has been roundly condemned for decades for its repressive policies toward the Palestinians. The question remains as to why the Arab states—who should have exercised solidarity with their suffering brothers—really treated them no better.

It would appear, based on the experience in Jordan, that there has been a certain level of fear regarding the Palestinians and the trouble that seems to follow them. Also, some people allege a political motive behind allowing the refugee problem to persist—that is, to keep the problem alive and to keep Israel under a cloud of international disapproval.

Whatever the causes and motivations, one thing is beyond dispute: The Palestinian refugee camps have been the source of much woe all around. They have produced a generation of Palestinians filled with rage and have become hotbeds for producing terror groups committed to the destruction of Israel.

An Explosion Waiting to Happen

It had been 20 years since Israel had occupied the Gaza Strip and the West Bank in the 1967 Six Day War, and tensions had been building for a long time. Palestinians in the towns of those occupied areas were fed up with what they considered harassment by Israeli Defense Forces (IDF)—constant identity checks, body searches, and verbal abuse from IDF officers. There was also the provocation of Israeli settlements in the occupied areas.

All it needed was a trigger, and an explosion was inevitable. That trigger came on December 8, 1987, in the form of a traffic accident involving an Israeli Army vehicle that killed four Palestinian workers. Just a day or two before, an Israeli shopper had been fatally stabbed in Gaza, and the rumors began flying that the traffic deaths had been intentional, in retaliation. Disturbances broke out the next day. A teenager threw a Molotov cocktail, and an IDF soldier shot him to death.

The resulting riots spread to the West Bank and Jerusalem and eventually came to be known as the first *Intifada* (uprising). It was a long period of ongoing violence—stoning of IDF soldiers and murdering of alleged collaborators. These years saw the formation of a new Palestinian organization more violent than the PLO—Hamas, an Arabic acronym for Islamic Resistance Movement.

This first Intifada was ruinous to the Palestinians economically, as frequent shutdowns and curfews in Gaza and West Bank towns deprived workers of access to jobs within Israel. It was also a public relations black eye for Israel, as the IDF was reduced to chasing, beating, and shooting impoverished Arabs through the Palestinian slums. In particular the sight of soldiers breaking the arms of stone throwers—a common practice—earned Israel a reputation as a bully.

> **Reality Check**
>
> The Tomb of the Patriarchs is the traditional site of the Cave of Machpelah, purchased by Abraham as a burial place for his wife Sarah (Genesis 23). Later, he, Isaac, Rebekah, and Jacob were also buried there. The modern site is venerated by Jews, Christians, and Muslims. Hebron was David's capital for seven years.

The first Intifada gradually faded and then ceased with the onset of the Oslo Peace Accords in 1993, which held out the promise of Palestinian self-rule. However, the next year violence from the other side changed the equation. Dr. Baruch Goldstein, a physician, entered the Tomb of the Patriarchs in Hebron (West Bank) and opened fire with an assault rifle, killing 29 Muslim worshippers and wounding many more. Goldstein was then beaten to death by the angry crowd.

What exactly triggered Goldstein's rampage may never be known, although Hebron was the site of a major massacre of Jews by Palestinians decades earlier. There were rumors that something like it was about to happen again. Also, Goldstein was a member of Kach, an extremist anti-Arab political party.

The results were clear. Up to that time, Palestinian violence had been directed mainly against the IDF and Jewish settlements. Now it would be directed against individuals and civilians. The next Intifada would be worse.

Changing Attitudes—Stop the Madness

One thing, however, appears to be changing—popular Palestinian support for political violence, especially that directed against civilians. When the second Intifada began in September 2000, an overwhelming majority of Palestinians supported the attacks and opposed a crackdown on the perpetrators.

By the end of the second year, that had changed. While Palestinians still supported attacks on soldiers and settlers in the West Bank, a small majority now also supported arresting militants and militia members to stop attacks inside Israel. What caused the change in attitude?

There appeared to be a growing realization that the costs were greatly outweighing the benefits. After more than two years of the Intifada …

- Some 2,000 Palestinians and 700 Israelis were dead.
- The Palestinian economy was in ruins.
- Israel had reoccupied the West Bank.
- Palestinian towns had become virtual prison camps as a result of travel bans.
- Most of the achievements of the Palestinian Authority had been wiped out.
- PLO headquarters in Ramallah had been reduced to little more than a pile of debris.
- Yasser Arafat himself had been reduced from an international statesman to a virtual prisoner hiding behind sandbags.

> **Word from the Wise**
>
> Who or what is the author of self-destructive behavior? "Satan, the god of this evil world, has blinded the minds of those who don't believe, so they are unable to see the glorious light of the Good News that is shining upon them." (2 Corinthians 4:4, NLT) Pray for those who are lost in darkness, unbelief, and self-destructive behavior.

Palestinians who had been intimidated into silence out of fear of appearing disloyal were beginning to find their voice. Some of them were saying the violence was counterproductive and needed to stop. Whether their voices would be strong enough to change anything was another question entirely.

Chapter 14

Oil and the New Arab World

We've already alluded to some reasons behind the growth of religious fanaticism and political extremism in the Arab world. Here's a fuller look in the form of a Top Ten List:

10. A loss of confidence in the Arab nationalism movement and pan-Arabism after the debacle of the 1967 Six Day War with Israel.

9. The collapse of the Soviet Union and the fading of the Marxist dream beginning in the 1980s.

8. A population explosion that has strained national resources and produced hordes of restless young men. Half the population of most Arab nations is under 25 years of age. (Both France and Iran experienced a youth bulge just prior to their famous revolutions.)

7. The failure of political institutions in the Arab world to make good on promises made after independence.

6. Enthusiasm for radicalism inspired by Khomeini's populist Islamic revolution in Iran.

5. Employment, refuge, and funding for militants provided by Saudi Arabia.

4. United States support of anti-Communist movements, such as the "good" militant Islamists in Afghanistan who eventually produced the Taliban. Thousands of Arab militants had nothing to do once the jihad against Moscow was over.

3. Israel's encouragement of alternatives to the hated PLO who turned out to be even worse—notably, Hamas.

2. The aforementioned Westofication and Coca-Colanization—in which Muslims fear their values are being overwhelmed and undermined by negative Western influences.

1. An explosion of petrodollars in the 1970s corrupted an entire generation and produced a cynical reaction to the royal families and the new fabulously wealthy elites.

Because of the number-one reason on this list, this chapter explores the central role that oil has played in the development of the modern Middle East. Oil influenced the shape of national boundaries and led to numerous armed conflicts. Oil dollars brought modernization and affluence, as well as corrupt regimes and violent reactions against those ruling elites.

An Earth-Shaking Discovery: Oil

Until the 1930s Saudi Arabia was a wretchedly poor country. Its economy was dependent on three primary things—the camel, the date palm, and the tax on foreigners coming for the annual hajj (pilgrimage to Mecca). Since becoming a wealthy oil nation, Saudi Arabia is the most influential Arab government in the world. Some say the several thousand males in the prolific Al Saud family now include 50 billionaires.

It's not just the Saudis. Kuwait has tended to lead the world in gross domestic product per capita, even ahead of the United States. Every year Arab leaders account for about 7 of the 10 richest heads of state in the world.

Americans tend to think they deserve some credit for saving the Saudis and Kuwaitis from aggression from the likes of Iraq's Saddam Hussein. To the average Arab, however, it is more a case of saving the Saudi and

Family Focus

Are you surprised that American efforts in the Middle East should be so unappreciated? Consider the merit of the Arab viewpoint. What would be your attitude toward your own government if leadership was not elected but passed on to family members?

Kuwaiti *royal families*. They all know the royal families guarantee the West cheap oil and billions in arms purchases in return for protection for them to stay in power.

The oil mega-fortunes also meant the final death knell to the pan-Arab dream. The haves simply had less and less incentive to merge their interests—and their fortunes—with the have-nots.

TIMELINE 1908–1991

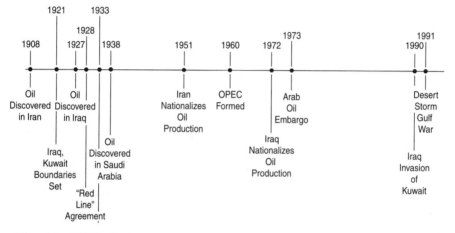

Oil and the Middle East.

An Orderly Stampede

The British first discovered oil in Iran in 1908 and then Iraq in 1927. Soon the British Navy was switching from coal to oil, and the Italians began to use it to fuel their military aircraft. Oil was soon to become a major ingredient and driving force in world geopolitics.

It may have been partly due to expectations of oil that Great Britain sought the League of Nations mandate for governing Iraq after World War I. When the national boundary lines were being drawn to divvy up the Ottoman possessions, England made sure that the line fell to include Mosul in Iraq rather than in Turkey. Mosul is now in the heart of Iraq's major oil-producing region.

Britain, France, and other Western powers pledged themselves to something called the Red Line Agreement in 1928, which basically insured an orderly *petroleum* stampede. Under its terms, oil exploration companies were not to seek major oil concessions in the old Ottoman territories (Middle East) without the agreement of all parties. It was a way to exploit the region cooperatively, create joint ventures, and avoid conflicts before they started. It also allowed American companies to participate in the Iraqi venture, called the Iraq Petroleum Company (now British Petroleum).

MidEast Dictionary

Petroleum is from Latin and Greek *petra* (rock) + *oleum* (oil); an oily, flammable liquid solution of hydrocarbons, yellowish-green to black in color, occurring naturally in the rock strata of certain geological formations; useful for fuel and other purposes when distilled.

Britain was preoccupied with its oil discoveries in Iran and Iraq and already had more oil than it knew what to do with. So, Britain let the Americans take the lead in Saudi Arabia, where the king, patriarch Abdul Aziz (Ibn Saud), was notoriously unapproachable.

Meanwhile, other major finds were being made in the Gulf region. Bahrain began pumping oil in 1932 A.D., and geologists cast envious eyes to the Saudi mainland, where they were sure they could see identical geological formations promising oil potential.

A Huge Find

Through a series of contacts through some rather oddball characters, the Americans managed to approach Ibn Saud in 1933, when the kingdom was just a year old. After lengthy negotiations, Ibn Saud granted a United States oil company the right to extract petroleum from his land in exchange for a couple of chests of gold coins and some other financial terms (total value said to be $250,000 to $300,000).

The king was pleased. Even if the geologists found no petroleum, they might find water, which was a precious commodity, too. However, if oil was found, he stood to receive 21 cents a barrel.

The company was the Standard Oil Company of California (Socal, now Chevron). Socal spent so much money the first several years in fruitless drilling that it sold a half interest to Texaco and called the joint venture Caltex. They concentrated their efforts at a place called Dammam Dome, a few miles inland from the Gulf adjacent to Bahrain and not far from Dhahran, which became an oil town.

The exploration team had almost given up after too many fruitless attempts when they finally struck it big at now-famous Dammam 7 in 1938, the same year as a major oil find in Kuwait. It was so big a find—perhaps a quarter of the entire world's oil reserves—that they also invited Mobil and Standard Oil of New Jersey (later named Esso and then Exxon) to share the cost of extraction and production. These companies together formed Aramco (Arabian-American Oil Co.).

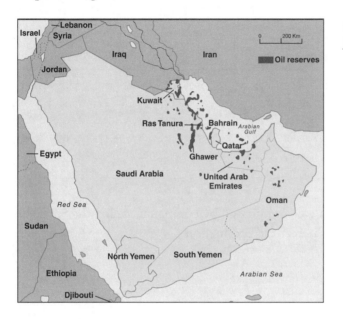

Saudi Arabia and its oil fields.

One Happy Monarch

The king again was pleased. His first check for 21 cents a barrel totaled out to more than $1.5 million. He had never seen such money. Soon the British, Germans, Italians, and Japanese were lobbying the Saudis for drilling rights. War was looming, and they all recognized the strategic military significance of this new resource. In the end, the Americans were granted a 60-year concession for new exploration.

Then World War II intervened, and production slowed as shipping became hazardous, particularly from the threat posed by German U-boats. There was also a shortage of tankers for commercial purposes.

After the war, oil production was fully unleashed. The Saudi yield exceeded everyone's wildest dreams. In the subsequent post-war economic boom, production of automobiles mushroomed, as did demand for oil, which jumped tenfold in the two decades following World War II.

The growing market for family automobiles was one factor. Others were the growing commercial airline industry, tractors and heavy agricultural equipment, and electrical generation.

> **Reality Check**
>
> Petroleum represents much more than just gasoline at the service station. The petrochemical industry produces a whole family of hydrocarbon products, including the very asphalt we use for blacktopping roads and all kinds of plastics. Others: cleaning agents and solvents, explosives, jet fuel, paraffin, kerosene, some medicines, naphtha, paints, synthetic rubber, wax, chemical fertilizers, synthetic fabrics, and detergents.

Petroleum production was dominated by companies called the Seven Sisters, accounting for nearly 80 percent of production:

- Socal
- Esso
- Texaco
- Mobil
- Gulf
- British Petroleum (BP)
- Royal Dutch Shell

The first four were the parent companies of Aramco in Saudi Arabia. Gulf was involved in Kuwait. BP was involved in Kuwait, Iraq, and Iran. Royal Dutch Shell was in Iraq, Iran, and Oman.

The Dark Side

There was a dark side to this economic boom. Stories of bribery were rampant. Members of the royal families would be educated in private schools overseas at oil company expense. Millions of dollars would go into the families, who treated their countries' oil resources as th

In 1951, Iran, which had been the leading oil producer in the early years, nationalized the Anglo-Iranian Oil Co. This outraged the British and triggere sympathetic boycotts and embargoes by the Western oil companies, who were used to doing business the way. Oil-producing countries, for example, had no say in the pricing of their own product.

The reaction against Iran produced a spectacular rise in the demand for Arab (non-Persian) oil, especially from Iraq, Saudi Arabia, and Kuwait. In Saudi Arabia, where oil revenues were already their main source of income, production jumped more than 40-fold. Multimillion-dollar palaces were built and camels traded in for air-conditioned Cadillacs.

Today the Saudi royal family is a political and economic powerhouse whose offspring are accustomed to wealth and privilege. In one case a 25-year-old prince built a $300 million palace in Riyadh and allegedly received a $1 billion commission on the kingdom's telephone contract with AT&T. In another case, the ski resort community of Aspen, Colorado, regards Saudi Prince Bandar fondly. Bandar has built a palatial home there and helped to underwrite the budgets of numerous local organizations.

of evil. How mu... for a high leader? "A just king gives stability to his nation, but one who demands bribes destroys it." (Proverbs 29:4)

Family Focus

What would be your priorities if your family controlled $1 billion? How would you use these funds? Would it change your lifestyle? No wonder Jesus said, "It is easier for a camel to go through the eye of a needle than for a rich person to enter the Kingdom of God." (Matthew 18:25, NLT)

The Oil Weapon: A Fraying Relationship

Over time, relations between the oil companies and their oil-producing hosts continued to unravel. The Seven Sisters were supposed to be splitting profits 50-50 with the oil producers, but the Arabs were not allowed to see the books and suspected the expenses were coming out of their half.

In 1960, the Seven Sisters unilaterally determined to reduce the price of oil by 10 cents per barrel. This move alone cost Saudi Arabia $30 million in lost revenue and wrecked the country's carefully crafted annual budget. The relationship was fraying.

Saudis and other oil producers met to devise a common strategy for dealing the oil companies. For its role in hosting the conference, Iraq allegedly incurred e wrath of the Western nations. There were rumors that Western intelligence agencies aided the rebellion of Iraqi Kurds in the north. The CIA was accused of a role in the overthrow of Iraqi strongman Abdul Karim Qasim by Saddam Hussein's Baath Party. If true, it would be a deep irony.

The resulting association was the Organization of Petroleum Exporting Countries (*OPEC*), which attempted to regulate the price of oil by controlling its supply. Tighter supplies would produce higher demand—and higher prices.

MidEast Dictionary

OPEC is a group formed in 1960–1961 to maintain a minimum price for oil; originally composed of some Gulf states plus Venezuela, it eventually expanded to include other members from Latin America, Africa, and Asia

Reality Check

By the 1990s oil prices were over $20 a barrel, and more recently over $30 a barrel. Some people are not aware that low oil prices are not necessarily good for the United States economy, as America is also an oil-producing nation and petroleum is a major industry.

The OPEC leverage turned out to be a double-edged sword that even worked occasionally to the advantage of the West. There were fewer radical moves, such as a state's nationalizing its oil industry, and more renegotiations of terms and phased acquisition toward full ownership of their production facilities.

The Saudis in particular strove to make things work. They generally cooperated to produce more oil and lower prices to offset inflation or to compensate for lost production, such as during the Iran-Iraq War. When oil prices collapsed and hurt United States producers in 1985, the Saudis pumped less and raised the price.

The other side of the sword appeared in 1973 when the Arab nations engaged Israel in the Yom Kippur War. Hostilities broke out just as OPEC was attempting to double the price of oil from $2.50 to $5 a barrel, partly to offset devaluation of the dollar. The oil companies were resisting, warning of devastating effects on the world economy. Meanwhile, Israel was hard pressed by the war, and the United States agreed to resupply Israel and provide a $2.2 billion emergency aid package.

Saudi Arabia turned on its old ally and led an Arab oil embargo against the United States and other Western nations supporting Israel. The impact was dramatic. Americans got a taste of hardship and crisis—long lines at filling stations, thermostats being turned down at homes and work places, and comprehensive energy conservation programs being adopted for the first time.

Politically, it was a shocker. Europeans were not hit as directly as America, but they denied landing rights to U.S. transport planes just in case, so as not to appear to be accomplices to America. Some in the Arab world found it immensely satisfying to see the Western world crawling on its knees. Muslim nations, tired of being dictated to by arrogant Westerners, were flexing newfound muscles.

Rather than doubling to $5 a barrel, oil prices the following year were raised to $11. The oil-producing nations had cut back production and virtually quadrupled the price. That move alone produced major long-term benefits for the Arab nations. This, too, was a shock to the West, but then oil had been a stable and cheap commodity for decades.

A Matter of Honor

For the Saudis the whole affair had been a matter of national honor. The Saudis were in a spot after the fiasco of the 1967 Six Day War. The blow to Arab pride reflected indirectly on the Saudis, the de facto leaders of the Arab world by virtue of their role as guardians of the holy places of Islam. Now, after the Yom Kippur War and the oil embargo, the score had been evened a bit.

Oil was also central to the 1990 Iraqi invasion of Kuwait and the subsequent Desert Storm war in 1991. Iraq had never been happy with its tiny neighbor to the south. It had objected in 1921 when Britain drew the boundary line to accommodate its old ally, the emir of Kuwait, leaving Iraq with very narrow access to the Gulf. Iraq continued to call for border adjustments and even challenged the legitimacy of Kuwait's sovereignty.

It almost came to blows the first time in 1961 as Britain was withdrawing from its former protectorate in Kuwait. Iraq's Abdul Karim Qasim threatened annexation, but Britain and some other Arab neighbors sent in troops to prevent an invasion.

> **Word from the Wise**
>
> Scripture warns repeatedly about the dangers of indebtedness. "Just as the rich rule the poor, so the borrower is servant to the lender." (Proverbs 22:7, NLT) Like Iraq, borrowers will sometimes go to desperate means to keep from going under. What are some other examples, even from people you know?

Iraq, Kuwait, and the Persian Gulf.

The next occasion came after the ruinous Iran-Iraq war. Iraq was deeply in debt to other Arab nations, owing billions to Kuwait it could not repay. Iraq demanded not only debt forgiveness but even more aid. Kuwait refused. By 1990, Kuwait was increasing its oil production. This lowered world prices and was particularly ruinous for Iraq, which desperately needed every penny.

Saddam Hussein accused Kuwait of stealing oil from their jointly operated Rumailla oil field and demanded $2.4 billion compensation. Hussein believed Iraq was owed at least that much as Arab "champion" against the Iranians. With their allegiance to Arab unity, the other states simply didn't believe Hussein would invade Kuwait. Even when he moved tens of thousands of troops to the border, they thought it was just a bluff. The moral apparently is that sometimes barking dogs really do bite.

Oil Politics

In 1972, the Iraqi government nationalized the Iraq Petroleum Co. By 1975, Iraqi oil revenues grew eightfold, from $1 billion to $8 billion. This considerably strengthened the hand of the Baath regime and its socialist agenda of controlling the major sectors of the economy.

After the Desert Storm war of 1991, its oil business came under United Nations sanctions. To prevent further purchase of armaments and weapons of mass destruction while Iraq's people starved, the so-called "Oil for Food" program was devised. Iraq could sell a restricted amount of oil each quarter with proceeds going to a special U.N. fund for food and medicine.

This did not, however, necessarily prevent abuse. Saddam's flamboyant sons, Uday and Qusay, have been accused of skimming millions from the program by insisting on kickbacks from purchasers. One way the allegations came to light was through dealers who paid their kickbacks and got nothing in return. It was the kind of trickery for which the term "kleptocracy" was coined, which means "rule by thieves."

Iraq has tried to build a coalition of other countries favoring removal of sanctions, enticed by the prospects of lucrative post-sanction deals. Russia, China, and France appeared to be the intended beneficiaries of this strategy. It was probably no coincidence that these three have been the biggest opponents of the United States' attempts to gain United Nations backing for the forced disarmament of Hussein's regime.

The Future

The major oil-exporting countries—largely the Gulf states—account for only a fourth of the region's population but generate three fourths of its gross domestic product. Only seven or eight percent of the region's gross domestic product is due to other industry such as manufacturing. In terms of Arab exports, oil accounts for 95 percent.

Yet, the benefits too often fail to trickle down to the average person in these states. Rarely do the oil profits go to public works and social services, schools, or health facilities. The royals may generously give of their fortunes to fund community projects, but these are more likely to be airports, armaments, and palaces than basic human services.

Except for Kuwait and the United Arab Emirates, the standard of living for most people in the region is

Family Focus

Imagine living in dire poverty while the royal family governing your nation was fabulously wealthy. How would you feel toward the government? How might a sense of equity and justice be restored?

surprisingly low, especially considering the vast oil wealth. In many ways Saudi citizens outside the royal family have the worst of both worlds—a very high cost of living but relatively low standard of living in terms of literacy, income, housing, health, and life expectancy. The government does provide subsidies, however, as a way of reducing the high costs of some things such as food, energy, transportation, health care, and education.

Petro-Islam

What the future holds is a matter of keen debate. One forecast held that the Saudi oil fields, vast as they are, could be exhausted at the current rate of production by 2077. Others believe the entire Arabian peninsula may sit over yet untapped reservoirs of petroleum.

The Saudis' greatest fear—especially since the Iranian revolution in 1979—has been regional instability. It is a conservative regime and, consequently, one that prefers reform to revolution. It's a mindset that sometimes has been termed "Petro-Islam." The term refers to a linking of foreign policy to religion with the goal of achieving Islamic dominance through shrewd financial strategies and economic dominance.

So, the Saudis are committed sponsors of political and financial organizations around the world that show Islam as a cohesive force that transcends nationality and culture to unite all believers in brotherhood. They have become major contributors to development projects throughout the Arab world, financial aid to poor Islamic nations, and major Muslim aid organizations such as the Organization of Islamic Conferences.

In a way, Petro-Islam is a strategy of buying power. Radical Islamists condemn the Arab royal families as corrupt sell-outs who have collaborated with the enemy, the Great Satan. The Saudis, however, seem to believe theirs is a more effective strategy in the long run.

Why fight your enemy, if you can just buy him out? It's an almost American concept. Perhaps that's why the Saudis and the Americans have had such a long-term relationship. Just ask Prince Bandar and the happy citizens of Aspen.

Age of Terrorism

As of this day and age, terrorism is considered to be premeditated, politically motivated violence aimed at intimidating and demoralizing civilians by clandestine agents or subnational groups; that is, not an army belonging to an officially recognized state or government.

Terrorism is not a new phenomenon. It has been around for centuries. Outright military conquest was not entirely necessary if enough people could be frightened into capitulating by a few acts of violence. A few groups—especially the Assyrians in biblical times and later the Mongols—became so expert at violence and terror that the mere mention of their name could incite panic.

In the Middle Ages, bodies infected with Black Death (bubonic plague) would be thrown over the castle walls to sow plague among the attackers. The British allegedly gave American Indians, who were assisting the French during the French and Indian Wars (1754–1767), blankets laden with smallpox.

Nor is terrorism today just a phenomenon of the Middle East. There are Basque separatists in Spain, Irish Republican Army terrorists in Ireland, and Shining Path guerrillas in Peru. That's not to mention extremist groups in America and individuals like Timothy McVeigh, who bombed the federal building in Oklahoma City. Bombs and bullets know no national boundaries.

When it comes to numbers, the Middle East has earned its reputation as the leader in terrorism. Of some three dozen prominent terrorist groups tracked by the U.S. State Department, 27 of them are Middle Eastern. Most of those are Arab or Islamic; one is Jewish.

Expanding Horizons

Originally, most of the Middle Eastern terrorist groups were generated in reaction to the establishment of the state of Israel in 1948, and their actions have been directed against the Jews. But increasingly—as the September 11, 2001 attacks on America demonstrated—the attacks are also directed against the West, especially the United States.

Sometimes the violence is directed against their own people. The Mujaheddin-e Khalq, for example, is a Marxist Iranian group working out of Iraq to overthrow the Islamic government of Iran.

Car and truck bombs have been a favorite technique. Suicide bombing grew into a major trend in the 1990s. Some Islamic extremists taught that the *shahid* (martyr) secured paradise not only for himself, but also for 70 of his relatives. More recently, the first several women joined the ranks of suicide bombers.

def·i·ni·tion MidEast Dictionary

Shahada means martyrdom; a *shahid* is one who sacrifices his life for Allah; most commonly practiced by use of an explosives belt, allowing the shahid to inflict maximum damage with careful timing and proximity to his target.

Terrorist violence against Christians also has been on the increase from radical Islamists. In late 2002, an American missionary was shot to death outside a health clinic in Sidon, Lebanon, and three Southern Baptist medical workers were gunned down in Yemen.

The trend generating the greatest apprehension, however, is the declared intention of terrorist groups to acquire weapons of mass destruction. These are what the U.S. State Department calls CBRN weapons—chemical, biological, radiological, and nuclear. With the vast destructive potential of such weapons, terrorism could become a fearsome force of unprecedented proportions.

Black September

Many have traced the roots of terrorism to the humiliation Arabs suffered in the 1967 Six Day War and subsequent difficulties. Many thousands of Palestinian refugees fully expected they would return to their homes at the head of victorious Arab armies massing to retake their land. It never happened.

However, they did manage one surprise victory in 1968. Arab guerillas from Fatah, Yasser Arafat's group, had been launching various attacks against Israel and in the process blew up a school bus, killing Israeli children. Incensed, Israel sent an armored column over the border into Jordan and attacked Karameh, where Fatah was based. To their surprise, the Israelis were driven back by a combination of freedom fighters, young boys blowing themselves up with dynamite, and reinforcements from Jordanian regulars.

This defeat tarnished the Israelis' aura of invincibility. Ecstatic Palestinians began lining up to join groups like Fatah and the Marxist Popular Front for the Liberation of Palestine (PFLP) by the score. There followed a wave of airplane hijackings and bombings that gave Jordan a bad name. Then Jordan's premier was assassinated. King Hussein was determined to eliminate the problem.

In September 1970, Hussein sent tanks, planes, and armored cars after the guerrilla fighters. In the resounding defeat, at least 4,000 of the Palestinians were killed. Their short-lived triumph had turned to ashes. The Palestinians called it Black September.

It was no accident, then, that the perpetrators of the next major terrorist attack called themselves the Black September Organization. This was the notorious attack on 11 Israeli athletes at the 1972 Winter Olympics in Munich, Germany. Two of the athletes died in the initial assault, and the rest were taken hostage.

The Black September terrorists demanded a getaway plane, but a shootout ensued at the airport with security forces. All nine Israeli hostages and five Palestinians were killed in the firefight. Three other terrorists were captured. They said they were just trying to bring world attention to the plight of Palestinians. They also had demanded the release of more than 200 Palestinian prisoners held by Israel.

Ironically, the three surviving terrorists were released just a few weeks later in exchange for passengers aboard a hijacked German jet. Over the next few years, *Mossad* methodically tracked down and assassinated 12 others believed to have had a part in the Munich attack. It was called Operation Wrath of God.

> **MidEast Dictionary**
>
> **Mossad** is the Israeli foreign intelligence service; it has been involved in many successful counter-terrorism operations, as well as assassinations, the invasion of Lebanon, and the Iran-Contra scandal in the United States; perhaps its greatest failure has been its unsuccessful attempts to eliminate Saddam Hussein.

The bottom line for the Palestinians was even greater bitterness and disillusionment. Not only had they lost their homeland to the Zionists; now their Arab brothers had turned on them. It was a bad recipe for the future.

Major Terrorist Incidents

After more than 35 years of terrorist violence, the incidents—especially those routinely perpetrated against Israel—would be far beyond cataloguing. The sections that follow are just several of the more dramatic ones.

TERRORISM TIMELINE 1948–2001

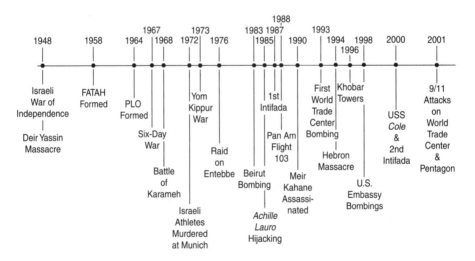

Decades of terrorist attacks.

Entebbe 1976

An Air France flight with 256 passengers flying from Tel Aviv to Paris was hijacked by terrorists and diverted to Libya for fueling for a much longer flight to Uganda, home of the brutal dictator Idi Amin. At a vacant terminal building in Entebbe, some 100 Israeli passengers were marked for execution if terrorists' demands were not met for the release of dozens of convicted terrorists.

The Israelis, who have had a policy of not negotiating with terrorists, secretly sent 200 special paratroopers in four transport planes. Entebbe was at the outer limit of the planes' range, but because Israel still held the Sinai Peninsula, the planes could be dispatched from farther south in Sharm El Sheikh. The daring raid was a dramatic success, safely rescuing all the hostages. It surprised the world and was a crushing blow to terrorist groups.

Achille Lauro 1985

Heavily armed terrorists from the Palestine Liberation Front hijacked the Italian cruise ship *Achille Lauro* off the coast of Egypt and held 400 passengers and crew hostage. They demanded the release of 50 Palestinian prisoners held by Israel. They also killed a disabled American tourist, Leon Klinghoffer, 69, and threw his body and wheelchair overboard.

 Reality Check

One who did not survive the raid was its leader, Lt. Col. Jonathan ("Yoni") Netanyahu, who was shot in the initial firefight. Jonathan was the older brother of Benjamin Netanyahu, who later became prime minister of Israel. The Jonathan Institute in Israel for the study of terrorism was named in his memory.

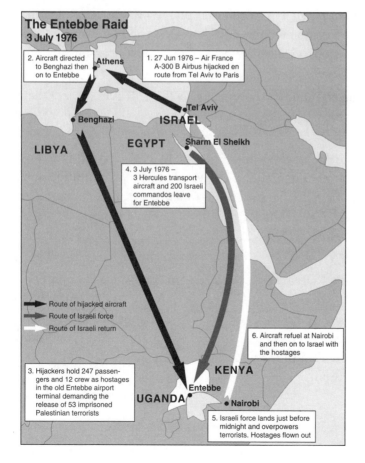

The Entebbe raid.

The Entebbe Raid
3 July 1976

2. Aircraft directed to Benghazi then on to Entebbe

1. 27 Jun 1976 – Air France A-300 B Airbus hijacked en route from Tel Aviv to Paris

Athens

Tel Aviv

Benghazi

ISRAEL

LIBYA

EGYPT

Sharm El Sheikh

4. 3 July 1976 – 3 Hercules transport aircraft and 200 Israeli commandos leave for Entebbe

Route of hijacked aircraft
Route of Israeli force
Route of Israeli return

6. Aircraft refuel at Nairobi and then on to Israel with the hostages

3. Hijackers hold 247 passengers and 12 crew as hostages in the old Entebbe airport terminal demanding the release of 53 imprisoned Palestinian terrorists

KENYA

Entebbe

UGANDA

Nairobi

5. Israeli force lands just before midnight and overpowers terrorists. Hostages flown out

While making their getaway in an Egyptian jet, the terrorists were intercepted by U.S. Navy F-14 fighters and forced to land in Sicily, where they were arrested. Italian authorities were backed up by members of Delta Force and Navy SEAL teams.

Reality Check

Youssef Magied al-Molqi, convicted of killing Leon Klinghoffer, disappeared one day in 1996 while on a 12-day furlough from a high-security prison in Rome. He had been serving a 30-year sentence. As is true throughout the European Union, Italy does not have the death penalty. He has not been found.

Pan Am Flight 103 1988

Sometimes called the air disaster of the century, Pan Am Flight 103 was blown up over Lockerbie, Scotland, by a bomb believed planted in Frankfurt, Germany, by Libyan terrorists (nobody was willing to claim responsibility; just raw anti-Americanism). The explosion killed all 259 passengers and 11 persons on the ground.

The casualties: By one account, 400 parents lost a child, 46 parents lost their only child, 65 women were widowed, 11 men lost their wives, 140 lost a parent, and seven lost both parents.

One defendant, Libyan Abdel al-Megrahi, got life in a Scottish jail with possibility of parole in 20 years. The other defendant, Lameen Fhima, was acquitted and re-turned to a hero's welcome in Libya. Ruler Muammar Gadhafi, still denying Libyan involvement, nevertheless had a camel sacrificed in Fhima's honor.

Embassy Bombings 1998

U.S. Embassies in Nairobi, Kenya, and Dar es Salaam, Tanzania, 450 miles apart, were blown up by bombs within minutes of each other. The explosions killed 224 persons, including a dozen Americans, and buried thousands of others under piles of tangled metal and concrete. Four members of Osama bin Laden's al-Qaeda terror-ist organization were convicted of the bombings in May 2001 in a tightly guarded Manhattan federal courtroom.

Other Attacks

Over time, attacks focused increasingly on Americans:

- Bombing of the U.S. Embassy in Beirut, 1983—63 killed, 120 wounded.

- Bombings of U.S. Marine and French paratroop barracks in Beiruit, 1983—300 killed.

- First bombing of the World Trade Center in New York, 1993—six killed, 1,000 wounded.

- Bombing of Khobar Towers in Dharan, Saudi Arabia, 1996—19 U.S. soldiers killed, 515 wounded.

- Bombing of the USS *Cole* in Aden, Yemen, 2000—17 U.S. sailors killed, 39 wounded.

- Hijacked airliner attacks on the World Trade Center, 2001—2,800 killed, scores wounded.

- Hijacked airliner attack on the Pentagon, 2001—189 killed, many wounded.

State-Sponsored Terrorism (Promoting the Cause)

State-sponsored terrorism is the same acts of violence carried out with the backing of another nation.

One of the most graphic examples is that of Saddam Hussein and the families of Palestinian suicide bombers. At a time when his own people were starving, Hussein was writing $25,000 checks to the families of each such "martyr." Smaller amounts would go for those otherwise killed or injured in some other connection to the Intifada (uprising). By one estimate Hussein had contributed some $10 million, mostly through the Arab Liberation Front, a small PLO faction closely aligned with Saddam's Baath Party.

Of the seven major state sponsors of terrorism identified by the U.S. State Department, five of them are in the Middle East. They are Iran, Iraq, Libya, Syria, and Sudan. (The other two are Cuba and North Korea.)

> **Family Focus**
>
> How are we to understand this strange phenomenon of suicide "martyrdom"? What drives young people to blow themselves up? Consider the beliefs they are taught; how does this differ from the concept of Christian martyrdom?

Making the list of state sponsors of terrorism results in various sanctions—a ban on arms sales and high-technology items, cut-off of foreign aid, and denial of all sorts of routine business relations. It's intended to pinch, and generally does.

Here are some of the documented terrorist activities.

Iran:

- Providing Lebanese Hezbollah and several Palestinian groups with funding, safe haven, training, and weapons.

- Some support to terrorist groups in the Gulf, Africa, Turkey, and Central Asia.

- Maintaining the death sentence and $2.8 million bounty on exiled Iranian author Salman Rushdie.

- Allowing some al-Qaeda operatives safe transit into and out of Afghanistan.

- The number-one most active state sponsor of terror in recent years.

Iraq:

- An unsuccessful 1993 attempt by the Iraqi Intelligence Service to assassinate former President George H.W. Bush and the Emir of Kuwait with a car bomb.

- Providing shelter, training, logistical assistance, and financial aid for three major terrorist organizations:

  The Mujaheddin-e Khalq Organization, which has committed terrorist acts in Iran and killed Americans.

  Several Palestinian terrorist organizations, including the Palestine Liberation Front and Abu Abbas, who masterminded the *Achille Lauro* hijacking.

  The Abu Nidal Organization, which has carried out attacks in 20 countries, including the United States, killing or injuring nearly 900 people.

- Was the only Arab-Muslim country that did not condemn the September 11 attacks against the United States. In fact, an official statement said the U.S. was "reaping the fruits of [its] crimes against humanity."

> **Word from the Wise**
>
> What is God's view of evildoing? The Bible says there are seven things God hates—"haughty eyes, a lying tongue, hands that kill the innocent, a heart that plots evil, feet that race to do wrong, a false witness who pours out lies, a person who sows discord among brothers." (Proverbs 6:17–19, NLT) Terrorists are guilty of these things, as are all sinners.

Libya:

- A Libyan intelligence agent was convicted of planting the bomb on Pan Am flight 103, killing 259 passengers, and 11 on the ground in Lockerbie, Scotland.

- A German court found the Libyan government responsible for the bombing of a West Berlin discotheque, killing two U.S. servicemen and one Turkish citizen and injuring 200.

- More recently, however, Libya has renounced terrorism and condemned the September 11 attacks on the United States.

Syria:

- Providing safe haven and logistics support to a half-dozen of the most extreme terror groups, including Hamas.

- Providing access to Lebanon's Bekaa Valley, under Syrian control, to major terrorists.

- Serving as the main conduit for Iranian-supplied weapons to Hezbollah.

- It has, however, cooperated in international efforts to eliminate al-Qaeda and does not allow attacks from Syrian territory.

Sudan:

- Serving as a safe haven for notorious extremists, including members of al-Qaeda and Hamas.

- Has begun to cooperate with international anti-terrorism efforts by investigating and apprehending some extremists.

> **Word from the Wise**
>
> How are believers to regard evildoers? The Bible says not to worry about them. "In a little while the wicked will disappear. Though you look for them, they will be gone. Those who are gentle and lowly will possess the land; they will live in prosperous security." (Psalm 37:10–11, NLT) God will bring ultimate retribution, a role that we are not called to play.

The Most Prominent Middle East Terrorist Groups

There are literally dozens of Middle East terrorist groups. The sections that follow describe a few of the more prominent ones.

The Palestine Liberation Organization (PLO)

The group that probably comes first to most people's minds is the Palestine Liberation Organization (PLO). The PLO, however, has officially renounced terrorism since 1988. This may be a technical distinction, as some of its affiliates are more directly involved in political violence. While no one really believes the PLO has totally "gone straight," it has concerned itself more in recent years with the creation of a Palestinian state.

The PLO was founded in 1964 as an umbrella group for various parties committed to Palestinian self-determination. It was deemed the official representative of the Palestinian people in 1974 by the Arab League. It even gained observer status in the United Nations.

Reality Check

The PLO for a time was headquartered in Beirut until driven out in the Israeli invasion of Lebanon in 1982. Then it was centered in Tunis, Tunisia, for a while until Israel bombed its headquarters there. Then it relocated to the West Bank. By the late 1970s, the PLO had won formal recognition from more than 100 countries, ironically far more than Israel.

Reality Check

When Israelis condemn Arafat as a man of blood, it is not so much because of the PLO as because of Fatah. Fatah had a secret life that its members took pains to conceal. The truth was that there never was a distinct organization called "Black September." In reality, Black September *was* Fatah, in disguise.

Yasser Arafat carries the title of chairman of the PLO executive committee and president of the State of Palestine. He was one of the only Arab leaders to support Saddam Hussein in his annexation of Kuwait and ensuing battle with the United States. Saddam had tried unsuccessfully to link his withdrawal from Kuwait to a demand for the withdrawal of Israel from the occupied territories. That support cost Arafat and the PLO dearly through the cancellation of financial grants and assistance from the oil-rich Gulf States.

Fatah

Fatah, which means "to liberate" in Arabic, is one of the oldest terror groups, founded in 1958 by Yasser Arafat and several others. Its membership soared after the battle of Karameh, in which Israel was driven back from Jordan. It has remained the largest of the 10 or so affiliates comprising the PLO. Over the years it has wavered between advocating the complete "liberation of Palestine"—code words for the destruction of Israel—and peaceful co-existence in an autonomous Palestinian state.

Hamas

Hamas, which is an acronym in Arabic for Islamic Resistance Movement, picked up much of the Arab nations' financial assistance that was withdrawn from Arafat. Just as the PLO is a broad, secular political movement, Hamas is a fundamentalist religious movement, seeking the creation of an Islamic Palestinian state. It is totally opposed to the peace process (endorsed by the PLO) begun in the 1990s in Madrid and Oslo.

> **Word from the Wise**
>
> Terror, so much a sign of our times, is defined as "intense fear." Believers are promised freedom from fear in the shelter of God. "Do not be afraid of the terrors of the night, nor fear the dangers of the day, nor dread the plague that stalks in darkness, nor the disaster that strikes at midday." (Psalm 91:5, NLT)

Hamas has advocated and practiced armed violence against Israeli settlements in the occupied territories. Consequently, membership in Hamas is illegal in Israel. Even the Palestinian Authority has arrested and jailed its members. It is responsible for the bulk of the suicide bombings. A martyr's death is celebrated like a wedding. "We offer candy, sweets, and cold drinks," said Hamas founder Ahmed Yassin, "because we know he'll be so high in heaven."

Hezbollah

Hezbollah, which means party of God (Allah), is a Lebanese radical Shi'ite group sometimes also known as Islamic Jihad. It is Iranian-inspired and seeks a Khomeini-style Islamic theocracy in Palestine—with the eradication of Israel. It has collaborated with Syria in its occupation of Lebanon. Hezbollah is virulently anti-American and has been involved in most of the kidnappings and killings of Americans in Lebanon, including the 1983 bombings of the embassy and Marine barracks.

Al-Qaeda

Al-Qaeda, which means "the base" in Arabic, is the creation of Saudi expatriate multimillionaire Osama bin Laden, originally to drive the Soviets out of Afghanistan. Working with the Afghan Taliban, al-Qaeda set up training camps there to produce

Reality Check

The United States has accepted bin Laden's challenge and has declared war on the terrorists. "Every nation in every region now has a decision to make. Either you are with us, or you are with the terrorists." President George W. Bush, September 20, 2001.

hundreds of armed terrorists and martyrs. In 1998 A.D., bin Laden declared war on America and said it was the duty of Muslims everywhere to kill Americans everywhere.

Al-Qaeda was responsible for the attacks on the U.S. Embassies in Kenya and Tanzania, Khobar Towers, the USS *Cole*, and the attacks on the World Trade Center and the Pentagon. The group's stated goal is the establishment of a pan-Islamic caliphate throughout the world by helping other extremist groups overthrow "non-Islamic" regimes and expel all Westerners from Muslim countries. Heading that list would be the U.S. troops in the holy land of Saudi Arabia.

Jewish Terrorism

Prior to statehood, Israelis armed themselves during periods of Arab violence in the 1920s and 1930s. Various groups formed for self-defense. One of them, *Haganah* (defense), became a professional military force. Others became militias not unlike the Arab terrorists they were fighting.

Irgun, an anti-British group during the mandate period, was responsible for blowing up the King David Hotel and the British offices, killing 91 people. It was also responsible for the 1948 massacre of the Palestinian village Deir Yassin, where more than 200 men, women, and children died. Its efforts were credited by some accounts with driving out perhaps 300,000 Palestinians just prior to Israeli statehood. Irgun's leader was Menachem Begin, who later became prime minister of Israel.

Lehi, also known as the Stern Gang, was another anti-British group that attacked British soldiers and bombed military installations. It allegedly also participated in the Deir Yassin massacre and continued to fight Arab Palestinians for several years after statehood. Its most famous leader was Yitzhak Shamir, also a later prime minister.

Kach (Hebrew for "thus") was an extremist anti-Arab group founded by American-born Orthodox rabbi Meir Kahane. Kach advocated restoration of the biblical Israel as an exclusively Jewish state and the expulsion of all Arabs. Kahane was assassinated in New York in 1990. Baruch Goldstein, who killed 29 Muslims in the 1994 Hebron massacre, was a member of Kach, which was outlawed as a terrorist organization. Kahane's son, Binyamin, started an offshoot called Kahane Chai (Kahane lives). Binyamin and his wife were killed in a 2000 drive-by shooting.

Then there's the behavior of Israel itself, which has dynamited civilian houses and conducted assassinations. In November 2001, for example, Israeli helicopters shot antitank missiles at a car with senior Hamas official Mahmoud Abu Hanoud, who was killed instantly. Many others have been dispatched similarly.

Technically, these incidents might not be called terrorism because they are carried out by the defense forces of a nation state. However, the tactics and the effects are the same. In addition, one of the results has been to further inflame a bad situation and alienate moderate Arabs.

Family Focus

What are the downsides of adopting the violent tactics of your enemy? What should be the Christian response for dealing with hatred and violence? Explore the different views on this topic held by Christians themselves.

The Challenge

The search for peace in the Middle East has been an elusive struggle for decades. It has not been without successes, but that day of final settlement of all hostilities is still not in sight. Here's what's been done to date—and what's still to be done.

We've looked generally at the basic beliefs of the three monotheistic faiths—Judaism, Christianity, and Islam. But have you ever wondered specifically how these beliefs compare, how they differ, and where they're similar? We look at that here.

We'll also begin to get a handle on that oft-heard question, "Why do they hate us so much?" Whether we agree or not, there are some serious issues. America wasn't chosen at random for terror attacks. We look at the nature of those attacks that have become almost unrelenting.

The biggest bad boy in the region for two decades has been Saddam Hussein, and we look at all the trouble he's been causing with his neighbors and with America. This is a story that's still developing at press time. We also look at the most recent challenges confronting the United States, including Osama bin Laden and the war on terror. It doesn't get any more current than this.

Chapter 16

The Peace Process

The lack of peace in the Middle East has not been for lack of trying. In this chapter we will look at some of the Herculean efforts that have been employed toward that end. It wasn't that long ago that the region appeared on the verge of a permanent solution.

Desperate Need for Peace

The desperate need for a Middle East peace process became painfully apparent shortly after the 1967 Six Day War created intractable issues that would take more than 30 years even to begin to solve. It wasn't just territories that the Arabs had lost; they'd also lost face, a most serious matter in the Middle East.

Alarmed by major Israeli gains at the expense of its neighbors Egypt, Jordan, and Syria, the United Nations passed Resolution 242. This famous document declared Israel's right to exist in peace within secure borders while insisting on Israel's withdrawal from the occupied territories. It became known as the "land for peace" formula and, though never implemented, is routinely invoked yet today in diplomatic and political debate.

For the next three years skirmishes continued between Egypt and Israel along the Suez Canal, called the War of Attrition. The United States tried to broker a settlement (the Rogers Peace Plan), but Egypt, still smarting over its loss of the Sinai Peninsula, insisted on Israel's withdrawal from occupied territories as a precondition. President Anwar Sadat eventually concluded only another war would settle things.

PEACE PROCESS TIMELINE 1964–2000

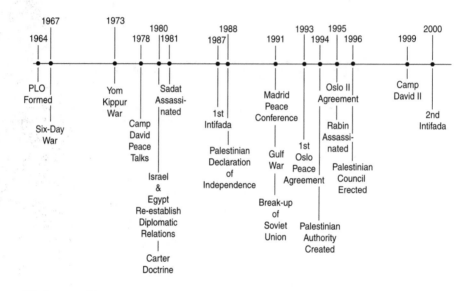

The long road to peace.

The 1973 Yom Kippur War caught Israel by surprise, and by the time the Israelis were able to push back the onslaught from the south by the Egyptians and from the north by the Syrians, the referee's whistle had blown the play dead. Casualties were high. More Egyptian soldiers actually died of thirst in the Sinai desert than from gunshots.

Israel was unhappy to be stopped short. Its forces had more than recovered lost ground; they were on their way to Cairo and Damascus. Egypt's Third Army was trapped by forces led by Ariel Sharon, and when the Soviets threatened to intervene, the United States put its forces on worldwide nuclear alert and then leaned hard on its ally, Israel. Henry Kissinger, secretary of state under President Richard Nixon, produced a disengagement agreement through his famous "shuttle diplomacy" parleys—negotiations between hostile countries or groups conducted by a mediator who travels back and forth between the parties.

The whole affair deeply unsettled Israel to be caught that unaware and pushed that close to disaster by the Arabs. An investigative commission criticized military leadership. The whole affair led to the collapse of the government of Prime Minister Golda Meir, who was replaced by Yitzhak Rabin in his first term in that post in 1974. The next year the United Nations General Assembly gave Israel another black eye by voting to condemn Zionism as a form of racism.

Nevertheless, there were some silver linings. Egypt's far better showing in this latest conflict allowed Sadat to feel that he could begin to negotiate with Israel from a position of honor. The shattering of Israel's myth of invincibility helped it to get over its psychological barrier to land concessions. By the time Menachem Begin became prime minister in Israel, there was a new political reality.

There's really no other way to explain how the Egyptian president who almost started a nuclear war and the Israeli prime minister who once led a vicious Jewish terrorism group could make history by going to Camp David, Maryland, in 1978 to talk peace.

Initial Steps

One of the fruits of the Camp David talks was a 1979 peace treaty between Egypt and Israel. For their efforts Begin and Sadat were awarded a Nobel Peace Prize. Israel agreed to return the Sinai Peninsula but kept the Gaza Strip. Egypt normalized relations with both Israel and the United States, which had been broken off under pro-Soviet leader Gamel Abdel Nasser. The United States in turn awarded record amounts of foreign aid to the two nations.

> **Word from the Wise**
>
> According to the Bible, believers are called to be peacemakers. "God blesses those who work for peace, for they will be called the children of God." (Matthew 5:9, NLT) What are some of the ways your family members can be peacemakers in the circles in which you live?

The Palestine Liberation Organization, however, was not a participant in the talks and refused even to consider Camp David Phase 2. This was an agreement called "A Framework for Peace in the Middle East," which would have provided for self-rule in the West Bank and Gaza, beginning as early as 1980. At that point, the PLO's demand was non-negotiable: All of the land had to be under Palestinian rule, not just the occupied territories.

Again, however, there were reasons for hope. Egypt and Israel exchanged ambassadors in 1980. The largest military threat against Israel was now a nation with which it was at peace. The region was to some extent being stabilized. The Yom Kippur War was the last major war involving Israel in the region. The process begun at Camp David served as an ideological foundation, a starting point for more fruitful peace efforts in the future.

Certainly, the Middle East remained a very dangerous place. Egypt's peacemaking with Israel was a source of later embarrassment for it as Israel continued to mix it up with its other Arab neighbors. Arab anger built as Israel invaded Lebanon—1978 and 1982—to strike at terrorist camps, bombed Iraq's nuclear reactor (1981), and formally annexed East Jerusalem (1980) and the Golan Heights (1981).

The Price of Peace

Egypt's peacemaking came at a price. For a few years it was a pariah among the Arab nations, expelled from the Arab League and even denied diplomatic relations in many Arab capitals. The feelings against Israel were that strong. In 1981, Sadat paid the ultimate price as his life was taken by an assassin's bullet.

Word from the Wise

The only real, true peace is found in Jesus Christ, and there will only be peace on earth when He comes again. "I am leaving you with a gift—peace of mind and heart. And the peace I give isn't like the peace the world gives. So don't be troubled or afraid." (John 14:27, NLT) How do you experience His peace in your own life?

On top of everything else was the Cold War, which tended to raise the stakes of any conflict in the Middle East by threatening to bring the United States and Soviet Union into conflict. Because of those stakes President Jimmy Carter, the peacemaker, drew a line in the sand in 1980. The line was around the Persian Gulf and the oil fields. It was called the Carter Doctrine. It stated:

"An attempt by any outside force to gain control of the Persian Gulf region will be regarded as an assault on the vital interests of the United States. It will be repelled by use of any means necessary, including military force."

Two years later, President Ronald Reagan expanded upon the Carter Doctrine by adding more specifically:

Family Focus

Were you aware of the Carter Doctrine (pledging to defend the Persian Gulf)? Discuss this U.S. policy, referring to Chapter 15 on oil, if necessary. Do you agree with this policy? Why or why not?

"An attack on Saudi Arabia would be considered an attack on the United States." The policy was abundantly clear and simple, and it remains the policy of the United States 20 years later.

New Catalysts for Peace: Algiers and Madrid Conferences

Meanwhile, several other attempts at a more comprehensive Middle East peace plan by two U.S. administrations and an Arab summit failed to get off the ground. Then, by 1987, a new challenge to peace was posed by the first Palestinian Intifada.

One event in 1988, however, changed the complexion of things. The Palestine National Council meeting in Algiers issued a Palestinian declaration of independence. This declaration may have been more form than substance, but it did for the first time pledge the PLO to renouncing violence and terrorism.

That development paved the way for the United States to begin low-level contacts with the PLO for the first time. In addition, that opened the door a crack wider for the Israelis, who had been unalterably opposed to direct contact with their old enemy. In 1991, the government of Yitzhak Shamir agreed to talks with a mixed delegation of non-PLO Palestinians and Jordanians.

 Word from the Wise

God calls people to reason with Him over a bigger issue than world peace. "'Come now, let us argue this out,' says the LORD. "No matter how deep the stain of your sins, I can remove it. I can make you as clean as freshly fallen snow. Even if you are stained as crimson, I can make you as white as wool.'" (Isaiah 1:18, NLT) Have you made peace with God in this way?

This was the landmark Madrid peace conference, co-sponsored by the United States and Soviet Union. Israel's neighbors Lebanon and Syria also participated. Madrid was significant for a couple of things: For the first time Israel appeared willing to accept the idea of land concessions under Resolution 242. Moreover, the Palestinians appeared willing to accept the idea of peace with Israel. Land for peace was now at least thinkable.

Undoubtedly the most significant thing about the Madrid conference was that it provided the catalyst for more substantive talks behind the scenes that no one would know about until much later.

Meanwhile, Saddam Hussein's invasion of Kuwait triggered the Gulf War in 1991. Saddam tried unsuccessfully to rally Arab support by turning it into an Arab-Israeli war. He lobbed missiles into Israel and tried to link his withdrawal from Kuwait to Israel's withdrawal from the occupied territories. None but Yasser Arafat and King Hussein of Jordan bought any of it.

Not only did Saddam lose the war, but Arafat lost Arab support for his cause as well as financial backing from the Gulf states. This probably made the peace process look more attractive to a more humbled and chastened PLO.

Also in 1991 came the disintegration of the old Soviet Union. This had the effect of freeing the United States from feeling compelled to defend Israel right or wrong against an Eastern bloc that was arming the Arabs and pursuing strategic advantage in the Middle East. Some would say it allowed the United States to become more objective about the Israeli-Palestinian dispute. It also might have made it more imperative for Israel to begin negotiating seriously.

Breakthroughs in Peace

Not that Israel was exactly leaping with joy over the peace process. Succeeding Menachem Begin as prime minister was Yitzhak Shamir of the conservative Likud Party. Shamir's election became more of a mandate for the status quo.

> **Word from the Wise**
>
> God has given His people a ministry of reconciliation. "All this newness of life is from God, who brought us back to himself through what Christ did. And God has given us the task of reconciling people to him." (2 Corinthians 5:18, NLT) How can you take steps toward reconciliation in your own life with those of other races or ethnic backgrounds?

Israeli settlements in the occupied territories actually increased under Shamir, only further inflaming the situation. This was also the period when the immigration of many thousands of Russian Jews to Israel was at its peak, and Israel was hard pressed to handle the influx. President George H.W. Bush attempted to apply political pressure by withholding promised financial aid for Soviet immigrant housing. Still, the hated settlements continued.

Israel's economy went into recession, and voters were unhappy. In 1992, the conservatives were voted out, and Yitzhak Rabin from the more liberal and pro-peace Labor Party was voted in. This would have major implications for the peace process.

The Madrid talks were actually still going on by 1993. Then rumors started to surface about secret back-channel negotiations going on in Norway. The rumors turned out to be true.

Oslo I

It had all started because of a study of living conditions in the West Bank and Gaza Strip by a group called the Norwegian Institute for Applied Social Science. The Norwegians developed relationships with both Israelis and Palestinians and suggested they go to neutral ground in Norway to discuss ways to reconcile their differences.

Secretly for 14 sessions over 8 months, Israelis and Palestinians for the first time held direct talks. The first Oslo agreement was called the Declaration of Principles on Interim Self-Governing Arrangements for Palestinians in the Gaza Strip and Jericho. The Declaration of Principles, for short, was almost more of a plan for a plan, an agenda of items to be resolved over the next five years between Israel and the Palestinians.

In this troubled environment, however, symbol is often as important as substance, and an important bridge had been crossed. The agreement was sealed on September 13, 1993 with a historic handshake and signing at the White House between Arafat and Rabin under auspices of President Bill Clinton.

One tangible outcome of this first phase of the Oslo accords was Israel's agreement to begin turning over control of the entire Gaza Strip to the Palestinians. Israel was not ready to do the same in the West Bank, but agreed to start with autonomy for Jericho. So, phase one became known as the Gaza-Jericho agreement.

The next year (1994) saw the creation of the Palestine Interim Self-Government Authority (PISGA), the creation of a Palestinian police force, and the withdrawal of Israeli Defense Forces from Gaza and Jericho. Israel also released some Palestinian prisoners.

These modest beginnings did have a positive ripple effect in the region. Jordan, which had technically been at war with Israel for 46 years, finally signed a formal peace treaty with its neighbor. This enabled Jordan to obtain precious water rights, additional Western aid, and eventual oversight of some Muslim holy sites in East Jerusalem.

Reality Check

Henry Kissinger once said, "In the Middle East you can't make war without Egypt, and you can't make peace without Syria." His words seemed only truer with time.

Jordan, long at odds with the Palestinians ever since Black September, began to reconcile with the PLO. King Hussein may have seen this as preferable to the greater danger posed by radical Islamic movements.

Lebanon was a different story. Peace there depended on relations with Syria, its occupier. Reconciliation with Syria was unlikely so long as Israel continued to occupy the Golan Heights with 13,000 settlers and control the water supplies. There was still a long road ahead. However, the center of gravity was shifting toward serious negotiation.

More Obstacles

Yitzhak Rabin, Shimon Peres, and Yasser Arafat were awarded the 1994 Nobel Peace Prize for their work in starting the peace process. In many ways, however, the hard work of peace was really just beginning.

There was the matter of some 140,000 Jewish settlers in the West Bank and Gaza. These were mostly very determined, conservative individuals who believed in biblical Israel as a Jewish state as an unalterable matter of principle. There was also the matter of language in the PLO charter opposed to Israel's very existence and vowing to "purge the Zionist presence from Palestine" by armed struggle. These were not matters lending themselves to easy solutions.

All along, the dispute had been couched in terms of Israel's occupation. Yet, that PLO charter had been written in 1964, three years before Israel acquired territories to occupy. Finally, the PLO Council voted in 1996 to remove this language from its charter, but many Palestinians continued to resist the idea of Israel's legitimacy. If the members of a group disagree among themselves, it is difficult to come to agreement with a third party.

Oslo II

Oslo Part 2 was formally signed in Washington in September 1995. It provided a timetable for Israeli withdrawal from the West Bank, first from the seven largest cities—Nablus, Jenin, Tulkarm, Qalqilya, Ramallah, Bethlehem, and part of Hebron— and then from 450 smaller Palestinian towns and villages. Eventually, all of the West Bank and Gaza was to be brought under Palestinian control by 1999.

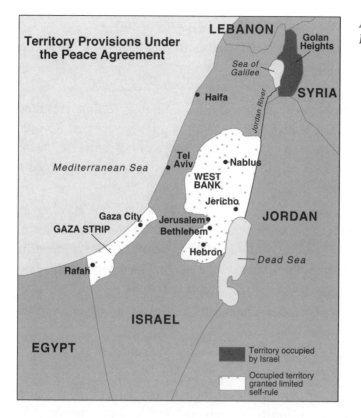

Territory Provisions Under the Peace Agreement

Areas returning to Palestinian control.

Israel released several thousand more Palestinian prisoners. A general election was held in 1996 to fill the 88-member Palestine National Council, and Yasser Arafat was elected president. Hamas and Islamic Jihad boycotted the election, while many of Arafat's Fatah associates won Council seats.

The November 4, 1995 assassination of Prime Minister Yitzhak Rabin was a blow to the prospects for peace. He was shot by a 27-year-old Jewish law student and anti-Arab political extremist who was opposed to the whole process.

Left unsettled at this stage of the process were some of the toughest problems of all. These included:

- The exact borders between Israel and Palestinians
- The political status of Palestine

Reality Check

Yigal Amir said he'd been prompted by God to shoot Rabin. The judge sentenced him to life, rebuked him, and quoted from Exodus 22:28: "Do not blaspheme God or curse anyone who rules over you." He said it was probably the worst crime a man could commit.

- The fate of Jewish settlers in the occupied territories
- What to do with Palestinian refugees who had left when Israel became a state
- The future of Jerusalem

By some accounts, there were nearly two million Palestinian refugees in Lebanon, Syria, and Jordan. The U.N. Relief and Works Agency reported 3.7 million registered with its agency. No one was predicting a change of heart among the zealous nationalist Jews who had been refusing to leave the settlements in occupied territories under any condition.

Governments in Israel, on the other hand, are somewhat like the weather. Wait long enough, and it's sure to change. In 1996. Likud hard-liner Benjamin Netanyahu, brother of the slain Entebbe hero, was elected prime minister. One of Likud's central policies was nonsurrender of the West Bank and Gaza. Netanyahu also opposed returning any portion of the Golan Heights to Syria.

Under the circumstances, the prospects for finishing the Oslo process did not appear encouraging.

Camp David II

Israel did begin withdrawing forces from the West Bank cities and turning over control to the Palestinian Authority as promised. However, a number of terrorist attacks, including suicide bombings with many casualties, appeared designed to disrupt the peace process. There were elements opposed to any dealings or compromise with Israel.

Between Netanyahu's hard-right government and the Palestinian extremists, the peace process was slowly grinding to a halt. The winds changed again, and in early 1999 Israelis voted Netanyahu out and voted in a peace candidate, Labor candidate Ehud Barak, a protégé of the late Yitzhak Rabin.

It seemed to be an opportunity for new life for the peace process after a three-year hiatus, and President Clinton committed himself to brokering the process in the waning months of his presidency. Israeli and Palestinian representatives, including both Barak and Arafat, held extensive negotiations in 2000 at Camp David, where 20 years before two other heads of state—Begin and Sadat—had made history. In the end, the issues proved too difficult, and the effort fizzled.

Clinton's approach was to seek concessions from Israel for full sovereignty over the West Bank and Gaza *and* the Temple Mount in Jerusalem in exchange for the Palestinians relinquishing their demand for the right of hundreds of thousands of refugees to return to their homes and land. Arafat's position was that this demand was not negotiable—and never would be.

Word from the Wise

Someday there will be no more disputes about national boundaries, shapes of negotiating tables, or locations of temples. The apostle John wrote of the Holy City, the New Jerusalem from heaven: "No temple could be seen in the city, for the LORD God Almighty and the Lamb are its temple." (Revelation 21:22, NLT) In the meantime, Christians are called the temples of the Holy Spirit.

Barak, however, was somewhat more flexible, reportedly willing to consider some form of shared sovereignty over the Temple Mount, where Solomon's Temple had once stood. Arafat was adamant on that point, too, insisting it was an exclusively Muslim site and denying any temple had ever existed there. Therefore, both sides went home empty-handed.

Intifada II

Barak's willingness to put the Temple Mount on the table did not sit well with many Israelis, for whom the very idea was sacrilegious. The growing controversy was already threatening to topple Barak's government when in September 2000 Ariel Sharon, a candidate to replace Barak as prime minister, took a little stroll on the Temple Mount.

Predictably, Arabs saw the event as a deliberate provocation, sparking a clash between stone-throwing Palestinians and Israeli troops that injured 30 people, mostly soldiers, who fired tear gas and rubber bullets into the crowd. The next day riots broke out in Jerusalem, igniting violence that went on for months, leaving hundreds dead. It became known as the al-Aqsa Intifada.

Sharon, a member of the Knesset and a war hero, had been forced to resign as defense minister in 1982 in the wake of atrocities in the Israeli invasion of Lebanon.

Now with one gesture he had signaled Jewish defiance of Arab claims upon the holiest spot in the Holy Land. What was worst of all in Palestinian eyes, Israelis then elected him to replace Barak.

This second Intifada put the peace process on the critical list. Israeli Defense Forces returned to the occupied territories, and it looked as if all the gains of recent years had been erased as violence escalated.

Amid criticism that he was neglecting the situation, newly elected President George W. Bush dispatched retired Marine General Anthony Zinni to the region to try to breathe new life into the process, but he, too, returned empty-handed. Next came efforts to revive the process under supervision of "The Quartet"—a collaboration of the United States, Russia, the European Union, and the United Nations.

Many believe that no serious progress will be made until the latest cycle of violence has run its course. Others point out that it was probably no coincidence that the first Intifada ceased when the Oslo breakthrough occurred and raised new hopes for peace. With so many missed opportunities, however, will people be willing to hope again?

Religions in Conflict

In this chapter we will examine the belief system of Islam. People are often surprised by its many striking parallels and commonalities with Judaism and Christianity. Yet, at the same time there are some very deep differences, as well.

"Islamianity"?

Can you identify the people of this religion? Here are six of the things they believe in:

1. One God who is all powerful.

2. Moses and Jesus.

3. The Bible as God's word.

4. Mary and the virgin birth of Jesus.

5. The second coming of Christ.

6. A religion of peace.

Yes, Christians would be one correct answer. These beliefs, however, are also claimed by Muslims. At least, that's one of the ways Islamic societies and committees for intercultural understanding have been positioning Islam in America, especially since the attacks of September 11, 2001. The idea is to emphasize in a period of religious strife and misunderstanding how much Muslims and Christians actually have in common.

Despite these superficial similarities, the differences between Islam and Christianity—and Judaism—are far greater. This would be a more accurate representation of Islam, the major faith of the Middle East:

1. One God—that is, no Son, no Holy Spirit—whose prophet is Muhammad.

2. Moses and Jesus as great prophets, but secondary to Muhammad.

3. The Bible, corrupted and distorted over the centuries, is superseded by the Quran.

4. Mary's conception was a direct miracle of the one God, supernaturally facilitated by the angel Gabriel (not the Holy Spirit).

5. Christ's return will be to proclaim Islam, marry, have children, and die.

6. The condition of peace is "Islam must rule."

 Reality Check

Sheikh AbdAllah Yussuf Azzam, the Muslim cleric who inspired Osama bin Laden, declared: "Jihad must not be abandoned until Allah alone is worshiped. Jihad continues until Allah's word is raised high." Bin Laden himself has said, quoting the *Hadith* (sayings): "I was ordered to fight the people until they say there is no god but Allah, and his prophet Muhammad."

In reality, there are worlds of differences between these religious systems. Nor is there likely to be such a thing as a hybrid "Islamianity" any time soon.

Religious Roots

It is true that Judaism, Christianity, and Islam have sprung from common roots in the Middle East. Christianity accepts all of the Old Testament—including all the prophets and all the teachings—in its entirety. It has added the New Covenant of Jesus Christ in the sense of fulfilling and completing this ancient belief system, as opposed to canceling or replacing it. Throughout the New Testament are statements like, "These things happened in fulfillment of the Scriptures …." (John 19:36, NLT)

The old sacrificial system of the Jews, involving various offerings of bulls and goats, was replaced by Christ's own sacrifice on the cross. Judaism itself was forced to abandon the sacrificial system upon the destruction of Jerusalem and the Temple just a few years later. Otherwise, Christianity absorbed the Old Covenant whole. They accepted its complete authority, but reinterpreted it in the light of Christ and his New Covenant.

Islam was another story. Historically, it is clear that Muhammad was exposed to the teachings of Judaism and Christianity. It is also clear that his mission was to deliver the Arab people from pagan polytheism into the knowledge of the one true God. In the end, however, Islam, unlike Christianity, did offer itself as a replacement for the Judeo-Christian belief systems.

Comparing Religious Beliefs

Islam developed its own distinct system of beliefs and practices that were intended to supersede those of Judaism and Christianity, while using those older systems as a familiar jumping-off point. In Chapter 4 we discussed the duties of Islam—the creed, ritual prayer, alms giving, the Ramadan fast, and the pilgrimage (Hajj). These duties are known as the *Din* or the five Pillars of Islam, plus Jihad.

Here we will look at Islam's belief system, called *Iman*, compared with beliefs in Judaism and Christianity. They are in six categories:

- God
- Angels
- Prophets
- Scripture
- Judgment
- Fate

First, we will consider the nature of God as seen through the different prisms of each faith.

God

Islam: There is only one God, indivisible, eternal, and absolutely sovereign, with no partners, associates, or any other being remotely of his stature. Possibly the greatest sin a Muslim can commit is to associate any other god with God.

His name—Allah—is known as the essential name of God. Muslims also revere the "99 names of God," but these are more on the order of epithets and attributes. Typical references to God as "Allah, the Merciful, the Compassionate," for example, employ the first two of the 99 names.

Many Muslims believe simply reciting the 99 names guarantees one entrance to Paradise. So, they developed a tradition of counting rosary beads as an aid to memorization in recitation. Some believe this practice originally came from the Buddhists and in turn was passed on to Christians through the Crusaders who lived in the Holy Land.

Conspicuously absent from the list of Allah's names is "love." The idea of a personal relationship with God is alien to Islam. Muslims hold that God is essentially unknowable. They do teach seven major attributes of Allah—life, knowledge, power, will, hearing, seeing, speech—all of which he possesses perfectly. God's life has neither beginning nor end, and he possesses all knowledge, total power, and so forth.

Judaism: God is one, a complete unity, and the creator of all things. The unity of God means he cannot be subdivided into constituent parts as can humans. God has no physical body and no gender in the human sense. But he is more than an impersonal supreme force in the universe. He is a person in the sense of having mind, will, and emotions, and it's in that sense that Scripture says man was created in his image.

Other attributes: God is infinite, eternal, omnipresent, omnipotent, omniscient, just, merciful, holy, and perfect. There are various Hebrew names for God, each a study in itself. The personal name for God—*Yahweh* (Jehovah)— is a Hebrew verb implying eternal self-existence and was God's answer to Moses' question about his identity in the desert at the burning bush.

Reality Check

There is also a tradition that there is a 100th name, the Great Name of God, which mystics have sought to learn for centuries. Muhammad taught that anyone calling upon God by this name would be given every desire. Another tradition holds that this name is known by the camel, and that is why the camel is such a proud, haughty animal.

Word from the Wise

The Jews immediately knew what Jesus was claiming when he said, "'(b)efore Abraham was born, I am.'" (John 8:58, NIV) This was an overt claim of eternal self-existence and divinity. They wanted to stone him because this was the name by which God had identified himself to Moses in the desert: "'I AM THE ONE WHO ALWAYS IS. Just tell them, "I Am has sent me to you."'" (Exodus 3:14)

Several other frequently used names are Elohim (God generically), El Shaddai (the Almighty), and Adonai (Lord). More often in Scripture it is simply expressed LORD.

Christianity: Christians adopted the Jewish concept of God with the addition of the concept of trinity or tri-unity—that is, God as three persons: Father, Son, and Holy Spirit. Jews do not accept the Son or Holy Spirit as distinct persons in the Godhead.

The Trinity is rank polytheism to the Muslims. Muhammad condemned it in the Quran: "They do blaspheme who say: Allah is one of three in a Trinity: for there is no god except One Allah. If they desist not from their word (of blasphemy), verily a grievous penalty will befall the blasphemers among them." (Sura 5:75) The belief is also denounced in inscriptions upon the Dome of the Rock on the Temple Mount in Jerusalem.

Christians claim full divinity for Christ, based on such Scriptures as Colossians 2:9 (NLT): "For in Christ the fullness of God lives in a human body." This is blasphemy to Islam. "Whoever joins other gods with Allah, Allah will forbid him the garden and the Fire will be his abode." (Sura 5:75)

The Quran also teaches that Christ instructed his followers to worship only Allah. In the Christian New Testament, Christ receives man's worship—which would be blasphemy if he were not divine. To the Muslim mind, it appears that Christians are deifying a man to the status of God, whereas Christians see it as God condescending to take on flesh and blood as Savior to redeem man by his own sacrifice.

def·i·ni·tion MidEast Dictionary

Jinn, in Muslim theology, is a race of supernatural beings created 2,000 years before Adam, equal to the angels but turned into demons after they rebelled against Adam; equivalent to the English word *genie*; also related, *genius* originally meant a guardian spirit attached to an individual.

Angels

Islam: As men were created from clay, angels were created from light. A third order of beings, *jinn*, was created from fire. Human prophets were considered superior to the angels. Satan was an angel who was turned into a jinn for his refusal to worship Adam.

Every human being is assigned two angels, one to record all his good deeds and another to record all his bad deeds for ultimate reward or punishment on Judgment Day. There are several orders of angels, including eight supporting Allah's throne, 20 in charge of hell, and four archangels (angel of high rank). One of the archangels is Gabriel, who appears in various roles in the Quran, sometimes in place of the Holy Spirit, as in Mary's conception.

The Arabic name for the devil is Iblis. He is in charge of a host of other devils (demons). Every human child is touched by the devil at birth; this is what makes the newborn cry out.

Judaism: The Hebrew Scriptures contain references to various orders of angels, including cherubim, seraphim, living creatures, and archangels. There appears to be a hierarchy, including "myriads" of common angels serving almost like foot soldiers, but such details are not spelled out. Circumstantially, seraphim appear to be concerned with worship and holiness, while the cherubim act as guardians of God's throne and ambassadors of God.

Satan was a fallen angel who rebelled against God and led a third of the heavenly host astray. Otherwise, Old Testament references to angels are tantalizingly sketchy. More details are contained in the books of the apocrypha, but those books are non-canonical and not necessarily reliable. The apocrypha are a dozen books from the Septuagint (Greek translation of the Hebrew Scriptures) that were accepted as scriptural by the Roman Catholic Church but not by Protestants. Martin Luther and the Reformation accepted these writings only for private study and edification.

Family Focus

Consider the Bible's statement that Christ is much higher than the angels. We may not be able to have a personal relationship with an angel, but we can with Christ. Nonetheless, angels are working on our behalf. "But angels are only servants. They are sent from God to care for those who will receive salvation." (Hebrews 1:14, NLT)

Christianity: Christ is "far greater" than the angels (Hebrews: 1:4, NLT). Angels make cameo appearances, as when Peter was miraculously freed from prison (Acts 12) and in the gospels when the angel at Christ's tomb asked the mourners why they were seeking the living among the dead.

Jesus himself referred to angels numerous times, as when he told Peter his Father would send more than 12 legions (3,000 to 6,000 troops per legion) if he were to ask. (Matthew 26:53, NLT) However, like the Old Testament, these accounts are tantalizing and sketchy. There is no serious attempt to instruct believers in any particular doctrines regarding angels. Most Christians have inferred that if this were a subject vital to their faith, Scripture would have provided such instruction.

Prophets

Islam: Muhammad claimed there had been 124,000 prophets in history, ending with himself. He was the last and greatest, the "Seal of the Prophets." Of those 124,000, 315 were apostles or messengers, and nine of those were of special importance—Noah, Abraham, David, Jacob, Joseph, Job, Moses, Jesus, and Muhammad. Jesus was simply the last great prophet until Muhammad. Islam teaches that Muhammad was a man, not divine, and not to be worshipped.

Judaism: Most of those prophets recognized by Islam came right out of the Old Testament. The Jews believed prophecy was the means by which God communicated with man, beginning with Moses and the Law. There were also false prophets, and the penalty for false prophecy was death. The batting average for a true prophet had to be 1,000. Miracles accompanied some of the prophets' ministries.

Prophecy did not mean foretelling the future so much as proclaiming an original word from the LORD (as opposed to a teaching from something already revealed).

Moses was the greatest prophet, and his Torah (or Pentateuch, the first five books of the Old Testament) was the greatest of all prophecy.

Christianity: Jesus treated the words of the Old Testament prophets as the word of God. Accordingly, Christians recognize the teaching of all the prophets—from the "former" prophets (Joshua, Judges, Samuel, Kings) to the "latter" prophets, both major (Isaiah, Jeremiah, Ezekiel, Daniel) and minor (Hosea, Joel, Amos, Obadiah, Jonah, Micah, Nahum, Habakkuk, Zephaniah, Haggai, Zechariah, Malachi).

Jesus was greater than Moses and, by implication, all the prophets. (Hebrews 3:1–6)

Family Focus

Prophecy is listed in the New Testament as one of the gifts of the Spirit for believers, (1 Corinthians 14:1, NLT) but there is disagreement among Christians about whether those gifts are for today. What do you believe? Why? How do you support that belief?

Scripture

Islam: One hundred holy books were given to the prophets prior to Moses (Adam, Seth, Enoch, Abraham). That leaves the *Tawrat* (Torah) given to Moses, the *Zabur* (Psalms) given to David, the *Injil* (gospels) given to Jesus, and the Quran (Recitation) given to Muhammad. But all that Muslims need to know of those lost books is contained in the Quran.

Muslims claim the books of the Jews and Christians—the Old Testament and the New Testament—were corrupted and distorted over the centuries and were therefore a mixture of truth and error. The Quran was given partly to remedy this problem. It replaces and supersedes all other Scripture.

Muslims have had to defend the Quran from charges that it contains errors, especially outright contradictions. Islamic scholars teach a "law of abrogation," which means a revelation that came from God at a particular time could be superseded or replaced—abrogated—by a new revelation given later. As the Quran is not laid out in chronological fashion as Muhammad received it, scholars must devote considerable study to determine which passages were of later vintage in the case of conflicts.

Judaism: The written Torah and oral Torah (teachings now contained in the Talmud and other writings) were given to Moses at Mount Sinai, every word dictated by God. There will be no other Torah. It is unchangeable. Over the centuries, trained scribes exercised rigorous discipline in copying texts, checking and rechecking for accuracy, and destroying old scrolls. This allowed some critics to claim that this destruction could have covered up major errors or alterations. But the discovery of ancient manuscripts—especially the much older Dead Sea Scrolls—refutes this.

> **Word from the Wise**
>
> Scripture tells us that Jesus makes God known by his life and words. "No one has ever seen God. But his only Son, who is himself God, is near to the Father's heart; he has told us about him." (John 1:18, NLT) What has Jesus told us about the Father?

Christianity: Jesus regarded the Scriptures as fully reliable. The New Testament teaches the inspiration ("God-breathed," 2 Timothy 3:16) and inerrancy (infallibility) of Scripture. As important as the Scriptures are, however, Jesus is greater. This is the reverse of Islam. Islam teaches that God's revelation to man was the Quran. Christianity teaches that God's ultimate revelation to man was Jesus Christ, the Word made flesh. (John 1:14, NLT)

Judgment

Islam: On the Last Day God will judge the world, and everyone's good deeds will be weighed in a balance scale against his bad deeds. Muhammad will be the defender and advocate of the righteous after Adam, Noah, Abraham, Moses, and Jesus decline, as unworthy of so great a task. All Muslims initially go to hell to have their remaining sins purged—much like the purgatory of Roman Catholicism.

Heaven consists of sensuous delights—beautiful gardens, beautiful women, flowing wine, luscious fruit, and so forth. God is nowhere pictured. There are seven divisions to heaven, and Allah's throne is still higher. There are also seven divisions to hell with progressively worse punishments. Infidels who say God is a plural being will be confined forever in the burning flames.

Judaism: Job, one of the oldest books in the Bible, speaks of a physical resurrection. "And after my body has decayed, yet in my body I will see God!" (Job 19:26, NLT) This subject is not a major focus of Jewish theology, and Jews today have a great diversity of views on the afterlife. Greater emphasis is on sound moral conduct in this life and preserving Jewish beliefs and culture.

Reality Check

Jews are supposed to be living expectantly for the Messiah. A declaration based on Maimonides' 12th Principle of Faith: "I believe with perfect faith in the coming of the mashiach, and though he may tarry, still I await him every day."

Two of the thirteen basic beliefs of Judaism, as set out by the great Jewish teacher Maimonides, however, concern the future coming of *Mashiach* (Messiah) and the resurrection of the dead. The righteous dead will live again in this Messianic era, a new spiritual and physical state of perfection sometimes called *Gan Eden*. This is a place of great joy and bliss that was foreshadowed by the Garden of Eden. The Mashiach will be a descendant of David, but not divine in any way.

The unrighteous go to a place of punishment or purification, depending on their sin, called Gehinnom or Sheol. Jewish tradition gives little attention to the actual process of judgment for the dead, other than defining righteousness as keeping the requirements of the Torah (Law).

Christianity: The idea of an in-between state like purgatory is nowhere taught in the New Testament. Those who have trusted in Christ alone for their salvation are promised a place in heaven with their Savior. Those who have rejected Christ as Savior will go to the "eternal fire prepared for the Devil and his demons"—hell. (Matthew 25:41, NLT)

One Christian view is that the first resurrection is when the dead in Christ are raised when Christ returns to earth. Believers will be judged and rewarded for their works. The second resurrection, 1,000 years later, is the resurrection of the unsaved for God's judgment, called the Great White Throne Judgment. Others believe we are now in the present 1,000-year spiritual reign of Christ and when He returns there will be one judgment and a new heaven and earth. Those whose names are not found in the Book of Life will be thrown into a lake of fire, called the second death.

> **Word from the Wise**
>
> Christians rejoice that their salvation does not depend on their deeds, and they do not face the second death. "I saw the dead, both great and small, standing before God's throne. And the books were opened, including the Book of Life. And the dead were judged according to the things written in the books, according to what they had done." (Revelation 20:13, NLT)

Fate

Islam: God determines everything in his absolute sovereignty, including evil. He leaves in error those whom he pleases and guides aright whom he pleases. No one can resist or even influence the Decrees of God, as this doctrine is often called. Sometimes it is called Predestination and it could be called determinism over free will.

Judaism: Moral choice is a major emphasis. People are born with a dual nature—impulses both to do right and to do evil. People, created in the image of God, however, also have the ability to think, reason, and choose. Free will is the ability to choose which impulse to follow. People are held morally accountable for their choices.

> **Word from the Wise**
>
> God gives people free will although this will is bound by sin. "'Today I have given you the choice between life and death, between blessings and curses ... Oh, that you would choose life, that you and your descendants might live!'" (Deuteronomy 30:19, NLT) Nonetheless, it's only God's grace that allows us to choose to do what is right.

Christianity: Christians are living examples of the tension between God's sovereignty and man's moral responsibility, while acknowledging the reality of both. Calvinists (based on the teaching of John Calvin) give greater emphasis to God's sovereignty; Arminians, (based on the teaching of Jacob Arminius) lean more to man's responsibility. Both would view outright determinism as incompatible with a God of love. It would, on one hand, remove personal responsibility for an individual's actions while, on the other hand, making God arbitrary and unjust for punishing individuals who had no real control or responsibility for their actions.

Other Issues

In addition to Islam's formal duties and beliefs, there are some additional issues that would distinguish it from other faiths, especially Christianity. Foremost among those issues are God the Father, the Crucifixion, and salvation.

God the Father: Christ's teaching of God as our Heavenly Father is totally alien to both Islam and Judaism. To Islam it would be outright blasphemy, since fatherhood implies offspring, which is one of the most offensive things of all to Muslims. It is not "seemly" to attribute offspring to Allah, according to the Quran.

Crucifixion: Islam also explicitly denies the central event of Christ's entire ministry—the Crucifixion. "But they killed him not, nor crucified him, but so it was made to appear to them…" (Sura 4:157) It was apparently inconceivable to Muhammad that almighty God could allow his true servant to be persecuted and slain. The explanation, then, must have been that Christ was raised up alive to God and it only appeared that he had been crucified.

Salvation: Both Islam and Judaism, as well as various other religions, teach salvation through certain forms of conduct, observances, rituals, religious activities, and good deeds. Islam especially takes this to great lengths in its complex Din, or duties. These resemble in many ways the legalism of the Pharisees that Christ condemned in the New Testament.

Christians call this "works righteousness"—the attempt to earn favor with God for salvation through external behavior. They would say this is one of the greatest distinctions of Christianity, which teaches salvation as a manifestation of an internal reality.

Word from the Wise

Some say mercy is not getting what we deserve; grace is when we do get what we don't deserve. "God saved you by his special favor when you believed. And you can't take credit for this; it is a gift from God. Salvation is not a reward for the good things we have done, so none of us can boast about it." (Ephesians 2:8–9, NLT)

The Case for Israel

To hear some people talk, all the problems of the Middle East are Israel's fault. It's not just Islamic extremists who question Israel's right to exist; many in the West ask the same thing. This chapter addresses that basic question: Why Israel?

Why All the Hatred Against Israel?

Just several days before jet airliners crashed into the World Trade Center and the Pentagon in September 2001, a dramatic event unfolded in South Africa that was largely obscured amid all the September 11th headlines. Delegates from many nations of the world attended the United Nations World Conference Against Racism in Durban. It became a forum for denouncing Israel.

One of the conference's official acts was a condemnation of Israel for the following *alleged* practices:

- Racism
- Genocide
- Ethnic cleansing
- *Apartheid*

The United States, knowing what was afoot, boycotted the conference. Secretary of State Colin Powell explained: "I know that you do not combat racism by conferences that produce declarations containing hateful language, some of which is a throwback to the day of 'Zionism equals racism' or supports the idea that we have made too much of the Holocaust; or suggests that apartheid exists in Israel; or that singles out only one country in the world—Israel—for censure and abuse."

> **def·i·ni·tion MidEast Dictionary**
>
> **Apartheid** literally means the state of separation; the official policy of racial segregation and discrimination against nonwhites practiced in South Africa.

Powell was referring to a 1975 U.N. resolution equating Zionism with racism that was on the books until it was finally repealed in 1991 under pressure from the United States. Clearly, something doesn't add up. Why all the hatred against Israel?

The standard answer is usually "because of the occupied territories." The statement suggests that if Israel would just give back what it's taken, the problem would be solved. Unfortunately, it's just not that simple.

The Occupied Territories

Of the five wars Israel has fought with the Arabs, it wasn't until the end of the third one—the Six Day War of 1967—that Israel even possessed territories to occupy. The War of Independence (1948) with all its Arab neighbors and the Sinai campaign in 1956 A.D. with Nasser's Egypt were fought for entirely different reasons: Israel wanted to exist, and its neighbors didn't agree.

> **Reality Check**
>
> Israel's existence was threatened in the 1973 conflict, the Yom Kippur War. Egypt and Syria penetrated some miles into Israeli territory in the south and the north before they were turned back. If they had penetrated that far into Israel with its pre-1967 borders (that is, without the Sinai Peninsula and the Golan Heights), it probably would have been all over for the Jewish nation.

"We will exterminate Israel," Nasser continued to threaten in 1959. Soon more Arab leaders were saying similar things. "Our goal is clear: to wipe Israel off the map," said President Abdul Salam Arif of Iraq. "The Arab struggle must lead to the liquidation of Israel," said Algerian President Houri Boumedienne.

It wasn't until the 1967 conflict that Egypt lost the Gaza Strip (and the Sinai Peninsula) to Israel, Jordan lost the West Bank, and Syria lost the Golan Heights. Up to that point the issue had been just the fact of Israel's existence.

As a result of the Oslo peace process, Israel agreed to turn over direct control of the West Bank and Gaza Strip to the Palestinians in exchange for an end to the ongoing conflict. The Israelis kept their end of the bargain and began handing over control to the Palestinian Authority. But when the result was not peace, but even greater violence, Israeli forces moved back in to the West Bank and Gaza Strip in recent years.

Events suggest that even the Palestinian refugee problem is not so much a cause as an effect of Arab enmity toward Israel. Over the years there have been too many missed opportunities, too many peace offers walked away from, too many roads not taken to believe that it's all Israel's fault. Words like "apartheid" to describe a democratic country with freedom of religion that provides all the benefits of citizenship—including seats in the Knesset—to its Arab minority seem to be outside the standard definition of this term.

It seems that to those who may not want the conflict to end, the occupied territory is not really the West Bank or Gaza. It's all of Israel. If that's the case, any end to conflict may indeed be a long time off.

Land and Religion

For all the talk about occupied territories, no true peace is likely to be achieved without a settlement of the conflict over Jerusalem and the Temple Mount. Nor is there likely to be a harder dispute to settle.

Jerusalem

When Jewish forces captured East Jerusalem from Jordanian control in 1967, jubilant soldiers hoisted the Israeli flag with the Star of David atop the Dome of the Rock on the Temple Mount. Moshe Dayan—the famous Israeli general with the black eye patch—ordered the flag taken down. The holy places of the Old City would be open to all three faiths— Jews, Christians, and Muslims. Israel magnanimously granted supervision of the Temple Mount and its two mosques to the *Waqf* while maintaining authority for security.

Such behavior was not out of the kindness of their hearts. Israelis were morally obligated by their beliefs from Old Testament times to accord fair treatment to the stranger or alien—ethnic minority—living among them. One such command in the Torah is stated in

MidEast Dictionary

Waqf is a Muslim religious trust, usually an endowment of property and often the name also for the trustees; in Jerusalem, it is the Muslim supreme religious council responsible for the Temple Mount.

Numbers 15:15-16: "Native Israelites and foreigners are the same before the LORD and are subject to the same laws. This is a permanent law for you. The same instructions and regulations will apply both to you and to the foreigners living among you."

Obviously, there have been many violations of this principle in the years since, but it is the guiding principle. By contrast, Arabs periodically republished and circulated this statement of Muhammad from the Hadith: "The resurrection of the dead will not come until the Muslims will war with the Jews and the Muslims will kill them … the trees and rocks will say, 'O Muslim, O Abdullah, here is a Jew behind me, come and kill him.'"

The Israelis found disturbing conditions from the Arab occupation of the Old City between 1948 and 1967:

- All 27 synagogues had been destroyed
- Hundreds of Torah scrolls, holy books, and priceless manuscripts had been burned
- The ancient holy Mount of Olives cemetery had been desecrated
- Tombstones had been broken and removed, some used as paving stones and some in construction of latrines
- An entire section had been bulldozed for a hotel road

Family Focus

How would you deal with intentional destruction of your church or desecration of your family's burial places? Would there be a temptation to strike back? Would you try to get away from the situation? What would a right response look like?

Only in recent years did Muslims begin talking of Jerusalem as the third holiest site of Islam, but it is not even mentioned in the Quran. It's just a tradition that Muhammad visited here—the so-called "night journey," when the prophet also visited heaven.

It's hard, however, to overstate the significance of Jerusalem to the Jews and to Israel. A psalmist who had lived through the Babylonian captivity 2,500 years ago wrote: "If I forget you, O Jerusalem, let my right hand forget its skill upon the harp. May my tongue stick to the roof of my mouth if I fail to remember you, if I don't make Jerusalem my highest joy." (Psalm 137:5–6, NLT)

The Temple Mount

If Jerusalem is the heart of Israel, the Temple Mount is its epicenter.

While there have been Intifadas and internal terrorist incidents, Israel has been at peace with its Arab neighbors since 1973—and that's no small feat under the circumstances. But if war should break out again, chances are it will involve the Temple Mount in some fashion. It was, in fact, one of the two main stumbling blocks resulting in failure of the most recent Camp David II peace talks between Israel and the Palestinians.

The Temple Mount is the 40-acre platform that once supported the great Temple of Solomon, built 1,000 years before Christ, and now houses the Dome of the Rock and the al-Aqsa Mosque. The Rock around which the famous mosque is built is special to both Muslims and Jews. To the Muslims it is the rock on which Muhammad stood before he was taken up to heaven. To the Jews it had several traditions—possibly the stone altar atop Mount Moriah where Abraham almost sacrificed Isaac, the cornerstone rock in God's creation, and possibly the "threshing floor" altar that Kind David purchased which could have been the site of the Holy of Holies of Solomon's Temple.

Word from the Wise

The Bible tells us that no Temple is necessary for us today because we have something far better. Christ is both the high priest and the sacrifice. "And so, dear brothers and sisters, we can boldly enter heaven's Most Holy Place because of the blood of Jesus." (Hebrews 10:19) We are also told that we ourselves are the temples of God, "…God's temple is holy and you Christians are that temple." (1 Corinthians 3:17, NLT)

Despite Israel's hands-off approach, Muslim sensitivities seem to be unfounded. No Jewish prayers have ever been allowed on the Temple Mount under Muslim control, and any suggestion of archaeological exploration or excavation has produced extreme reactions.

The Jews walk on eggshells here, knowing the potential explosiveness of the situation. This is where, after all, the second Intifada began as a result of Ariel Sharon's visit in September 2000. The Wakf responded by barring non-Muslims from the Temple Mount, which they call *Haram al-Sharif*—the Noble Sanctuary. The Muslim reaction seems to center on fears that at any moment the Jews might decide to destroy the mosques so they can rebuild their Temple, as some actually have threatened.

The sensitivities have even led to attempts to rewrite history. Palestinian and Muslim leaders—notably Yasser Arafat and the current mufti of Jerusalem—now maintain that there never was a Temple on the Temple Mount. They say there is absolutely no evidence of any Jewish presence there, which may account for the prohibition on excavations that could show otherwise.

> **Reality Check**
>
> Hedging their bets another way, some claim that even if Solomon's Temple had been on the Temple Mount, the mosques were there first. The only problem with that is Muhammad wasn't even born until some 1,500 years after Solomon and his Temple. The official date for the start of Islam was 622 A.D.—a big difference.

Getting to the Root

Some have concluded that the Arab-Israeli conflict is less a dispute over land than over religion and race. If the idea of a Jewish state is racist, it raises interesting questions about Arab nations where Islam is the official state religion, sometimes painfully enforced, and where other religions are suppressed. Is this racism, too?

What if in its moment of victory in 1967 Israel had declared Jerusalem the holy city for Jews only, off limits to Muslims, Christians, and other gentiles? How would that be different from Mecca, the Saudi holy city, which is off limits to Jews and Christians? Is this being done by the Muslims for political reasons?

The Jews didn't do that in Jerusalem because officially, Israel was established as a democratic secular state. There are probably many reasons for this double standard and here are the big ones:

The Land Itself

When a national homeland for the Jews was conceived by the League of Nations in 1920, it was originally much larger, including what is now Jordan. Under the British Mandate Jordan became one more independent Arab nation, leaving Israel with one fourth of the original land and, upon statehood, many thousands of unhappy Palestinians.

Many of them have asked if the Jews were being compensated for the Holocaust, why wasn't the land taken away from Germany (which had perpetrated the Holocaust under Hitler)? Of course, the Holocaust was only one factor in the creation of Israel, which had been envisioned long before that. Europeans, especially the British, who had botched the post-World War I territorial settlements by making conflicting promises to both Jews and Arabs, were probably the real culprits, but it was the Jews and Arabs who were stuck living there with each other.

The Cold War

For years the old Soviet Union and Eastern Bloc were encouraging Arab nationalism and liberation movements, especially among groups like the PLO and others. There was also a good deal of mischief-making, such as when the Soviets allegedly passed along phony intelligence prior to the 1973 war alleging the Israelis were about to attack their Arab neighbors. The United States felt compelled under such circumstances to defend its interests in the Middle East, including Israel, which was then branded as an imperialist tool.

So a negative history began to be created that took on a life of its own with help from the outside—like the proverbial helper who throws gasoline on a fire. No matter now that the Cold War is long over. After years of fighting, the Palestinians and Jews have more than enough of their own grievances against each other. They don't need other nations stirring the pot.

Reality Check

A major issue toward the end of the Cold War was emigration of Soviet Jews to Israel. The United States pressured Moscow to let the Jews go as a condition of improved relations (détente), while the Arabs pressured hard against it. It resulted in a major population increase for Israel, as some 200,000 Jews a year came over in the early 1990s.

Shame and Honor

The passage of time heals many things, but in the case of issues of shame and honor, it may actually make things worse. Concepts of shame and honor are deeply ingrained in Arab culture. It's why in the Gulf states there are so many foreign workers: Many Arab males find it difficult to do menial labor or work as a subordinate under someone who is not their tribal superior. It is a culture where offenses must be avenged or the aggrieved party—the victim—bears a mark of shame.

This is a social psychology that the West often has failed to appreciate, but it explains much. It was the reason, for example, that Egypt was finally willing to talk peace with Israel once it had done respectably in the 1973 war and could negotiate from a position of honor. It may help explain the phenomenon of suicide bombers who would rather die than live in dishonor. It also helps explain the general hostility that's rooted in colonialist domination in the past and a lack of Western prosperity in the present.

Religious Hostility

Islamic fundamentalism teaches that non-Muslim lands must be subjugated. This is especially true for any territory once in Muslim possession but no longer; it must be recovered. Muslims of this persuasion believe they are not permitted to make peace with non-Muslims or with a non-Muslim country until its inhabitants surrender to Allah. They are considered *Dar al Harb* (house of war).

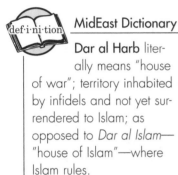

MidEast Dictionary

Dar al Harb literally means "house of war"; territory inhabited by infidels and not yet surrendered to Islam; as opposed to *Dar al Islam*—"house of Islam"—where Islam rules.

Family Focus

Discuss your beliefs about the state of Israel. What should be done about the big issues of Jerusalem, the Temple Mount, the Palestinian refugees, and the occupied territories? How would you answer someone who challenges Israel's right to exist? On what do you base your opinion?

Some Muslims refuse to believe that Jews by themselves could have so successfully established a strong state like Israel; so, they must have been only tools of the West, who really did it.

The Jews have also been accused of controlling the financial and political systems in America—as they allegedly did in Europe before Hitler—and so, in this case it's the Jews who are the masterminds. This way of thinking is also held by some Christians and is part of anti-Semitism.

Israel's Claims

Israel, once cooperative, has soured on the peace process and, once divided politically, is now handily electing hardline politicians like Ariel Sharon. Under pressure from the United States and others to make peace, Israelis ask if America should be compelled to negotiate with Osama bin Laden and Saddam Hussein. And PLO Chairman Yasser Arafat is just as adamant in the opposite direction.

When speaking to exclusively Arab audiences, Arafat's tone changes. He speaks of the peace process as a temporary step toward weakening Israel enough to push it yet closer to ultimate demise.

In 1996 he spoke on "The Impending Total Collapse of Israel." Once a Palestinian state is created, Arafat predicted, a million of the wealthiest Jews will move to the United States. Once that happens, the Jews will become a minority in their own country, and the process will accelerate—ultimately resulting in a "united Palestine under total Arab-Muslim domination."

It's a pretty unlikely scenario, but probably good for fund-raising, and it does give an insight into Palestinian motivations. The Arabs have underestimated the Israelis before, and they're not going to go away that easily. For a number of reasons, the Israelis believe Israel is rightfully theirs.

Continuous Presence

There's a popular myth that after an absence of nearly 2,000 years the Jews suddenly reappeared in Palestine, stole the land, and Israel was born. That's not quite what happened. While many Jews were scattered around the world in the diaspora, many others remained in the Holy Land. By one account there were 40 Jewish communities for centuries from Galilee in the north to the Negev in the south and on both sides of the Jordan.

They were there, in fact, in sufficient numbers to make a significant impact in history. In 614 A.D. the Persians with Jewish help, conquered Jerusalem and allowed the Jews to resettle in it. In 628 A.D. the Byzantines defeated the Persians, and the Jews were persecuted and subjected to forced conversions. The Jews initially were allies of the Muslims in the Islamic invasion beginning in 634 A.D., but after a few years they were again persecuted. In the 12th century they were persecuted during the Crusader invasions.

Clearly, the Jews were a major presence through the centuries. It was only during the period from 1948 to 1967 A.D., under Jordanian control, that the Jews were excluded from the West Bank—Judea and Samaria.

Legal Possession

The homeland was created by the League of Nations following World War I, followed by actions of the United Nations following World War II. Over those years Zionists were busily buying up land in Palestine for settlement.

Much of the land was desolate. During the centuries of Ottoman rule, people had been taxed on trees—and so, people cut them down. The Jews began planting trees, irrigating the land, and draining swamps. As the land became less barren and business and commerce developed, more Arabs moved into Palestine, too. Many turned right around and left again during the 1948 Israeli War of Independence, and then the trouble began with the refugee problem.

Wars

Israel acquired land by war. But again, these territories were captured from Egypt, Syria, and Jordan in a conflict in 1967 that Israel did not start but was forced to fight. Israel returned the Sinai Peninsula in a peace settlement with Egypt, which relinquished claims to the Gaza Strip.

Israel and Syria have yet to come to terms on the Golan Heights. In another peace settlement, Jordan relinquished claims to the West Bank, but now this is hotly disputed territory between the Israelis and Palestinians. The West Bank—ancient Samaria and Judea—is in many ways the heart of Israel.

> **Word from the Wise**
>
> The apostle Paul predicted a time would come when all of Israel would turn to God. Meanwhile, he said, there's all the more opportunity for non-Jews to hear the Good News and be saved. "Some of the Jews have hard hearts, but this will last only until the complete number of Gentiles comes to Christ." (Romans 11:25, NLT)

Divine Providence

Perhaps most important of all, many Israelis see the hand of God in their return to the land of Israel as a nation once more. There were the covenants with Abraham and David in Scripture promising both the land and an eternal kingdom. There were also dire warnings and curses in Deuteronomy and Leviticus that disobedience and idolatry would result in the loss of these benefits, at least temporarily—which the Jews experienced for centuries in the diaspora.

There were many other places in Scripture—especially from the prophets Isaiah, Jeremiah, and Ezekiel—that clearly foresaw a time in the last days when the Israelites would be restored to their land. Evangelical Christians were seeing it, too. Some of them were fond of saying, "If you want to see a miracle of God today, just look at Israel."

Clash of Civilizations II

Increasingly, the collision of Islamic extremism with the West has come to mean a collision with the United States. This chapter focuses on the increased targeting of Americans over the past two decades.

America Held Hostage

Some say America's war on terrorism didn't begin September 11, 2001, but in April 1980 in Operation Eagle Claw. This was the attempted rescue mission of 52 Americans being held hostage by the Ayatollah Khomeini's Iran. It was a tragic scene in what some have called the most humiliating episode in American history.

As the days turned into weeks and months since Iranian militants seized the hostages at the U.S. Embassy in Tehran, President Jimmy Carter's administration was forced to consider increasingly aggressive responses. They'd already warned Iran's leaders in a private back-channel communiqué of "extremely grave" consequences if even one hostage was harmed. At that point the threats to put the hostages on trial as spies stopped. But they remained hostages.

TIMELINE 1979–1988

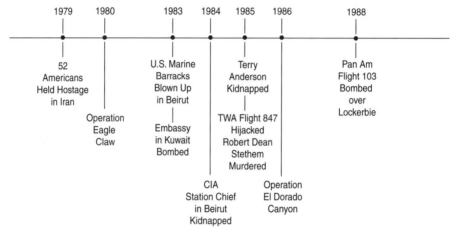

America takes center stage.

Iran was adamant in its demands:

- The return of the Shah, who was receiving medical treatment in New York at the time (later moving to Panama and then Egypt)
- A deposit of $24 billion to insure the eventual return of frozen Iranian assets in the United States
- The return of the Shah's wealth to Iran as stolen funds
- An admission of guilt for past United States actions in Iran
- An apology and a promise not to interfere in Iranian affairs in the future

The United States was equally adamant about not caving in. The Carter administration discussed a number of options, including limited military strikes on "economic" targets, seizing some portion of Iranian territory, mining its ports and harbors, and mounting some type of rescue mission. The last option was considered the least risky in terms of potentially triggering a wider regional conflict, but the hardest one to pull off.

Secretary of Defense Harold Brown conferred with a high Israeli military official who had been involved in executing the 1976 raid on Entebbe. A key difference was that these hostages were not conveniently held at an airport where they could be snatched in a lightning strike, as in Uganda (described in Chapter 15). It would be a highly difficult and complex operation. Secret plans began to be formulated.

The Rescue Mission

An ugly mood had been building in Tehran for some time. Young Islamic revolutionaries had been demonstrating against the United States, burning the American flag, and chanting, *"Magbah Amerika!"* (Death to America). Finally, on Nov. 4, 1979, a huge crowd surrounded the U.S. Embassy and forced their way in, taking diplomatic staff members and Marine guards captive. The official rules of engagement prohibited the Marines from firing weapons under such circumstances. For 444 days, Americans were tormented by threats and the sight of blindfolded hostages being paraded for show.

It became clear early on that the dispute would not have a quick or easy resolution. The new Islamic regime in Tehran was not fully operational as a government; much less did it have control over the radicals holding the hostages. But the regime's ideological sympathies were clear. Ayatollah Khomeini declared: "This is not a struggle between the United States and Iran. It is a struggle between Iran and blasphemy."

The Islamic regime despised America for its intervention in Iranian affairs, particularly its propping up the Shah and his brutal secret police, the Savak. It was also a general loathing of the corrupting influence of Western culture. It was Clash of Civilizations II.

On the night of April 24, 1980, the United States dispatched a clandestine force of eight Sea Stallion helicopters and six C-130 transport planes from various locations, including the USS *Nimitz* carrier in the Persian Gulf. Flying at low altitude and without lights, the force was to approach Tehran in the north of the country in several stages, including refueling at an abandoned airfield in the desert prepared by special forces. It almost worked.

Unfortunately, three of the helicopters became disabled, partly due to severe dust storms they encountered at that altitude, and the mission was aborted in the middle. A minimum of six helicopters were needed to extract all 52 hostages. Worse, during refueling one of the choppers collided with a C-130, which burst into flames. Eight crew members were killed and five wounded.

Operation Eagle Claw.

The wreckage and the disabled helicopters were abandoned in the desert, and the mission was scrubbed. It was yet another American humiliation as the president was forced to announce the failed mission the next day.

Word from the Wise

With all the hatred among religious, racial, and ethnic groups, one thing in the world that never fails is God's love. His unfailing love is a major refrain throughout Scripture. "The unfailing love of the Lord never ends! By his mercies we have been kept from complete destruction .... Though he brings grief, he also shows compassion according to the greatness of his unfailing love." (Lamentations 3:22,32, NLT)

Lessons Learned

After the discovery of the United States' intentions, the Iranians moved the hostages to a secret location to prevent any repeat rescue attempts. About eight months later Khomeini's regime was ready to release the hostages after the death of the Shah in Egypt and outbreak of war with Iraq. Few of their demands had been met, other than a release of frozen assets and immunity from civil lawsuits resulting from the captivity. The United States also pledged not to intervene in Iran's affairs. But the damage had been done. America had been humiliated, made to look like an incompetent, helpless giant.

The political fallout was considerable. Secretary of State Cyrus Vance, whose counsel against the military mission had been rejected, resigned. Carter himself was weakened politically and was defeated for re-election by Ronald Reagan.

In retrospect, some believe the rescue mission was scrubbed prematurely. In a couple of cases, the mechanical problems were merely warning light indicators that might have been false alarms. Many believe the surprise assault on the embassy would have been a dramatic success, and the daring rescue would have worked.

Reagan administration officials let it be known that they never would have approved negotiating for the release of hostages, implying military action instead. This school of thought holds that there may be casualties in the short term, but otherwise the nation will be vulnerable to endless additional threats in the long term.

Also questioned was the U.S. State Department's policy of not allowing the Marine guards to defend the embassy and its personnel. It was standard operating procedure for all embassies out of concern that firing on local people would only further inflame an already volatile situation.

> **Family Focus**
>
> What do you think? Do you agree with the policy of negotiating with extremists rather than responding with force? How would you respond in a terrorist situation, knowing some civilian lives probably would be lost?

To this day, at least one of those Marines wishes they had been able to defend themselves. Ex-Marine Rodney Sickmann has been quoted as saying the guards might have died defending the embassy, but it would have sent a stronger signal to those tempted to consider it open season on Americans. He believes America's troubles with terrorism today can be traced back to those events in 1979 A.D.

Terror Turns Deadly

The Reagan administration soon discovered that standing tall against Islamic extremism and international terrorism might be easier said than done.

In April 1983 a suicide truck-bomb attack on the U.S. Embassy in Beirut, Lebanon, killed 17 Americans and dozens of Lebanese and injured scores of others as the seven-story building collapsed around them from the enormous explosion. Among the dead were the CIA's Middle East director and other key operatives.

Six months later a similar suicide truck-bomb attack killed 241 U.S. Marines when their Beirut barracks was blown up. A simultaneous attack on French troops a mile away killed 59. The attacks were nearly identical in method, and the terrorist group Islamic Jihad claimed responsibility for both. The troops had been there as part of a multinational peacekeeping force brought in to try to restore order during Lebanon's long civil war.

Reality Check

Mughniyah's cousin, Mustafa Youssef Badreddin, was part of a pro-Iranian group also conducting operations against Iraq. He was given the death sentence, but ironically when Iraq invaded Kuwait in 1990, Iraqi forces unwittingly released Badreddin and the other 16 accomplices.

It was the largest loss of life in a single day for the Marines since the battle of Iwo Jima in 1945. The United States withdrew its forces from Lebanon several months later and confined its operations to firing offshore from a carrier battle group.

In December 1983 the U.S. Embassy in Kuwait was bombed, killing six and injuring 80. Seventeen people were arrested and convicted in the attacks, including the cousin and brother-in-law of a very big fish—Imad Mughniyah, a senior Hezbollah officer who would turn out later to be a major operative. Over the next several years the release of the "Kuwait 17," as they came to be called, would become a key demand of terrorist kidnappers and hijackers.

More U.S. Hostages

Then began a series of kidnappings that eventually totaled 30 Westerners held hostage at various times. One of the first was William F. Buckley, CIA station chief in Beirut, in March 1984. He was reportedly tortured and eventually killed the next year, though it was a few more years before his remains were found wrapped in blankets on a roadside near Beirut International Airport. Marine Lt. Col. William

Higgins, head of the U.N. peacekeeping forces in Lebanon, was also abducted and killed after lengthy interrogation and torture.

Some details of Buckley's treatment were confirmed by Terry Anderson, the Middle East bureau chief of the Associated Press, who was taken captive in March 1985 and was confined for more than six years. Anderson won a court judgment for $100 million against Iran, determined to be the sponsor of these terrorist activities, under a federal law passed in 1996 allowing American victims of terrorism the right to sue foreign governments in U.S. courts. Collecting on the judgments, however, is another matter.

Anderson was one of 18 Americans taken hostage in Beirut. In his lawsuit Anderson said he was half starved, beaten, taunted, and humiliated, regularly threatened with death, and forced to witness the mistreatment of fellow prisoners. He said he was forced to look on helplessly while Buckley was killed just a few yards away. Actually, Anderson, an ex-Marine and a Christian, was one of the fortunate ones able to pick up his life and move on after his release. Many others suffered crippling psychological scars.

This, too, was to have major political fallout for a U.S. administration when it was eventually discovered that the release of some of these hostages had been purchased through major arms sales to Iran, which was then at war with Iraq. This became known as the Iran-Contra Scandal and was most damaging to the Reagan administration, which had made such a point of not negotiating with terrorists or paying ransom.

Family Focus

Imagine being imprisoned for years by terrorists without knowing what might happen. Upon his release, Terry Anderson said he forgave his captors because his faith required it. How do you think his faith might have helped him survive better than some others? How would you have coped?

Reality Check

The U.S. Navy today has a ship named after one of the terrorist victims, Marine Col. William Higgins. It now also has a guided missile destroyer named in honor of a sailor, Petty Officer Robert Dean Stethem.

Flight 847

Robert Dean Stethem, a 23-year-old Navy construction diver, was returning home from an assignment in the Middle East in June 1985 when TWA Flight 847 was hijacked in Athens, Greece, by Hezbollah terrorists. They demanded the release of more than 700 Lebanese taken prisoner by Israelis during their withdrawal from operations in southern Lebanon. Ironically, the United States—unbeknownst to the hijackers—had been pressuring Israel to release such prisoners, which was considered a violation of the Geneva Conventions.

It did not go well for Robert Dean Stethem when the hijackers discovered there was a Navy man on board. After many hours of being beaten and tortured, the terrorists finally told the other passengers to put their heads down and close their eyes. They then shot Stethem in the head and dumped his body out onto the airport tarmac in Beirut.

Reality Check

The Flight 847 hijackers held 39 American hostages for two more weeks, eventually releasing them when Israel released some of its prisoners. There was some uncertainty about the hijackers' identities, but investigators discovered one intriguing clue. Fingerprints in the men's lavatory were identified as belonging to Imad Mughniyah—a senior Hezbollah officer.

Despite the beatings, Stethem refused to denounce the United States or to identify other military personnel onboard. His body was so disfigured that he had to be identified by fingerprints. Stethem was posthumously awarded the Purple Heart and Bronze Star for heroism and bravery.

Stethem's family might not be good subjects for an empathetic discussion of the need to understand the motivation of terrorists or why Muslim extremists hate the United States. At Stethem's memorial service his brother Kenneth, a retired Navy SEAL, invoked the memory of the Iran hostage crisis just six years before. "We had war declared on us by terrorists in 1979," he said, "but we decided not to show up."

Operation El Dorado Canyon

Iran clearly was behind much of the Lebanon-based terrorism of groups like Hezbollah. It continues to be one third of President George Bush's "Axis of Evil," but it wasn't the only player in the 1980s. Another major mischief maker was Muammar Ghadafi's Libya. In this case, however, the mischief was somewhat shorter-lived.

Libya was operating training camps that churned out thousands of new terrorists each year. It was surely no coincidence that terrorist incidents around the world climbed tenfold in the 1980s. Intelligence reports indicated Libya had provided $100 million to finance Palestinian terrorist actions against Israel.

In March 1986 the United States challenged Gadhafi by conducting "freedom of navigation" exercises in international waters bordering the Gulf of Sidra that Gadhafi claimed for Libya. As expected, Libya began challenging the U.S. warships and firing on its planes. That gave the Americans the excuse they needed to bomb the missile site and sink two of the Libyan naval attack vessels. But Libya still wasn't impressed.

In April 1986 a terrorist's bomb exploded aboard TWA Flight 840 over Greece, killing four Americans. Three days later a bomb exploded in La Belle Discotheque in Berlin, killing two American service men and injuring 79 other Americans. United States and West German intelligence indicated it was the work of Libyan terrorists. The Reagan administration decided it was time to strike back.

The mission was dubbed Operation El Dorado Canyon. This time Libya itself was going to be hit. The United States was forced to use British bases and add thousands of miles to its operation when allies France, Germany, Italy, and Spain lost their nerve and refused to allow use of their air space. The Air Force and Navy coordinated a nighttime attack on five sites in Benghazi and Tripoli, including military targets and terrorist training camps. All the targets were hit, and only one attacking aircraft was lost.

Reality Check

Why the attack was called Operation El Dorado Canyon was never publicly explained. There is a well-known gold mine with that name near Las Vegas, and the operation did strike gold, in a sense, considering its effectiveness. It was the first U.S. bomber attack from Great Britain since World War II and was also recognized as the longest fighter combat mission in history.

Gadhafi's own headquarters was hit, but not his residence. Nevertheless, there were claims that the leader's young adopted daughter had been killed. In any case, Gadhafi appeared to soften his tone thereafter, and there was a dramatic decrease in the number of Libyan-sponsored, anti-American terrorist activities. One major exception: the 1988 bombing of Pan Am Flight 103 over Lockerbie, Scotland, that killed 259 passengers and 11 on the ground. Libyan terrorists were implicated.

Otherwise, it seemed to be a case of message received.

Imad Mughniyah

There may have been a lull at the end of the decade of the 1980s, as three major sources of mischief turned their attention elsewhere for a time—Libya, presumably because of Operation El Dorado Canyon, and Iran and Iraq, who were at war with each other. But there were disturbing signs for the future as attacks became more sophisticated and the perpetrators harder to catch.

A case in point was Imad Mughniyah. The Lebanese Shi'ite had left something more than fingerprints behind in the 1985 hijacking of TWA Flight 847. Someone also got a picture. It turns out that Mughniyah may have been the one who beat and executed Robert Dean Stethem. Federal investigators tracked him to France in 1986, but he eluded their grasp. Intelligence reports indicated Mughniyah had had plastic surgery.

Mughniyah would turn out to be one of the world's most elusive terror masterminds, relentlessly—and fruitlessly—pursued for years by the United States and others. But as investigators began piecing the evidence together, a chilling portrait emerged. After connecting him to some major terrorist strikes in more recent years, authorities now believe that in addition to Flight 847, Mughniyah was also the man behind:

- The 1983 Beirut embassy bombing
- The 1983 double truck bombings of the United States and French compounds in Beirut with massive casualties
- Most of the abductions of Western hostages in Lebanon in the mid-'80s.
- Personally interrogating, torturing, and possibly killing the CIA's William Buckley

Word from the Wise

We need to pray continually that the Lord will thwart the efforts of terrorists. King David expressed deep concern about the workers of iniquity in his kingdom. "But I am in constant prayer against the wicked and their deeds …. Keep me out of the traps they have set for me, out of the snares of those who do evil." (Psalm 141:5,9, NLT)

Meanwhile, a war was being fought between the Soviets and Islamic mujaheddin warriors in Afghanistan in the early 1980s. This is where a Saudi expatriate named Osama bin Laden gained much of his experience in military tactics, as well as building a following of like-minded Islamic extremists who would branch out into other forms of combat and terrorism after the Soviets had been driven out.

Bin Laden would go on to play a major role in terror attacks that followed in the 1990s. And in retrospect, when investigators realized the extent of Mughniyah's involvement in some of these activities, it began to look like between the two of them, bin Laden and Mughniyah would account for 90 percent of the incidents of international terror.

Eye of the Hurricane

After the collapse of the old Soviet Union in 1991, the United States found itself alone as the one so-called superpower. It also began to find itself increasingly the primary target for Muslim rage and terrorism around the world.

As mentioned previously, looking for underlying reasons or trying to understand the root causes of extremist rage and violence could be a futile exercise. Clearly, for some outrages and atrocities, there can never be an excuse. Nevertheless, there are some issues that at least could be considered triggers and pretexts for violent actions.

Most often mentioned is America's penchant for interventionist involvement with other countries. In the Middle East, some people have very long memories. To name a few examples:

- America's support of the Shah of Iran through actions of the CIA and his brutal Savak secret police in the 1950s
- Supporting coup attempts in Syria and backing a corrupt king in Libya in the 1960s
- United States support of Israel through financial aid and armaments when its survival was at stake in the 1970s
- Supporting Israel's invasion and occupation of southern Lebanon as well as support for the Christian militias there in the 1980s

By 1990 America would have a new cause for concern: Iraq's invasion and occupation of Kuwait. It would put America even more in the eye of the hurricane.

Iraq

Saddam Hussein made Middle East mischief for many years. This chapter looks at this legacy of conflict and misadventure that has marked the nation of Iraq under his aggressive leadership.

Two Faces of a Leader

Twenty years ago, Iraq wasn't looking too bad. Geopolitically, it was a counterweight to Iran, which was fast becoming something like America's worst nightmare. So, when Iran and Iraq went to war in 1980 A.D.—even though Iraq was the aggressor invading Iran—choosing sides wasn't a tough call for the United States. It was Iraq hands down. The situation was like the old aphorism, "The enemy of my enemy is my friend."

While even then its dictator, Saddam Hussein, would never be mistaken for Albert Schweitzer, there was reason for hope that with time the regime could be brought into the fold of moderate Arab states. Iraq was using its bounteous oil revenues to improve the standard of living for its people. It was beginning to show what a secular, progressive Arab state could accomplish in public health, education, and infrastructure—roads, water systems, electrification. On the surface at least, the people were relatively well off.

IRAQ TIMELINE 1975–1991

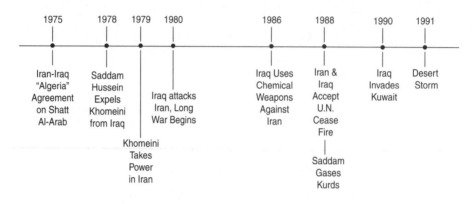

Iraq overshadows the Middle East.

It was no secret that Hussein was basically a thug who fought his way to power over a pile of bodies, taking the Soviet Union's Joseph Stalin as a role model. The Baath regime itself was a socialist cadre intent on running a *totalitarian* system that only tried to make the state look like a republic. But then, this *was* the Middle East, after all. Under the circumstances, almost *anything* seemed better than the rising tide of Islamic fundamentalism.

MidEast Dictionary

Totalitarianism is rule by a government or state in which one party or group maintains complete control under a dictatorship and bans all others.

An indication of how favorably disposed the United States was to Iraq came in 1981, when Israel bombed Iraq's nuclear plant and the United States led a chorus of international protest against its old Middle East ally. America at that time was not nearly so alarmed about the prospects of weapons of mass destruction in Saddam's hands. Then during the Iran-Iraq war, Iraq accidentally fired on the USS *Stark* in the Persian Gulf in an apparent case of mistaken identity, killing 37 U.S. sailors. An apology sufficed to end the matter.

Reality Check

Mistakes do happen. In July 1988, the United States shot down an Iranian civilian airliner with a heat-seeking missile, mistaking it for an Iranian F-14. All 290 persons onboard were killed. The USS *Vincennes* was engaged in a battle with Iranian gunboats in the Strait of Hormuz when the plane approached too closely and did not respond to radio challenges to back off.

Saddam Confronts

The name Saddam means "he who confronts" in Arabic. It would turn out to be most appropriate, as Iraq under Saddam made a habit of confronting its neighbors. He became known largely by his first name to avoid confusion with another notable Hussein, the King of Jordan.

Trouble began between Iran and Iraq while the Shah was still in power. The strategic Shatt al-Arab, the confluence of the Tigris and Euphrates in the last few miles before emptying into the Persian Gulf, separated the two countries and had been Iraq's under an old treaty. After the British left, the Shah stopped paying transit fees to Iraq for use of the waterway. So, Iraq started supporting opposition groups within Iran. In response to that, Iran started providing support to opposition Kurds within Iraq.

A compromise eventually was reached in which Iraq agreed to share the waterway and Iran agreed to stop aiding the Kurds. But when Ayatollah Khomeini came to power in 1979, the situation deteriorated again, as Khomeini provided aid and encouragement to Iraq's majority Shi'ites in the south. This had great potential for disruption within Iraq, run by a Sunni regime. The Baath party always worried about potential uprisings from the Shi'ites, who were both more numerous and more inclined to follow religious leaders, particularly at a time when religious fervor was at a high pitch.

Saddam apparently had great designs to be the next Nasser, the new champion of pan-Arabism, and began looking for pretexts to go to war with his Shi'ite Persian (non-Arab) neighbor. Later actions indicated he believed he would have no trouble rallying the support of other Arab nations. When his secret police uncovered assassination plots against government ministers by Iraqi Shi'ite extremists, Saddam began preparing for war.

Iran-Iraq War 1980–1988

Saddam escalated tensions by abrogating the 1975 Algeria agreement with Iran that had established joint operation of the Shatt al-Arab and claiming all of it for Iraq. Both sides began trading artillery fire across the border, and before long they were conducting air strikes against each other. Finally, on September 23, 1980, Iraq sent troops into Iranian territory, invading Khuzestan, an oil-rich border region with a majority Arab population. It was now full-scale war.

The Shatt al-Arab separating Iran and Iraq.

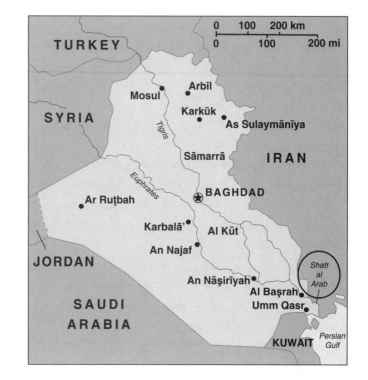

At the outset odds-makers undoubtedly would have picked Iraq. It commanded one of the world's largest armies—some say the fourth largest—and was well equipped with Soviet tanks, Russian MiG and French Mirage fighter jets, and other substantial weaponry. Iran was in disarray from its recent revolution with little of its military leadership still intact. It was equipped with American tanks and planes, but with little hope of obtaining replacement parts.

After all, Iran was still holding 52 hostages of the Great Satan, and U.S.-Iran relations were a bit strained. The United States attempted to influence things even further in Iraq's favor by sharing military intelligence with Saddam's regime. Yet, with all that, the Iraqis still faltered in their drive. The Iran campaign turned into a Vietnam-style quagmire.

Perhaps Saddam underestimated the Ayatollah's determination. Back in 1978, as part of his fence mending, Saddam had acceded to a request from the Shah of Iran to expel Khomeini from the Shi'ite holy city of An Najaf in southern Iraq. That's when Khomeini went into exile for a year in Paris before making his triumphant return to replace the Shah. No doubt the Ayatollah remembered well the Iraqi leader who had given him the boot.

Word from the Wise

Saddam Hussein was full of schemes, but often it seemed he just outsmarted himself. Much about the Iraqi leader's life illustrates the biblical principle of reaping. "Don't be misled. "Remember that you can't ignore God and get away with it. You will always reap what you sow! Those who live only to satisfy their own sinful desires will harvest the consequences of decay and death. But those who live to please the Spirit will harvest everlasting life from the Spirit." (Galatians 6:78, NLT)

The Iranians had several factors in their favor. They had air superiority with their American bombers, allowing them to go on the offensive into Iraqi territory, especially in the early going while they still had parts. They also managed to put up formidable resistance to the Iraqi invaders through a combination of Revolutionary Guard forces and the human wave assaults of the Basij martyrs—many of them children—who served as cannon fodder. The Iranians showed a clear willingness to sustain far heavier casualties than their enemy.

Some of those Iranian casualties did not come from conventional weapons fire. By 1986, thousands of Iranian combatants were showing unusual symptoms— respiratory problems and burns instead of bullet holes. There were an estimated 10,000 or more casualties from Iraqi chemical weapons, including mustard gas and nerve agents. It was an ominous sign of things to come.

Eventually, the superpowers began to be drawn in as the conflict threatened the movement of oil supplies through the Persian Gulf. The United States began to reflag some foreign tankers, especially the Kuwaitis, as Iran and especially Iraq began trying to cut off the other's oil commerce. Other Western nations helped in the tanker escort operation. It was during one of these operations that the USS *Stark* was hit by an Iraqi missile.

> ### Word from the Wise
>
> Saddam Hussein appeared to have a particular gift for creating hellish conditions on earth. It reminds us that even worse times are in store in the last days. "And another horse appeared, a red one. Its rider was given a mighty sword and the authority to remove peace from the earth. And there was war and slaughter everywhere." (Revelation 6:4, NLT)

Finally, the United Nations Security Council issued a cease-fire resolution in 1988. Iraq, realizing it had bitten off too much, had been willing to end the conflict for some time. Iran, however, continued to hold out, insisting on Saddam's ouster as a condition of peace. But then Iran started to lose some decisive battles. Iraq used more chemical weapons. The two began attacking each other's cities with missiles, and Iran began to fear a chemical missile attack.

Eventually, they agreed to the cease-fire. The toll had been horrendous. Iraq suffered upward of 400,000 casualties; Iran, something close to a million.

There were other casualties as well. It came out later that while the Iran-Iraq war was going on, Saddam had been fighting an internal war with the Kurds. The Iraqi Kurds had been agitating for independence through the creation of an autonomous region. Some were accused of being Iranian collaborators.

Saddam's cousin, Ali Hasan al-Majid, headed an ethnic cleansing operation called al-Anfal, meaning "the spoils." Al-Majid became known as "Chemical Ali" for his use of chemical and biological weapons on Kurdish towns and villages. Perhaps the worst attack occurred in the northeast at Halabja in March 1988. As many as 12,000 people are believed to have died in three days of attacks. Human rights groups allege that overall more than 180,000 people are missing and presumed dead with some 1,200 villages destroyed.

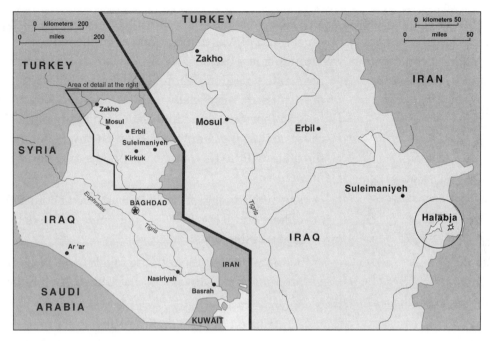

The Anfal chemical and biological campaign.

The Invasion of Kuwait

Although Saddam Hussein told the Iraqi people they'd won, the Iran-Iraq War was essentially an incredibly expensive stalemate. That was not entirely by accident. During the conflict the United States, Soviet Union, France, and others tended to supply aid to whichever side looked to be losing at the time. No one wanted to see a big winner come out of this contest, especially Iran with its revolutionary Islamic brand of ideology.

The Need for Debt Relief

Oftentimes the roots for the next war can be found in the circumstances of the last one. That certainly would be true in this case. In many ways the Iran-Iraq War created a monster. The bad news was that it left Iraq enormously in debt—by more than $300 billion, according to one estimate. The worse news was it also left Saddam Hussein with a million-man army, the largest in the region, with battlefield experience in a shattered economy. It was a bad combination.

Iran was pumping oil vigorously to replenish its war-drained coffers. But Iraq's oil production was way down because of war damage, and even the reduced amount it could market was bringing less because oil prices were down. Saddam desperately needed debt relief. He owed billions to various Gulf states, especially Saudi Arabia and Kuwait. He figured they owed it to him as the champion of the Arab cause against the common Persian enemy. Saddam began threatening little Kuwait next door. His grievances were numerous:

Family Focus

Dig beneath the surface here. Why would a big war machine and a shattered economy be a bad combination? Consider Iraq's situation in light of precedents such as pre-World War II Germany. A dangerous combination of strength and weakness. Are there any parallels?

- Kuwait, his biggest creditor, was owed about $50 billion, and Kuwaitis were not interested in debt rescheduling.

- Saddam blamed the collapse in oil prices on overproduction by Kuwait and the United Arab Emirates.

- Kuwait was allegedly "stealing" oil from the Rumailla oil field on the Iraq-Kuwait border.

There was also an historical issue involving Kuwait's legitimacy. When the national boundaries were drawn in the region after World War I, the British had carved themselves a piece of the pie around the emir of Kuwait, who had prime Gulf frontage. The British continued to administer this territory until 1961.

But earlier under Ottoman rule, things were different. Iraq consisted of three provinces around three major cities—Mosul, Baghdad, and Basra. Kuwait was loosely considered part of Basra. In Saddam's view, that's the way it should have stayed.

Green Light to Invade?

Nobody, it seemed, really believed Iraq actually would attack Kuwait. The very idea of attacking a brother Arab state was somewhat shocking. Saddam's moving 30,000 troops to the border in July 1990 was viewed as saber rattling to get his way by intimidation. Warning signs were definitely being missed.

No one would end up with more egg on its face than the United States. Iraq had broken off relations with Washington after the 1967 Arab-Israeli War and restored relations in 1984 in the middle of the Iran-Iraq War. On July 25, 1990, Saddam

Hussein met in Baghdad with U.S. Ambassador April Glaspie in a session that has been widely blamed for inadvertently giving Saddam a green light for invasion.

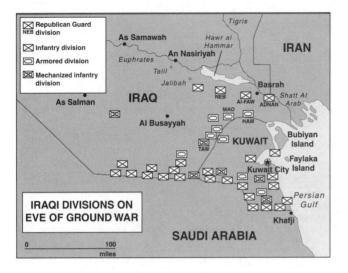

Iraq invades Kuwait.

They discussed Iraq's military buildup along the Kuwait border. A careful reading of the transcript of that meeting indicates Saddam was hinting darkly that Iraq intended to have either the Shatt al-Arab or Kuwait. While not mentioning Kuwait by name, in retrospect it appears that's what he meant by referring to "the whole of Iraq." He believed Kuwait should be Iraq's 19th province.

Then Glaspie uttered the words that have been blamed for the misunderstanding: "We have no opinion of the Arab-Arab conflicts, such as your border disagreement with Kuwait." Glaspie disputed this account, basically saying those words were taken out of context. But Saddam was able to claim, whether sincerely or not, that the Americans never offered an objection to his Kuwait adventure.

A week later, August 2, 1990, Iraq invaded. Saddam's troops easily rolled over Kuwait and massed along the border with Saudi Arabia. The fat was in the fire.

Desert Shield

At the request of Kuwait and the United States, the United Nations Security Council took up the matter, condemned the invasion, and demanded an immediate withdrawal. President George H.W. Bush condemned the "naked aggression" and warned of possible United States action. Several days later he made the famous declaration: "This will not stand, this aggression against Kuwait."

Coalition forces push Iraq out of Kuwait.

On August 8, Saddam officially annexed Kuwait and several weeks later proclaimed it the 19th province of Iraq. Meanwhile, Kuwaiti forces retreated across the border into Saudi Arabia, where they would wait to fight another day. The Saudis, greatly alarmed, asked the United States to provide troops to defend their country from possible Iraqi attack. President Bush immediately dispatched a number of F-15 Eagle fighters to the kingdom, and Desert Shield was underway.

The UN Security Council imposed a trade embargo on Iraq and declared the annexation of Kuwait illegal. A U.S.-led naval blockade halted shipments of Iraqi oil. Desert Shield appeared to have halted further aggression, but the occupation of Kuwait appeared to be an accomplished fact without stronger counter-measures. In short, it was a stalemate.

Had Saddam overplayed his hand? At this point, it wouldn't appear so. He had obtained his objective and virtually doubled his oil reserves overnight. Now there would be no question of shelling out $50 billion to Kuwait—the situation was now reversed. Sure, there was a lot of saber rattling, but Saddam apparently figured he could weather the storm until it passed.

Any idea of a U.S.-led coalition involving brother Arab states seemed pretty far-fetched at the time. Besides, even if Bush could pull a rabbit out of his hat, Saddam had a few more tricks of his own—including an ace in the hole called Israel.

Desert Storm

It took months, but with patient diplomacy the Bush administration began to knit together an unlikely coalition of three dozen countries from Europe, Asia, and the Middle East willing to confront Saddam's aggression. Only Jordan and the PLO actively sided with Iraq. It must have come as some surprise to Saddam, who had not counted on that degree of consensus and determination.

The UN eventually endorsed the use of force and in December set a deadline of January 15, 1991, for Iraq to leave Kuwait. On January 12, the U.S. Congress approved going to war against Iraq. Rather than withdraw, Saddam directed Iraqis to prepare for the "mother of all battles." It would not be the last of his bluster and bombast about blood and fire and death awaiting the allies. It turned out to be quite the other way around.

Desert Shield graduated to Desert Storm on January 17, when the coalition air attack began against targets in Kuwait and Iraq. Bush told the nation that the goals of the war were to liberate Kuwait and to destroy Iraq's chemical arsenal and its nuclear weapons potential.

Bush authorized a call-up of one million National Guardsmen and other reservists. The United States had deployed more than 500,000 troops to the Gulf, primarily in Saudi Arabia, while other coalition partners sent 160,000 troops.

Weeks before, Israel's government had distributed gas masks to its people in the face of Saddam's threats against it. By attempting to turn the conflict into an Arab-Israeli dispute, Saddam had hoped to drive a wedge into the U.S.-backed coalition against him. He was gambling that Arab nations especially would not want to be part of a coalition involving the United States and Israel. Now, Saddam began to make good on those threats, launching dozens of Soviet-made Scud missiles into Israeli territory.

Had Israel responded to the attacks in customary military fashion, Saddam no doubt calculated he could split the coalition by turning it into another Arab-Israeli war. In this he miscalculated. The Bush administration persuaded the Israelis to hunker down and refrain from retaliating. Meanwhile, U.S. forces moved Europe-based Patriot missiles into the theater to defend Israel. The Patriots were effective in intercepting the Scuds and minimizing the damage to Israel. Saddam's ploy had failed.

Iraqis Take It on the Chin

While the air war continued on, the first real ground battle occurred at the end of January 1991 as Iraqi forces crossed over from Kuwait and seized the Saudi town of Khafji. Saudi troops repelled them two days later.

After the Iraqi forces were sufficiently softened up by aerial bombardment, the coalition ground campaign officially began on February 24 under the command of U.S. General Norman Schwarzkopf. The Iraqis, taking massive casualties, began to fold quickly. Not that the wounded beast didn't still have a few tricks left. On the second day of the campaign, an Iraqi Scud missile slammed into U.S. barracks near Dharan, Saudi Arabia, killing 28 U.S. soldiers. But the day after that, February 26, Saddam tried to blunt the offensive by announcing plans to withdraw from Kuwait.

> **Reality Check**
>
> Some think the poor showing Iraqi forces made against the coalition with its Soviet equipment and tactics was not lost on Eastern bloc nations. According to this view, the resulting demoralization may have even hastened the disintegration of the Soviet Union and the Warsaw Pact later that same year.

He was too late. Already coalition air forces were pounding the route between Kuwait City and turning it into a "Highway of Death." Some 10,000 Iraqi troops were killed. By the next day coalition forces were entering Kuwait City and re-hoisting the Kuwaiti flag. The U.S. 1st Armored Division pursued Iraqi forces across the border and fought a major engagement with the celebrated Iraqi Republican Guard, decisively defeating them.

Later that same day, February 27, President Bush declared Kuwait liberated and suspended military operations just 100 hours after they had begun and six weeks after the air war was launched. Coalition forces had flown more than 100,000 sorties while losing 75 aircraft. Casualties were remarkably light. The United States suffered 148 battle deaths, 145 non-battle deaths (accidents), and 467 wounded, while other coalition members lost a handful each.

Iraq, on the other hand, may have lost 100,000 soldiers plus 300,000 wounded, 150,000 deserted, and 60,000 taken prisoner. Forty-two entire divisions were rendered combat-ineffective—that is, they could no longer fight.

Particularly disastrous were its major armored division losses with Soviet tanks and outmoded tactics. The Iraqis lost 4,000 tanks, compared with the coalition's four.

Aftermath

It was not a cheap war. The cost to the U.S.-led coalition has been estimated between $60 billion and $70 billion. At least three fourths of that was borne by countries other than the United States, primarily Kuwait, Saudi Arabia, other Gulf states, Germany, and Japan.

Kuwait suffered major damage from the Iraqi occupation, not the least of which were the 500 oil wells that Saddam's forces set on fire on their way out and that took months to extinguish.

Iraq's ethnic groups paid a steep price, too, as Saddam struck back hard against uprisings by the Kurds in the north and Shi'ites in the south, many of whom may have thought Saddam was finished.

They were not alone. President Bush and most of the Arab allies also expected that Saddam's days were numbered because of the humiliation and destruction he had brought upon his nation. Many have asked why the U.S. coalition had shut down its war effort and not gone on to Baghdad and directly confronted Saddam Hussein. The answer probably has three parts:

- UN resolutions had not authorized it.
- Coalition members would have split over it.
- The smart money was on Saddam being overthrown, anyway.

Family Focus

Do you agree with the decision not to take the war to Saddam in Baghdad? Discuss how it most likely would have played out if this had been done.

When it became clear that Saddam was entrenching himself at the expense of his enemies, the U.S., British, and French established "no-fly" zones in the north and south of Iraq to protect the Kurds and Shi'ites, primarily from helicopter gunship attacks. Iraq also was saddled with some significant terms in the cease-fire agreement it was forced to sign. Besides making reparations to Kuwait and acknowledging its sovereignty, Iraq was required to destroy its longer-range offensive missiles.

And the United Nations established the UN Special Commission (UNSCOM) to disarm Iraq of any weapons of mass destruction.

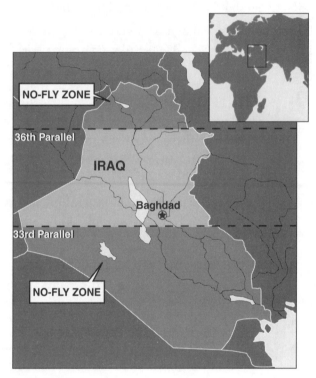

Iraq's "no-fly" zones.

Clearly, his adversaries had underestimated Saddam, and that would come back to haunt them.

The Future

For many people the big fascination with the Middle East is its centrality. It seems this region is always in the thick of things. Human history basically started here, and there are serious reasons to believe it could end here. The fact of Israel's existence means the beginning of the end to many who study biblical prophecy. The subject certainly has made millions in the entertainment industry as a story line for fiction. Still, it's serious business. And it may come as a surprise that there are Jewish and Islamic End Times scenarios, too—complete with their own Antichrists and Messiahs.

Feeling a little bit lost by now? Feeling overwhelmed by too many trees to see the forest? Never fear. Finally, we pull it all together in a kind of focused review called Frequently Asked Questions. You don't have to take all these answers as the last word by any means. At best, they're merely an attempt to make some judgments and form some conclusions—upon which reasonable minds certainly may differ. You don't have to agree. We offer them in the spirit of encouraging you to think and reflect on all these things for yourself. You've learned a lot, you know ….

America in the Crosshairs

In this chapter we look at how America was forced to deal with the reputation it had acquired as an easy mark for militant Islamists. The United States had to demonstrate that it did have the stomach for the fight, even if it did mean taking casualties.

Terror Attacks of the 1990s

By the 1990s, certain elements were laying traps in hopes of ambushing America and even beginning to bring the battle for the first time to America's shores. As well, the United States was clearly on a collision course with Iraq.

The Somalia Trap

The United States and its coalition may have won a resounding victory in the 1991 Persian Gulf War, but there was a hidden cost. America, already despised by Muslim extremists for its support of Israel and other issues, graduated to enemy number one, especially with the demise of the other superpower, the Soviet Union the same year.

IRAQ TIMELINE 1975–1991

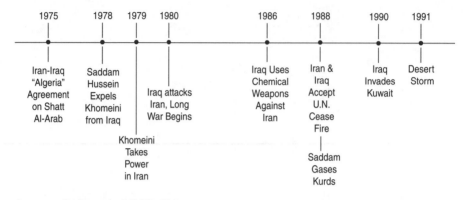

Iraq overshadows the Middle East.

In much of the Muslim world the Gulf War became known as *al-Azma*—"the Crisis"—second only to *al-Naqba*—"the Holocaust"—when Israel was established. Radical Muslims deeply resented seeing the Arab world divided, and the majority siding with Israel's great ally, the United States. It deepened feelings of resentment toward allegedly corrupt regimes like Saudi Arabia and Kuwait, which in their view could only survive by being propped up by the corrupt West.

Extremists recalled how the Americans bailed out of Lebanon after their Beirut barracks were bombed in 1983. Inflict enough casualties, they believed, and the Americans could be forced out elsewhere. Perhaps they could be driven out of Saudi Arabia and the Gulf states, too. Somalia, on the strategic Horn of Africa, became the testing ground for this hypothesis.

There was no more zealous advocate of this theory than Osama bin Laden, who had seen it work in Afghanistan, where the Soviets had been driven out by the Mujaheddin in 1987 after years of resistance. Several years later bin Laden was now in Sudan, which had become a radical Islamic hotbed.

By 1992, thousands were sick and dying of starvation in Somalia while competing warlords used control of food as a weapon to break and defeat each other's people. Responding to the humanitarian crisis, President Bill Clinton committed U.S. troops to head a United Nations effort to ensure food deliveries, save lives, and break the warlords' stranglehold on the people. Little did they know that there were others laying a big trap for the Americans.

The U.S. Paper Tiger

U.S. forces soon discovered that soldiers made poor policemen, as much of the action involved various problems and disputes among factions of the civilian population, and even among individuals, rather than conventional military engagements. This provided more fodder for militant Islamists, and the Iranian government began accusing the United States in numerous reports of attacking civilians.

Meanwhile, it was no coincidence that an anti-American coalition—reportedly of Iraqis, Sudanese, and Iranians—had formed in Sudan with a goal of making Somalia become to America what Afghanistan had been to the Soviets—a graveyard. There were Arab Afghan fighters, primarily from Egypt and Algeria, plus Iranian-backed Lebanese Hezbollah guerrillas and Iraqi fighters. Bin Laden's job reportedly was providing logistical support through his al-Qaeda organization as the forces mobilized in Somalia in support of warlord factions—principally General Muhammad Farrah Aidid—against the Americans.

The fact that Sunnis and Shi'ites were now working together was a significant development. It was probably a measure both of how broadly Khomeini's brand of militancy had influenced global Islam and the degree of hatred they shared toward their common enemy, the Great Satan. By 1993, the lingering humiliation of the Gulf War was still fairly fresh. This cooperation is also significant to remember when skeptics discount any idea of a connection between al-Qaeda terrorists and Saddam Hussein's Iraq because of religious differences.

Finally in September, the Somalis managed a spectacular ambush of U.S. Blackhawk helicopters over Mogadishu. The televised spectacle of dead U.S. servicemen being dragged through the streets of the capital by a howling mob shocked Americans and satisfied the extremists' goals of unacceptable casualties. Several months later, the Americans again were gone.

Bin Laden had been proved right. "This convinced us that the Americans are a paper tiger," he said later.

World Trade Center I

The conflict was brought to American soil in the first World Trade Center bombing in February 1993. Six were killed and hundreds injured in the blast from an explosives-laden truck parked in the underground parking garage. Two notables who were arrested and convicted were Sheikh Omar Abdul Rahman and Ramzi Yousef, whom some law enforcement and terrorism experts called one of the most dangerous men on earth. Yousef is now serving a 240-year term at the Supermax maximum-security federal penitentiary in southern Colorado.

Investigators also implicated Yousef, a Kuwaiti and a virtuoso bomb maker, in unsuccessful plots to assassinate President Clinton and Pope John Paul II in 1994 in the Philippines. There have even been allegations of a Yousef connection in the April 1995 bombing of the federal building in Oklahoma City, but nothing proven. Nor has a direct link been made between Yousef and bin Laden beyond some strong circumstantial evidence, including the fact that Yousef trained in Afghanistan during bin Laden's tenure there.

 Word from the Wise

Ramzi Yousef is a caged lion who can no longer destroy. The apostle Peter wrote of one who is to be feared far more. "Be careful! Watch out for attacks from the Devil, your great enemy. He prowls around like a roaring lion, looking for some victim to devour. Take a firm stand against him, and be strong in your faith." (1 Peter 5:8–9, NLT)

Khobar Towers Bombing

Equally mysterious were the circumstances behind the June 1996 truck-bombing of the Khobar Towers military housing complex in Dharan, Saudi Arabia, which killed dozens, including 19 U.S. Air Force personnel, and blinded, maimed, and injured hundreds. It had all the markings of a very professional operation. A tanker truck had been loaded with 5,000 pounds of military-class high explosives with a sophisticated directional charge that could have been devised only by explosives experts.

Someone obviously was out to sting both the Americans and the Saudis, but it appeared that that someone might actually be inside the Saudi royal family. Allegations centered on Prince Abdallah, who was in the midst of a power struggle within the house of Saud as to who would succeed the ailing King Fahd. Abdallah was said to be conspiring to create an incident to embarrass his rivals, who were responsible for domestic internal security.

Supposedly, Syrians were recruited to stage a small terrorist incident, but when the Syrians got Iranians involved, things got out of hand. What was supposed to be a small embarrassment turned into a very large and horrible disaster.

Embassy Bombings

Bin Laden's al-Qaeda was clearly implicated in the August 7, 1998, U.S. embassy bombings in Dar-es-Salaam, Tanzania, and Nairobi, Kenya, killing 224 persons, including 12 Americans. More than 5,000 were injured, mostly Africans. A U.S. federal grand jury has indicted 13 individuals, including bin Laden, in the incident.

Reality Check

Sheikh Omar Abdul Rahman, a blind Muslim cleric, also was convicted for his involvement in the East Africa embassy attacks. He'd already been indicted in the World Trade Center bombing and was accused of plotting bombings of the Lincoln and Holland tunnels and the United Nations building as well as assassinations of prominent Americans.

On August 27, 1998, President Clinton announced a military response called Operation Infinite Reach. Five U.S. warships in the Arabian Sea and two in the Red Sea began launching dozens of Tomahawk cruise missiles at suspected enemy targets. Eighty missiles altogether pounded a pharmaceutical plant in Sudan and a terrorist camp associated with bin Laden in Afghanistan. The Sudan factory was suspected of manufacturing the deadly nerve agent VX.

The administration also believed that bin Laden had been behind Ramzi Yousef's attack on the World Trade Center. Then in 2000 al-Qaeda was implicated again in the bombing of the USS *Cole* in port in Yemen, which killed 17 sailors.

Clinton called bin Laden "perhaps the pre-eminent organizer and financier of international terrorism in the world today."

September 11, 2001: The Day Everything Changed

So it didn't take too long to guess who might be the most likely culprit when Americans awoke on September 11, 2001 to find their country under attack. In the coming days and weeks any question was erased that the attacks had been anything but the work of Osama bin Laden and al-Qaeda.

Summary of the attack:

- An American Airlines Boeing 767 and a United Airlines Boeing 767 en route from Boston to Los Angeles were hijacked—with full fuel loads for maximum devastation—by men armed with box cutters to take out crew members.

- These two airliners were flown just minutes apart into the north and south towers of the World Trade Center in Manhattan.

- Shortly afterward, an American Airlines Boeing 757, en route from Washington, D.C., to Los Angeles, crashed into the Pentagon.

- A fourth hijacked plane, United Flight 93 headed from Newark to San Francisco, crashed in a field near Shanksville, Pennsylvania.

- Both World Trade Center towers collapsed, and a section of the Pentagon was destroyed.

- All 266 persons aboard the planes were killed. The total number of dead and missing was 3,038.

Some brave Americans aboard Flight 93, having heard about the other three incidents via cell phone conversations in the midst of their own hijacking, took matters into their own hands. They apparently rushed the cockpit, knowing death was imminent anyway, and battled the hijackers unarmed. Details are unknown, except that this plane otherwise would have proceeded to Washington, as it was headed, and been used against yet another target, possibly the White House or Capitol building.

To say the attack was shocking would be an understatement. Americans had not experienced anything so devastating since Pearl Harbor, and many thought it was worse. Experts considered it the ultimate in *asymmetrical warfare*—that is, the attempt by a subnational or terrorist group to even the score with a superior force by use of unconventional means.

Several years prior, bin Laden had made a big show of declaring war on America. At that time, he was not taken all that seriously. Now everything had changed. Now President George W. Bush was declaring war on terrorism—and on bin Laden and al-Qaeda. The United States would go after them, and Bush said, "We will make no distinction between the terrorists who committed these acts and those who harbor them."

> **def·i·ni·tion** **MidEast Dictionary**
>
> **Asymmetrical warfare** is a form of conflict undertaken when the sides are so mismatched that the weaker side would have no chance of prevailing in a direct (conventional) military confrontation; instead, the weaker side seeks to achieve a political objective by imposing costs—pain, death, and terror—on the stronger side's civilian population, thus weakening the stronger side's political will.

Operation Enduring Freedom

Specifically, those who had been harboring them were Mullah Muhammad Omar and his beyond-extreme Islamic Taliban government of Afghanistan. And it seemed the Taliban were not about to turn over their al-Qaeda guests, least of all to the United States. So the United States went in after them.

Operation Enduring Freedom began on October 7, 2001, four weeks after the September 11 attacks. As in Desert Storm, there were weeks of devastating aerial bombardments on al-Qaeda and Taliban strongholds before ground forces began to move in. Air Force and Navy bombers flew 200 sorties a day from Diego Garcia in the Indian Ocean and from carriers in the Arabian Sea.

This was different, however, from Desert Storm, when 3,000 sorties a day were flown to hit a similar number of targets. Army General Tommy Franks, head of U.S. Central Command, said about 10 aircraft had been needed in Desert Storm to take out one target, while in Operation Enduring Freedom a single aircraft could take out two targets on average.

Reality Check

The long arm of political correctness reached even into this first engagement in the war on terror. Originally called Operation Infinite Justice, the name was changed out of concern that it might be offensive to Muslims, who consider only Allah to be infinitely just. One thing that was not changed, however, was the war itself, despite complaints from some about prosecuting a war during Ramadan.

The difference was the leap in technology and munitions in 10 years that allowed a much heavier use of precision-guided "smart" bombs. The United States also used more specific types of bombs such as "daisy cutters," to explode just above ground and level everything in their path, and "bunker busters" to burrow deeply into this cave-filled region and destroy underground fortifications. They were all designed to make an enemy cry "uncle," and they were most effective.

New Day in Afghanistan

Eventually, the theater was ready for ground forces to move in and begin taking the cities from Taliban control. It involved a coalition of forces from:

- Australia
- Canada
- Denmark
- France
- Germany
- Norway

It was led by the United States and worked closely with the coalition of anti-Taliban Afghan militias called the Northern Alliance.

Soon city after city began to fall. Hamid Karzai was sworn in as prime minister of the Afghan interim government on December 22, 2001, just days before the fall of the capital, Kabul. Major engagements were fought in the end in eastern Afghanistan, notably Operation Anaconda and an assault on mountain enclaves in Tora Bora, where bin Laden was thought to be holed up. He was never found. Some thought he had been killed, but later intelligence indicated he probably slipped away, perhaps into the rugged border area with Pakistan.

In all, only 10 Americans were killed in the fighting, a remarkable feat. Al-Qaeda suffered heavy losses. Scores of Taliban and al-Qaeda "detainees" were spirited away to a makeshift prison facility called Camp X-Ray at the U.S. naval base at Guantanamo, Cuba. There they would be questioned for whatever intelligence information they could provide.

> **Word from the Wise**
>
> Jesus promises a true freedom that no army, president, or political system can provide. "And you will know the truth, and the truth will make you free .... So if the Son sets you free, you will indeed be free." (John 8:32, 36, NLT) It is freedom from sin and death in order to spend eternity with Him.

Vulnerability at Home

Back home there was a growing realization that the American way of life—including the belief that transoceanic distances insulated the United States from outside threats—had changed fundamentally. There was also recognition that much work needed to be done.

While the war was being prosecuted in Afghanistan, a domestic terrorist was delivering little packages of anthrax powder to numerous offices around the country, especially targeting U.S. Senators, Congressmen, and news media workers. These crimes were never solved despite massive investigations. There were indications of a woeful lack of coordination and even communication among U.S. intelligence and law enforcement agencies that made America particularly vulnerable to attack.

President Bush declared a U.S. war on terrorism—and put other nations on notice that they must choose which side of that war they were on. He announced creation of an Office of Homeland Security to coordinate all federal counter-terrorism efforts and intelligence gathering. He and Attorney General John Ashcroft announced aggressive steps to shut down and prosecute radical Islamic financial networks operating in the United States under the guise of charitable organizations.

Family Focus

Over the decades America's openness and tolerance had allowed it to become one of the best places in the world for anti-American militants to produce inflammatory films and videos, raise thousands of dollars, distribute their propaganda, and continue to build global networks of hate and violence. Some argue that this kind of hate literature is the equivalent of shouting "fire!" in a crowded theater. Its defenders say it's protected religious expression. How would you approach the problem of balancing our civil liberties with our security needs?

The chilling fact was that investigators needed to look no farther than their own backyard to find major evidence of terrorist-financing networks.

Literature preaching hatred—and even advocating the killing of Jews and Christians—was being freely produced under the cover of First Amendment protections. There was even evidence of sites in the United States being used for military training, firearms practice, construction of explosive devices, and assembling of arsenals by Muslim extremists. Lax immigration policies regarding dangerous individuals prompted some to claim that it was easier to come to the United States as a terrorist than as a refugee.

All of these issues needed to be addressed regardless of opposition from civil libertarians concerned about the prospect of repressive measures being established in the name of domestic security. President Bush and others were compelled to warn against the very real possibility of inappropriate overreactions against Muslims by misguided individuals.

Bush Doctrine

A set of post-September 11th policies began to take shape that became known as the Bush Doctrine. It included two already announced policies plus one new one:

- Those who harbor terrorists will be treated no differently from terrorists themselves.

- States must choose which side they are on in the war against terror.

- The United States would no longer wait for threats to materialize into actual strikes but would preemptively strike first.

Under this doctrine there would now be zero tolerance for situations that once might have been overlooked until the threats became tangible. By then, the administration believed, it would be too late. Thousands could be dead.

The best case in point was Saddam Hussein, who'd kept on ticking despite his licking in Desert Storm. Worse, Saddam essentially had sent UN weapons inspectors packing in 1998 after years of obfuscation and bare toleration. The response from the United States and Great Britain at the time had been a four-day missile attack on strategic Iraqi sites called Operation Desert Fox. But now Saddam was free of the onerous inspections for banned weapons of mass destruction—for a time. The lesson seemed to be that if you stalled long enough, you could wear down the paper tiger.

Word from the Wise

Scripture speaks of a security that is not found through laws or force of arms. It is in the Lord Himself." Happy are those who fear the LORD .... They do not fear bad news; they confidently trust the LORD to care for them. They are confident and fearless and can face their foes triumphantly." (Psalm 112: 1, 7–8, NLT)

However, after the attack on America, Saddam Hussein found his free pass had expired with a new U.S. administration with a new attitude. President Bush decided to reopen the Iraq case, to the consternation of some who believed efforts would be better spent continuing to pursue bin Laden and the terrorists. The administration's response was that it was doing that, too, but there was at the same time a clear and present danger from Iraq, which could be a dangerous source of weapons of mass destruction in the hands of terrorists.

"He will be stopped," Bush said of Saddam.

My Dog Ate My Weapons Report

Upon their withdrawal in 1998, inspectors from UNSCOM (United Nations Special Commission) charged Iraq had not properly accounted for at least 4,000 tons of ingredients used to make chemical weapons. Under United Nations Resolution 1441, Iraq was required to provide full and accurate disclosure of its weaponry and to cooperate immediately, unconditionally, and actively with weapons inspectors. Nevertheless, when weapons inspections resumed in 2002 under threat of war from the Bush administration, the results were frustrating.

Reality Check

UNSCOM was replaced under this new round of inspections by UNMOVIC—the UN Monitoring, Verification, and Inspection Commission. And with increasing concerns about a possible Iraq nuclear weapons program, it was also subjected to inspections by the IAEA—the International Atomic Energy Agency.

Secretary of State Colin Powell charged that Iraq's reports were incomplete and inaccurate, providing no accountability for the disposition of its banned weapons. Specifically, weapons inspectors found that Iraq had failed to account for its production of the deadly nerve agent VX, plus 6,500 chemical bombs, and about 1,000 metric tons of chemical agent. Iraq also had acquired the materials to produce much more anthrax than it declared, among other deadly biological agents, including botulin toxin.

Iraq had been pursuing a policy dubbed by the U.S. administration as "cheat and retreat"—that is, telling a new lie to replace the old lie when confronted with hard evidence. This time the paper tiger was showing some teeth.

The day after the first anniversary of the September 11 attacks on America, President Bush addressed the UN General Assembly with harsh words for Iraq and challenging words for the international body to stand up to the Iraqi threat or risk becoming irrelevant. He accused the Iraqi regime of systematic abuses against its own people, including "arbitrary arrest and imprisonment, summary execution and torture by beating and burning, electric shock, starvation, mutilation, and rape."

"He blames the suffering of Iraq's people on the United Nations," Bush said, "even as he uses his oil wealth to build lavish palaces for himself and to buy arms for his country." He might have added, paying millions of dollars to the families of Palestinian suicide bombers.

The Road Ahead

Still, the international community was not entirely convinced—or, possibly, unwilling to admit it lacked the nerve to start another fire that might get out of hand. France, Germany, and Russia in particular threatened to block action on any new UN resolution authorizing use of force against Iraq.

The fear was that things would go badly. There could be major terrorist attacks. Muslim nations might be provoked to even greater extremism. The region could be destabilized. Saddam might employ the "Samson" strategy—that is, setting his oil fields on fire (as he had in Kuwait) and destroying his own country in the face of defeat. Then again, some of these "allies" may have been more worried about their own private relationships with Saddam and the money he owed them.

Yet, the hawks could make a strong argument in the opposite direction. Disarming or bringing down Saddam Hussein could eliminate a major source of weapons of mass destruction and have a chilling effect on state-sponsored terrorism. The Iraqi people would be liberated, and a vibrant, rebuilt state of Iraq could be a force for democratic, free-market reform throughout the region. The oil cartel would be weakened, and the price of oil would be reduced considerably. Repressive regimes would have a much harder time defending their own corrupt agendas by simply attacking the West.

Family Focus

To which of these views of the dangers and prospects of another war—or the larger war against terror—do you subscribe? Why? Discuss. And is your family prepared for the worst? Visit on the web www. whitehouse.gov and go to the Homeland Security area—"Are You Ready?"— that gives advice on wise precautions for Americans during national emergencies and terrorism attacks.

In the end, President Bush, failing to win United Nations endorsement, unilaterally launched a major military attack on the Saddam Hussein regime in March 2003 called Operation Iraqi Freedom. The United States and its coalition partners, notably the United Kingdom, declared that their mission was not conquering but "liberating" Iraq. Only time would tell whether the ultimate outcome—including unanticipated problems and unintended consequences—would be closer to those best-case or worst-case scenarios. Probably, the truth would fall somewhere in the middle.

Chapter 22

The Middle East in Prophecy

The Middle East is widely known as the cradle of civilization. Many fear it could also become civilization's grave. This chapter explores the central role of this region in all the prophetic belief systems of Jews, Christians, and Muslims.

End Times Fever

Shortly after the September 11 attack on America, there was a noticeable increase in interest in spirituality and prophecy. This included revived interest in the sixteenth-century French astrologer, Nostradamus, and other far-out topics. Books on biblical prophecy, already a healthy segment of the prosperous Christian publishing industry, gained even further steam.

The dawn of a new millennium in 2000 had at least temporarily added to the ranks of doomsayers, and then came this new wave of religious terrorism. Events in America and the Middle East seemed headed for ever-larger disasters. People were both frightened and curious: Could we be living in the End Times? Was Judgment Day or *Armageddon* just around the corner?

MidEast Dictionary

Armageddon literally means "mount of Megiddo"; a strategic valley in Israel where the armies of the world will be gathered for the central battle at the end of the Tribulation resulting in the final overthrow of evil.
Eschatology literally means the "study of last things"; the branch of theology dealing with such things as death, immortality, resurrection, judgment, and the end of the world.

In the 1970s, the mother of all best-sellers was *The Late Great Planet Earth* by Hal Lindsey. Then, by 2001, the runaway best sellers were the *Left Behind* series by Jerry Jenkins and Tim LaHaye. It had to be more than coincidence that these two publishing phenomena were actually fictional and non-fictional flip sides of the same exact story, the meaning of the End Times—or *eschatology*. People are naturally and innately curious about what the future may hold.

Skeptics then and now have tended to counter that such apocalyptic scenarios have been around for centuries and are just nonsense. At the end of the first millennium in 999 A.D., hundreds of people took to the mountains in full expectation that the end was at hand. During World War II there were people who thought Hitler was the Antichrist.

Yet, there was now one significant new factor that made all the difference: Israel.

Signs of the End Times

Always until May 14, 1948, there had been a major piece missing from any End Times scenario. That was the day Israel was reborn as a nation. According to prophetic passages in the New Testament, the end could not come until certain events took place in Israel, including the special event called the *Abomination of Desolation*. There are various views on this subject among different sects of Protestants and Catholics. Some interpret these events as things that have already occurred in the past. Many others, especially evangelicals, however, believe that these are things yet to be fulfilled, perhaps in this very generation.

MidEast Dictionary

Abomination of Desolation is also known as the desolating sacrilege; the act of setting up an idol for worship in the Holy Place of the Temple, thereby defiling it and ending the holy sacrifices.

Some have argued that this prophecy was already fulfilled by one of the Seleucid (Syrian) rulers who set up an image of Zeus and sacrificed a pig in the Temple in Jerusalem *before* the time of Christ. Others argue that this was a direct description of the Antichrist *after* the coming of Christ. They base their argument on passages in the Old Testament book of Daniel and on the words of Christ himself: "And the Good News about the Kingdom will be preached throughout the whole world, so that all nations will hear it; and then, finally, the end will come. The time will come when you will see what Daniel the prophet spoke about: the sacrilegious object that causes desecration standing in the Holy Place ...." (Matthew 24:14–15, NLT)

Word from the Wise

Though there will be much suffering before the end comes, John the apostle had a vision of what was to come after the old heaven and earth had passed away. "And I saw the holy city, the new Jerusalem, coming down from God out of heaven like a beautiful bride prepared for her husband .... It was filled with the glory of God and sparkled like a precious gem, crystal clear like jasper." (Rev. 21:2, 11, NLT)

Family Focus

How do you feel about Israel? Do you see it as an accident of history that's been causing a lot of trouble? Do you wish it would just go away? Or do you see God's hand in these events? How does this affect your view of God's involvement in the world yet today? Discuss.

This entire chapter of Matthew consists of Jesus' detailed answer to the disciples' direct question about what signs would mark his coming again and the end of the world. Jesus responds with a list of signs—wars, famines, earthquakes, persecution of believers. Then he speaks of the Gospel being preached around the world and the Abomination of Desolation as the immediate prelude to "a time of greater horror than anything the world has ever seen or will ever see again." (Matthew 24:21, NLT)

This so-called Great Tribulation, as it is described in the book of Revelation, sounds almost like a modern nightmare involving weapons of mass destruction. But note that the trigger event, the act of desecration, occurs in the Temple—in Jerusalem. And Jesus in the same passage had just told the disciples that the Temple was about to be "so completely demolished that not one stone will be left on top of another!" (Matthew 24:2, NLT)

Obviously, someone was going to have to rebuild that Temple that the Romans would destroy in order for these events to occur. But first, the Jews would have to get their country—and Jerusalem—back ....

Israel: Blessing and Curses

During Moses' time God had promised great blessings to Israel and rewards for obedience to his commands—fruitfulness of the land, peace, prosperity, freedom, protection from its enemies. But the LORD also gave dire warnings of punishment and curses for disobedience—disease, drought, famine, defeat by their enemies, expulsion from the land, being scattered among the nations.

These blessings and curses can be found in Leviticus 26 and Deuteronomy 28. God also promised a time when he would re-gather Israel from the nations where they had been scattered.

In fact, most of these things have happened. Israel enjoyed a great kingdom under David and his descendants, the people fell into idolatry and disobedience, they were defeated by their enemies and scattered throughout the world—and now they have been re-gathered and restored in this generation.

Enemies of Israel

Israel continues to be surrounded by enemies. Scripture also indicates dire consequences for Israel's enemies. God identifies them by name in a remarkable passage: "They devise crafty schemes against your people, laying plans against your precious ones. 'Come,' they say, 'let us wipe out Israel as a nation. We will destroy the very memory of its existence.' This was their unanimous decision. They signed a treaty as allies against you—these Edomites and Ishmaelites, Moabites and Hagrites, Gebalites, Ammonites, and Amalekites, and people from Philistia and Tyre. Assyria has joined them, too, and is allied with the descendants of Lot." (Psalm 83:3–8, NLT)

These are Arab peoples associated with specific places in the land of Israel and its immediate neighbors—Jordan, Syria, and Lebanon. Today they would be called Palestinians. It shows how ancient are the hatreds. The Edomites, for example, descendants of Jacob's brother Esau, provoked God's anger by refusing to allow the Israelites to pass through their land (southeast of the Dead Sea in modern Jordan) on their way to Canaan.

More than 3,000 years later, re-gathered Israel encountered the same sort of hostilities from descendants of these same peoples and was compelled to fight a war for independence—not from a colonial power, but from its neighbors. The ancient hatreds continue to this day in the ongoing hostilities of terrorism and Intifada.

A Word from the Prophet

The prophet Ezekiel foresaw a future time when the ruined cities of Israel would be re-inhabited by the Jews and the desolate land would become fruitful again. He also declared God's wrath against the Edomites and others for their violence against Israel, promising great punishment: "Your continual hatred for the people of Israel led you to butcher them when they were helpless, when I had already punished them for all their sins .... For you said, 'The lands of Israel and Judah will be ours.

We will take possession of them ....' I will punish you for your acts of anger, envy, and hatred .... My jealous anger is on fire against these nations, especially Edom, because they have shown utter contempt for me by gleefully taking my land for themselves as plunder." (Ezekiel 35:5, 10–11, 36:5, NLT)

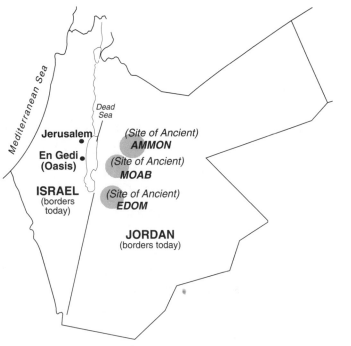

Israel's cousins—Ammon, Moab, Edom.

In turn, the prophet warned, these people would be dealt with in the same fashion. God promised them "a bloodbath of your own." (Ezekiel 35:6) This may refer to a slaughter that is yet to come or possibly even to the recent bloodshed in ongoing Arab-Israeli hostilities. Upwards of 2,000 Palestinians have been killed in the al-Aqsa Intifada alone.

Word from the Wise

In the end, all of the saints will declare the justice of all God's judgments. He is both just and merciful and perfect in all His ways. "Great and marvelous are your actions, Lord God Almighty. Just and true are your ways, O King of the nations. Who will not fear, O Lord, and glorify your name?" (Revelation 15:3, NLT)

The Temple

Some of the Jews today are well aware of their covenant promises to the land of Israel through Scripture from the time of Abraham. Israel today is a secular state. Until recently, at least, only a minority of ultra-Orthodox even thought in terms of reclaiming Jerusalem's Temple Mount and rebuilding the Temple. Obviously, this would be in direct conflict with the Muslims, who have two mosques on the site and are trying to claim the entire structure exclusively.

Things, however, are changing. Once the Israelis saw the Temple Mount nearly negotiated away during the Camp David follow-up to the Oslo peace accords, positions hardened. In the face of this threat and the Intifada, the Jewish peace movement faltered and faded, and voters twice elected a prime minister, Ariel Sharon, who has made the Temple Mount a non-negotiable item.

It is hard to see how the Temple could be rebuilt without a total outbreak of Arab-Israeli war. Yet the prophet Isaiah left no doubt that it would happen, if you accept the view that modern Israel is part of an ongoing fulfillment of prophecy: "In the last days, the Temple of the LORD in Jerusalem will become the most important place on earth. People from all over the world will go there to worship. Many nations will come and say, 'Come, let us go up to the mountain of the LORD, to the Temple of the God of Israel. There he will teach us his ways, so that we may obey him.' For in those days the LORD's teaching and his word will go out from Jerusalem." (Isaiah 2:2–3, NLT)

> **Family Focus**
>
> Considering that the Muslims have closed the Temple Mount to non-Muslims, how do you suppose the Jewish Temple could ever be rebuilt? What would become of the Dome of the Rock and the al-Aqsa Mosque that now stand in the way? How do you suppose this issue might figure into the final conflict of the End Times?

Jewish Eschatology

The Old Testament prophets also spoke of that terrible time of the end with the great horrors to which Jesus referred. They often referred to it as the Day of the LORD or "the time of Jacob's trouble." The prophet Zechariah said the nations would be gathered against Jerusalem and would attack the Holy City, causing half of its inhabitants to flee.

Then the LORD himself would descend onto the Mount of Olives just east of the city and strike the attackers with a devastating plague. "And the Lord will be king over all the earth. On that day there will be one Lord—his name alone will be worshiped." (Zechariah 14:9, NLT)

Ezekiel prophesied of a great attack against Israel in the last days by a mysterious people called Gog and Magog. Some speculate these are people from the north, possibly Russian; others believe it just means various nations from far off. In any case, God deals them a crushing defeat.

Daniel prophesied that the archangel Michael, the special protector of Israel, would defend the nation from catastrophe. "Then there will be a time of anguish greater than any since nations first came into existence." (Daniel 12:1, NLT)

Other major portions of Jewish eschatology are found in the extra-biblical writings called the *Talmud*. Here are found various signs foreshadowing the coming of the Messiah.

These signs include the re-gathering of Israel, soaring inflation, and a decline in truth, wisdom, faith, scholarship, piety, and respect for elders. The Messiah—a non-divine human being—will rule over the nations of the earth as God's appointee. He will be called *Mashiach ben David*—Messiah son of David—a descendant of King David who will rebuild the Temple and restore Jewish religious observance to the re-gathered nation.

Reality Check

How can there be an Antichrist, if the Jews don't believe in Christ in the first place? It may sound strange, but "Christ" is just the Greek equivalent of the Hebrew "Messiah" or anointed one. So, Anti-Messiah might sound more accurate, but it's actually all the same thing.

There is even an "Antichrist" figure, Armilus, who will oppose the Messiah at the time of the end. This Armilus will arise to conquer Jerusalem and battle with Mashiach ben David. There are several versions of this story, including one describing him as an actual son of Satan. Some believe he will be a Roman. In one account he is finally destroyed by Mashiach ben David; in another, God kills him.

Islamic Eschatology

Islam, too, has a vision of the End Times that puts a different spin on things. There is an Islamic false Messiah named *al-Dajjal* and an Islamic version of the Gog and Magog battle as a final war between Muslims and Jews for Jerusalem.

Jesus will return to defeat al-Dajjal and thousands of Jews who become followers of this great deceiver, according to the Hadith. Muslims will defeat Christians in battle, and Allah will destroy all non-Islamic nations. Jesus will eradicate all swine on earth, break all crosses, and establish Islam as the true world religion. Forty years later Jesus will die and be buried beside Muhammad in Medina.

Other Islamic signs of the end include a decrease in religious knowledge and prayer and an increase in immorality, worldliness and materialism, wars, and women becoming prominent in public affairs. The major signs are the emergence of al-Dajjal and battles with Jews and Christians.

Muslims also have an Islamic version of Messiah. Sunnis call him *Muntazar* (the "awaited"). Shi'ites expect *Imam Mahdi*, the twelfth imam, who has been in a suspended state since hiding himself in a cave below a mosque in Samarra, Iraq. This site, now blocked by a gate, is one of the most sacred sites in Shi'a Islam, where the faithful gather to pray for the Mahdi's return.

The Shi'ite Mahdi was born in 868 A.D. and became imam while a small child in 874 A.D. upon the death of his father, Hasan al-Skari, the eleventh imam. He disappeared entirely in 939 A.D. and is believed to exist in a supernatural state while awaiting the time of his return.

> **Word from the Wise**
>
> Christians should be as eager as Andrew to share their knowledge of the true Messiah with others. "Andrew, Simon Peter's brother, was one of these men who had heard what John said and then followed Jesus. The first thing Andrew did was to find his brother, Simon, and tell him, 'We have found the Messiah' (which means the Christ)." (John 1:40–41, NLT)

Other characteristics of the Mahdi:

- Will return on Judgment Day to fight evil, save the world, and usher in equality and justice.
- Has the ability to appear and disappear at will.
- Will do battle with evil forces in one final, apocalyptic battle.
- Will repair the Mosque, reconstruct Mecca, and bring a new Book with new teaching, restoring Islam to its original purity and integrity.
- Will rule the world under a perfect, universal government to guide humanity and bring about a perfect spirituality—including the conversion of Jews to Islam.

Christian Eschatology

There is an old saying in Christendom: "The Old Testament is the New Testament concealed; the New Testament is the Old Testament revealed." The Christian view of the End Times is such a case, building on Old Testament prophecies, such as those concerning the Messiah and the Abomination of Desolation, and filling in the gaps. In some cases the prophetic statements almost don't make sense otherwise.

It would be Jesus' coming again, for example, that Zechariah had in view when he described the Lord descending onto the Mount of Olives outside Jerusalem. Then Zechariah 12:10 (NLT) makes perfect sense: "They will look on *me whom they have pierced* and mourn for him as for an only son. They will grieve bitterly for him as for a firstborn son who has died." (Emphasis added.) Clearly, this "pierced" one is seen as a reference to the crucified Christ.

Word from the Wise

The hymn writer Matthew Bridges captured the eternally sacred nature of Christ's wounds:

Crown Him the Lord of love;
Behold His hands and side,
Those wounds yet visible above
In beauty glorified.

But Christ will not return as the lamb of God but as the Lion of Judah, in power and victory.

The last verses of the Gospel of Luke depict Christ's ascension into heaven from the vicinity of the Mount of Olives. Then the Book of Acts picks up the story again at that point with two angels asking, "Men of Galilee, why are you standing here staring at the sky? Jesus has been taken away from you into heaven. And some day, just as you saw him go, he will return!" (Acts 1:11, NLT)

The order of events is different from the Jewish interpretation. That is, rather than Mashiach ben David coming (the first time) and rebuilding the Temple, the sequence is the rebuilding of the Temple, the coming of the Antichrist who desecrates the Temple, the Great Tribulation, and then the coming of Jesus the Messiah (the second time).

One of the clearest references to the Messiah in the Old Testament, for example, is the prophet Daniel's reference to the "Anointed One" in Daniel 9. In this account the Messiah is "cut off" or killed, "appearing to have accomplished nothing, and a ruler will arise whose armies will destroy the city and the Temple." (Daniel 9:26, NLT) This is quite different from the Talmudic Messiah who comes on the scene much farther down the road, but it is quite consistent with the New Testament Christ.

Signs of the End in Christianity

There are several versions of End Times scenarios, probably the most popular of which is the one portrayed in the *Left Behind* series. Technically, it is called the dispensational, pre-Tribulation, pre-millennial interpretation of prophecy—or the "Beam Me Up, Scotty" brand. That means the church will not go through the *Great Tribulation* because Christ will return first to rescue believers—the "rapture"—and then come again to rule 1,000 years on earth from Jerusalem.

Not everyone agrees with this scenario. Some believe the church will go through the Tribulation. Others believe most of these events are historical and have already occurred, except for the return of Christ *after* 1,000 years of a church age—a view called "postmillennialism." Yet another view holds that there will be no such 1,000 years of universal peace and righteousness, a view called "amillennialism."

From Old Testament prophets and New Testament Gospels and epistles come these signs of the end:

- The re-gathering of Israel
- Nations rising against each other in war
- Famines and earthquakes in many places
- Persecution of believers
- False messiahs proliferating
- Temple worship restored
- The Abomination of Desolation
- The gospel preached to all the nations
- Disturbances in the heavens

def·i·ni·tion MidEast Dictionary

Great Tribulation, in the premillenial version, the seven-year period following the rapture of the church during which the Antichrist will rise and the Temple will be rebuilt; the second half of this period is a time of divine judgment climaxed by the battle of Armageddon and then the millennial kingdom of Christ.

One thing that all three systems have in common is that many of their Signs of the End either have already occurred, are in process, or appear that they could be imminent. That's probably one more reason so-called Jewish, Muslim, and Christian fundamentalism is on the rise at the same time. There's a growing sense that time may be short.

Chapter 23

Frequently Asked Questions

The Bottom Line

Here are some of the most central questions—with answers—for understanding the Middle East conflict. Much of the material here has been discussed in earlier chapters. Now it is time to bring it all together. Numbers in parentheses refer to chapters of this book containing the full explanation of a particular point.

Understanding the Rage

Why do they hate us so much?

This was the question heard so often after the September 11 attack on America—"they" being Muslim extremists. The conventional wisdom was that America's interventionist foreign policies had brought this on and that Americans should work harder to understand the root causes of such extremism. Perhaps if America just minded its own business, pulled its troops out of Saudi Arabia, and abandoned Israel, the violence would stop.

Perhaps. Recent history suggests, however, that such demands are never-ending and the truth is not so simple. America has many vital interests and many friends in the Middle East—Egypt, Jordan, Afghanistan, and most of the Gulf states, especially Kuwait. (Chapters 9–12) The lesson of World War II was that isolationism is not the answer. America, in this view, must be constructively engaged in the world, including the Middle East, in the interest of peace, freedom, and democracy.

Why the hatred is intensifying is no great mystery. The extremists used to despise the Soviets at least as much, but with the disintegration of the Soviet Union in 1991 America was left as the lone superpower—and the prime target of this wrath. (Chapter 21) Even some longtime allies in Europe have distanced themselves from America for this reason, fearing their own irrelevance in America's growing shadow. George W. Bush, in this view, could be as great a danger as Saddam Hussein.

Keen observers have noted that Arab societies that bang the drum most loudly against America and Israel tend to be ones who themselves have the most to hide. Painting someone else as a villain to deflect attention from your own failures is a classic ploy. Culturally, however, the United States is on a slippery slope, and there is a sincere Muslim abhorrence of materialism, carnality, immorality, and other objectionable things from America that appear to be engulfing the world in a multimedia flood.

Clearly, America needs to be healed of its sickness. As Christians here in the United States we should humbly heed this judgment and realize that to some extent we are guilty of these sins just as is the rest of our culture. It should cause us to repent and reach out in loving service to Muslims as fellow creatures made in the image of God.

For Americans there is also the issue of the questionable morality of giving in to terrorist demands. It's a shortsighted strategy that might buy some relief in the short run, but even more grief in the long run. Ironically, history strongly suggests that America has fared far better when it has stood tall and strong against aggression than when it has retreated and appeared to be a paper tiger. (Chapter 21) Nonetheless, we shouldn't adopt an arrogant or superior attitude. We'll continue to alienate other cultures to our way of life if we continue to do this.

Therefore, yes, Americans should work harder to understand the roots of Muslim anger and extremism. And they should also remain strong in the face of intimidation and aggression.

Israel vs. Palestine

Who really owns the land?

By most measures the land does belong to Israel now—by history, by continuous presence, by international law, by war, and by divine providence. Nonetheless, as this has created a huge Palestinian refugee problem, some just solution needs to be found. When the Ottoman Empire was defeated and dismantled at the end of World War I, the land was up for grabs. Under a League of Nations mandate, the British designated it as a national homeland for the Jews. (Chapters 8, 13) To appease the Arabs, the larger Jordanian territory was allowed to separate and become an independent Arab state.

The United Nations recognized Israeli statehood in 1948. Historically, the Jews have been there far longer than anybody else. The Israelites first occupied the land as early as 1400 B.C., about 2,000 years earlier than the Arabs, who arrived in the area in the seventh century A.D. during the Islamic conquests. Only the Canaanites—a Hamitic people unrelated to the Arabs—predated the Israelites. Scripture says God gave the land to Israel in the Abrahamic Covenant (Chapter 2) and commanded the Israelites to conquer Canaan completely and to drive out the inhabitants.

Of course, all of this is a matter of enormous dispute. Muslim scriptures contradict the Jewish claim to the land. Others have tried to refute the biblical argument entirely. That's why some say the dispute is not so much about land as it is about religion.

What is Palestine and who are the Palestinians?

There was never a real country called Palestine. This was the name given by the Romans to eradicate Jewish identity from this province after they expelled the Jews from Jerusalem in 135 A.D. (Chapter 2) It existed for many centuries as a southern region of Syria under the administration of successive conquerors, including the Byzantines, the Islamic Empire, and the Ottomans. (Chapter 13)

The Palestinian people themselves are actually a conglomerate by intermarriage of Arabs and many different peoples from the larger region, as opposed to a true ethnic group. This included Canaanite, Philistine, and Bedouin peoples along with myriad others—Turks, Greeks, Syrians, Egyptians, Sudanese, Druze, and Armenians.

Why can't they solve the Palestinian refugee problem?

This is the right-of-return issue. Israel is a democracy, and accepting hundreds of thousands of Palestinians as citizens would be tantamount to demographic suicide. (Chapter 13) It would put Jews into minority status. The Palestinians, on the other hand, are just as opposed to dropping this demand. Presumably, a Palestinian state could avert the political problem by conferring Palestinian rather than Israeli citizenship on the refugees.

The refugee camps in the West Bank and Gaza Strip provide substandard and unhealthy living conditions for some 400,000 Palestinian refugees. They are also hotbeds of anti-Israel violence and terrorism. But neither do Israel's neighbors— Jordan, Syria, and Lebanon—want to take on more of the burden of this population. At times, it has appeared that the issue has been allowed to fester just to keep Israel under the whip of international disapproval.

The United States and Israel

Why does the United States always support Israel?

It doesn't always. The United States has opposed and rebuked Israel numerous times, notably for its strike on the Iraqi nuclear facility in 1981 (Chapter 9) and more recently for building Jewish settlements in the occupied territories. However, it is true that the United States has been Israel's biggest and longest-standing ally.

The United States shares many values with Israel and supports its right to exist. America sees Israel as the lone democracy in the region, which deserves its support. Both share an abhorrence of terrorism, to which each has fallen victim increasingly over the years. Not that Israel is a perfect democracy or that Christians and Muslims share the same degree of religious freedom as they do in the United States. Overall, however, the many areas of similarity tend to make the two nations natural allies. Politically, U.S. governments have tended to reflect the pro-Israel attitude of great numbers of American Jews and Christians.

Another reason for America's pro-Israel alignment involved the Cold War. America felt the need to lend virtually unconditional support to its friends, particularly Israel, in the face of an Eastern bloc that was arming Arab states and seeking strategic advantage in the region. (Chapter 16) Since the disintegration of the Soviet Union, the United States has become less one-sided in its policies and has even pressured Israel to give up the occupied territories, negotiate with the Arabs, and even allow the creation of a Palestinian state.

Isn't the real problem the Jews?

Not entirely. Without Israel there would still be major problems in the Middle East. The longest modern war between Iran and Iraq (1980–1988) had nothing to do with Israel. (Chapters 1, 20) The longest civil war was between Christians and Muslims in Lebanon (1975–1990). (Chapter 9) The Gulf War in 1991 involved Iraq, Kuwait, and a coalition of nations led by the United States—not involving Israel.

Israel was involved in anti-terrorist military actions in southern Lebanon in the late 1970s and early 1980s, and it has been the target of two internal Palestinian uprisings called Intifadas. Other than that, Israel has been largely at peace since the 1973 Yom Kippur War. The conflicts in the region have mostly involved its Arab neighbors.

Petroleum and Politics

Isn't the whole conflict really over oil?

Oil doesn't have anything to do with Israel's interests, which are mainly survival. The vast wealth produced by oil is what re-energized a demoralized, fragmented Arab world decades ago and reawakened nationalistic aspirations. (Chapter 14) It also made the Gulf region to be of major strategic interest to the West. As for the United States, the Carter Doctrine in 1980 A.D. declared that security of the Persian Gulf was in America's vital interest, and it would defend the Gulf by any means necessary from any would-be invader. (Chapter 16)

It certainly was oil that made the region strategically vital to the United States, but this had nothing to do with the Arab-Israeli conflict per se. The only significant oil Israel possessed was in the Sinai Peninsula, which Israel gave back to Egypt in the peace process. It had more to do with the Cold War, and America's fear that the Soviet bloc might seize the oil weapon to use against the West.

What happened to the Arab "oil weapon" against the West?

This oil weapon—the Arab oil embargo—was used for the first and last time during the 1973 Yom Kippur War, when Israel's back was against the wall and the United States angered the Arab states by resupplying its ally with war materiel. The embargo was quite effective at the time, at least in terms of causing stress and disruption. (Chapter 14) It probably did little, however, to endear the oil-producing states to Americans.

Since then, the oil weapon has lost much of its clout for the simple fact that the Organization of Petroleum Exporting Countries (OPEC) no longer controls the world oil market as tightly as it did then. It didn't take long for fractures to begin to divide OPEC members. Small producers wanted to pump as much oil as they could to maximize profits, while large producers wanted to limit production to keep prices up.

This inherent conflict made consensus on production quotas difficult, let alone enforcing embargoes. Then non-OPEC producers, such as Norway and Russia, began realizing large production volumes, even further diluting the market by producing and selling entirely as they saw fit.

The Peace Process

Why can't they just settle things and make peace?

Israel has made peace with others—notably Egypt and Jordan—and evidences a desire to live in peace. The peace movement among Israelis has been a strong political force for years, at least until recently, when it began to appear fruitless and voters began electing hard-liner politicians again.

The Oslo peace process began a framework for peace that offered much hope. The West Bank and Gaza Strip were moving toward autonomy. (Chapter 16) There were others on the Arab side, however, outside the PLO—notably Hamas and Hezbollah—who did not want to see any agreement or compromise with Israel. They instigated a new cycle of violence that has stalled the entire process.

Also, the Oslo follow-up at Camp David failed to achieve a needed breakthrough, primarily because of two insoluble issues—the Palestinian right of return to their homes and land and control over the Temple Mount in Jerusalem. The Palestinians would not relinquish their right of return, and Israel would not relinquish total control of the Temple Mount. And so, the process remains stalled.

Isn't the dispute really over the occupied territories?

Only on the surface. Israel fought three wars with the Arabs before they even had the territories. (Chapter 18) The Palestinian Liberation Organization was formed in 1964, three years before Israel acquired the territories in war. Israel made peace with Egypt in 1979 and agreed to return the Sinai Peninsula. (Chapter 16) Once the PLO formally renounced terrorism, Israel negotiated turning over rule of the Gaza Strip and the West Bank to the Palestinian Authority.

That process has been interrupted by the Intifada uprising by the Palestinians. Israel and its friends tend to believe the occupied territories have been more of a pretext than a root cause. The real issue, in this view, is Israel's right to exist.

Isn't the solution a separate Palestinian state?

That may happen, but it still wouldn't solve the other two major problems involving the Palestinian right of return and the Temple Mount. Besides, Israel probably has good reason to be wary of Palestinian independence. It may be more of a step in bad faith toward war than toward peace. There have been too many other statements to Arab audiences casting Palestinian statehood as just an interim strategy to weaken Israel further.

The goal of total "liberation of Palestine" has not been forgotten. Many Arabs believe creation of a Palestinian state will encourage thousands of wealthy Jews to leave the country. The Jews then could lose control by becoming a minority in Israel. (Chapter 18) Yasser Arafat himself calls the ultimate goal a "united Palestine under total Arab-Muslim domination." In other words, no more Israel.

Coming to Grips with Islam

Is it true that Islam is a religion of peace?

That's half true. Islam is also a religion of warfare and conquest that was birthed in a warrior culture in seventh-century Arabia. Islam means "submission." It attempted to subject the entire world to Allah, and but for a few strategic battles it nearly succeeded. (Chapters 6, 7)

Islam borrowed much from Judaism and Christianity, which are known for high standards of ethical treatment of other human beings created in God's image. But note that God made some exceptions—such as the command that the Israelites eliminate the Canaanites by putting everything to the sword. This was not considered murder.

There is a parallel in Islam. While Muslims are required to treat their fellow man humanely, things change in the case of jihad. If a people are offered the chance to convert to Islam and refuse, holy war may be declared and casualties may result. The fact that this has been little practiced in recent history (except for incidents in Sudan and Nigeria) has not erased it from the Quran. Osama bin Laden's demand that Americans convert to Islam was no fluke—it was a justification for declaring jihad.

The statement that "Islam is a religion of peace" came from President George W. Bush shortly after the September 11 attack for understandable political reasons. It was part of a message to Muslims and non-Muslims alike. There was a real danger of an anti-Muslim backlash by non-Muslims, and Bush was counseling Americans not to mistake all Muslims for violent extremists. It was also a signal to mainstream Muslims not to let their religion get hijacked by extremists.

Why don't more Muslims condemn terrorism and violence?

Actually, more are beginning to do so. There is evidence that a small majority of Palestinians now no longer support political violence. (Chapter 13) Until recently violence was unquestioningly supported as a legitimate response to Israeli oppression. Speaking out against it would have involved the risk of being labeled disloyal or, worse, a collaborator. Now many are concluding that the costs to the Palestinians themselves of Intifada and other violence outweigh the benefits. On the other hand, virtually no Muslim clerics have spoken out publicly against the September 11 attacks on America.

How do Muslims justify suicide? Isn't suicide against their religion?

This is a huge debate within Islam. Yes, suicide for a Muslim would be a sin, but the terrorists call themselves "martyrs," not suicide bombers. This is highly controversial among more mainstream Muslims, many of whom don't agree with the martyr argument. They say martyrs happen; you don't choose to become one. Martyrdom happens at the hand of your oppressor, not your own hand. There's also a distinction between religious martyrdom and political acts.

This debate illustrates a broader problem in Islam with its relative lack of concrete, objective standards to which everyone agrees. Christians and Jews, of course, have many scriptural disagreements among themselves and with each other. But because Muhammad's revelation was progressive—his teachings evolved—Islamic scholars employ the "law of abrogation" to interpret the Quran. (Chapter 17) This means a certain amount of picking and choosing what to believe. So, Muslims tend not to judge or condemn other Muslims, even extremists.

How about the West's violent history in the Crusades?

Two wrongs can never make a right, and that's the underlying logic here. That is, in this view the September 11 attack, the torture and execution of Robert Dean Stethem (Chapter 19), the killing of Jewish toddlers in an Israeli settlement, and countless other atrocities are no worse than what Christians did in the Crusades. It's a free pass for endless justifications and rationalizations. Nothing, apparently, is too hideous or heinous to excuse.

Never mind that the Crusades were 900 years ago. Never mind the many centuries of Muslim oppression and atrocities in Europe and then the Holy Land that eventually triggered the military response of the Crusades. Never mind the tens of thousands of Christians who were murdered and sold into slavery (a practice that continues today in Sudan). (Chapter 7) The brutality of the Crusades was shameful and inexcusable, and not even these lesser-known crimes against Christians should be used to justify it. And by the same token, neither should the Crusades be used to justify any human barbarism and butchery today.

However, in another sense it would be wrong to draw a complete moral equivalence between the two sets of misdeeds. There is one significant difference: When Muslim extremists mistreat, brutalize, and kill people, they do so with at least the arguable endorsement of their religion. When Christians commit these acts, it has been in utter disobedience to Christ, the Prince of Peace who taught his followers to turn the other cheek.

Unfinished Business

Why wasn't Saddam Hussein eliminated years ago?

Operation Desert Storm in 1991 was so successful in large part because of the support of the international community and the multilateral military coalition formed to liberate Kuwait. Once that was accomplished, the mission was complete. (Chapter 20) Had the United States pressed the attack further, the coalition probably would have unraveled.

Also, United Nations resolutions authorizing the use of force were limited to the liberation of Kuwait. At the time most people thought defeating Iraq there would cause Saddam Hussein to lose power or be overthrown. President Bush said he thought Saddam would be gone in six months. They were wrong.

What's Likely to Happen Next?

One can only guess. There are plenty of best-case and worst-case scenarios from which to choose. One thing that can be safely said, however, is that whatever future course the region takes regarding war and peace and terrorism, the United States is likely to be at the center of the action. After two decades of a more passive policy sometimes called "containment and deterrence," the United States is now engaged proactively in the region to the point of police action, military intervention, and nation building. It already has left its mark indelibly in places like Kuwait, Afghanistan, and now Iraq. For better or worse, the Middle East is slowly being changed.

At one extreme, skeptics warn that such intervention will inevitably reap the whirlwind in terms of greater Muslim and Arab anger and resentment. They had predicted, for example, that invading Iraq (Operation Iraqi Freedom) likely would trigger the use of weapons of mass destruction, major terrorist attacks, torching of the oil fields, soaring oil prices, and long-term hatred of the United States. So far, however, little of that has materialized, but the long-term effects are still unknown.

At the other extreme are those who believe strong American intervention will bring greater stability to the region, if not outright peace and prosperity. Bush administration officials advocate a vision that is sometimes called the "democracy domino theory." In this view, a strong, free, prosperous, and democratic Iraq, for example, will become, in Mr. Bush's own words, "a dramatic and inspiring example of freedom for other nations in the region." Just as a strong and prosperous Hong Kong has inspired massive economic reforms in an envious People's Republic of China, so should other nations in the Middle East desire to emulate a democratic, free-market Iraq. At least, that's the theory. Undemocratic regimes like Saudi Arabia's should be quaking in their boots.

The problem, of course, is that so far it's only a theory. Afghanistan is now a democracy, but it will always be a relatively poor country. Iraq, blessed with great resources including vast oil reserves, should be a much better test. By all rights, it could become a shining city on a hill once its great riches stop being spent on lavish presidential palaces, military adventurism, and suicide bombers. With massive American aid, Germany and Japan rebounded from their defeat in World War II to become mighty economic powers and prosperous societies. Those, however, are much more stable and homogeneous societies. The question is whether the same can be accomplished in a country as unstable and fractious as Iraq.

Meanwhile, the chances for peace in the region may have been enhanced, at least in the short term. The Bush administration speaks hopefully of a so-called "demonstration effect," in which military action in Iraq, in effect, draws a dramatic psychological line in the sand. In this view, what's been demonstrated is that in this new world order there is a high price to be paid for international misbehavior. Then perhaps the next dictator considering making mischief will think again.

When it comes to the Middle East, no one really knows whether the future holds the best-case or the worst-case scenario. Again, the truth is likely to be found somewhere in the middle.

Appendix A

Glossary

Abbasid   Second major Islamic dynasty, ruling in Baghdad until the Mongol invasion, 750-1258 A.D., descendants of Muhammad's uncle, Abbas.

Abomination of Desolation   Also known as the desolating sacrilege; the act of setting up an idol for worship in the Holy Place of the Temple, thereby defiling it and ending the holy sacrifices.

Abrahamic Covenant   God's unconditional six-fold promise of blessing and nationhood to Abraham; the patriarch would be the father of a great nation that would be a blessing to all the nations, and its land would extend from the river of Egypt *(Wadi el-Arish)* to the Euphrates River, according to several passages in Genesis.

Abrogation   Principle of interpretation of the Quran by Islamic scholars to resolve conflicts or contradictions by identifying the more current, operative statements.

Agape   From the Greek—A divine, altruistic love far beyond simple affection or human romance.

Ahmadi   A small but zealous, evangelistic sect whose founder claimed to be a prophet on the order of Muhammad sent to purify Islam.

Alawite   A mostly Syrian offshoot of Shi'a that incorporates jihad and reverencing of Muhammad's cousin Ali as its sixth and seventh pillars of faith, as well as a few Christian and Zoroastrian traditions.

Allah   The god of Islam, a contraction in Arabic from two words *(al-ilah)* literally meaning "the god"; there are 99 names for Allah, but he is considered basically unknowable.

Andalusia   Al-Andalus, Arabic name for the Iberian Peninsula (Spain and Portugal), which the Islamic Empire largely controlled until 1492.

Antichrist   The great antagonist of Christ, expected to spread universal evil before the end of the world but finally to be conquered at Christ's second coming.

Apostasy   A falling away from faith or from God, often from the influence of false teachers.

Arab   Semitic people originating in Arabia now widely scattered throughout surrounding lands.

Arabian Peninsula   Countries of Bahrain, Kuwait, Oman, Qatar, Saudi Arabia, United Arab Emirates, and Yemen.

Arianism   A heretical teaching, named after the Alexandrian theologian Arius (originally from Libya), that held that Jesus was a created being and not of the same substance as God the Father.

Ark of the Covenant   A rectangular box of acacia wood overlaid with gold and carried on poles, containing the two stone tablets inscribed with the Ten Commandments, a pot of manna with which God had fed the Israelites in the desert, and Aaron's rod that had miraculously budded; the ark was ultimately placed in the Holy of Holies in Solomon's temple.

Armageddon   Literally, "mount of Megiddo"; a strategic valley in Israel where the armies of the world will be gathered for the central battle at the end of the Tribulation, resulting in the final overthrow of evil.

Armilus   Counterpart of the Antichrist in Jewish eschatology, who will unsuccessfully oppose the Messiah in the time of the end.

Aryan   Of Indo-European or Indo-Iranian descent, from a root meaning noble or superior; term popularized by the Nazis in the 1930s to mean a Caucasian of non-Jewish or non-Semitic descent.

Ashkenazi   Primarily European Jews influenced by Western culture.

Ashura   An annual Shi'ite religious observance re-enacting the tragedy of Ali, a descendant of Muhammad, who was killed in his quest to become caliph, which started the Shi'a split in Islam; its emotional observance involves much weeping and wailing and even self-flagellation to the point of bloodshed.

Assyria   Ancient empire contemporary with competing kingdoms of Babylon, Egypt, Israel, and Judah; roughly equivalent to modern Iraq and Syria; conquered the northern kingdom of Israel (Samaria) in 722 B.C.

Asymmetrical warfare   A form of conflict undertaken when the sides are so mismatched that the weaker side would have no chance of prevailing in a direct (conventional) military confrontation; instead, the weaker side seeks to achieve a political objective by imposing costs—pain, death, and terror—on the stronger side's civilian population, thus weakening the stronger side's political will.

Ayatollah   Highest-ranking religious leader among Shi'ite Muslims.

Baath Party Literally, "renaissance" in Arabic; an international Arab movement that advocated public ownership of major industries and natural resources and constitutional, representative government with guaranteed civil rights for citizens, such as freedom of speech, at least on paper.

Balfour Declaration British document in 1917 A.D. under League of Nations mandate that declared England's support for the creation of a national homeland for the Jews in Palestine.

Basiji Members of Iranian *Basij* or volunteer corps; generally old men and young boys inducted during the Iran-Iraq war to serve as cannon fodder, enticed by the promise that death in the war would mean automatic acceptance in heaven.

Bedouin An Arab of any of the nomadic desert peoples of Arabia, Syria, or North Africa.

Berber Earliest known inhabitants of North Africa, hamitic peoples with their own separate languages, many living as desert nomads, herdsmen, and traders; related to the term "barbarian" (foreigner).

Black September The devastating September 1970 attack by forces of Jordan's King Hussein against Palestinians that killed at least 4,000 of them and stopped their terrorist activities; also the name taken by a terrorist group that massacred Israeli athletes at the 1972 Munich Olympics.

Burkha All-enveloping head-to-toe veil worn by Afghan women under the Taliban allowing only the eyes to be seen.

Bush Doctrine Anti-terrorist policies of President George W. Bush, which holds nations accountable for harboring terrorists or siding with them and reserves the right to strike preemptively at a terrorist threat before it materializes.

Byzantine The Eastern empire that split with Rome in the fourth century A.D. with its capital at Constantinople until conquered by the Islamic Empire in 1453 A.D.; synonymous today with the Greek Orthodox Church.

Caliph Literally, "successor"; successor to Muhammad as head of Islam, abolished by Ataturk after the end of the Ottoman Empire; *imam* is the equivalent for Shi'ite Muslims.

Canaan Earliest name for the Promised Land, named for one of the main tribal inhabitants, who took their name from Noah's grandson and Ham's son, Canaan.

Carter Doctrine Declaration by U.S. President Jimmy Carter in 1980 that America considered the Persian Gulf to be in its vital interests and would defend it from any invader by military force, if necessary.

Colonialism Political control by one power over a dependent area or people for economic exploitation, natural resources, new markets, or influence; the most active colonialists were countries of Western Europe from 1500 to 1900.

Conservative   The branch of Judaism that strives to preserve many traditional ways in the midst of the modern world, a middle way between Reform and Orthodox.

Coptic   The ancient Christian church of Egypt, which still uses the Coptic language, derived from ancient Egyptian and written with the Greek script; in the fifth century the Roman church condemned the Coptics as heretical because of their belief that Christ had only one nature, not two (monophysite doctrine).

Core   Major division of the Middle East consisting of the Fertile Crescent plus the Arabian peninsula.

Crescent   Central core countries of the Fertile Crescent—Iraq, Syria, Lebanon, Israel, and Jordan.

Crusades   From Latin *crux* for cross; military expeditions European Christians undertook from the eleventh to thirteenth centuries to recover the Holy Land from the Muslims.

Al-Dajjal   In Islamic eschatology, a deceiver who will come in the last days, much like Antichrist, and gather many Jewish followers until he is defeated by Jesus.

Dar al Harb   Literally, "house of war"; territory inhabited by infidels and not yet surrendered to Islam; as opposed to *Dar al Islam*—"house of Islam"—where Islam rules.

Davidic Covenant   God's promise to David that he would make his throne an everlasting kingdom, ultimately fulfilled in Jesus, Son of David.

Dead Sea Scrolls   One of the greatest archaeological finds of all times, a collection of Old Testament books and other writings found in the caves of Qumran; nearly identical with modern texts but 1,000 years older, they helped confirm the reliability of the Old Testament as the word of God.

Deobandi   An ultra-conservative brand of Islam observed by the Taliban of Afghanistan, named after the town in India where it originated.

Desert Shield   The 1990 multinational military buildup in Saudi Arabia opposing Iraq's occupation of Kuwait.

Desert Storm   The 1991 war against Iraq fought by the United States and a coalition of other countries to liberate Kuwait from Iraqi occupation; followed Desert Shield, an operation to protect Saudi Arabia from invasion.

Dhimmi   A non-Muslim living in Muslim territory and subject to special taxation and some restrictions.

Diaspora   The scattering or dispersion of the Jews since the time of the Babylonian captivity and the destruction of Jerusalem.

Druze   A breakaway Islamic sect whose beliefs are secret, primarily in Syria, Lebanon, and Israel; members do not really consider themselves Muslims and many even serve in the Israeli armed forces.

Edom A region south of the Dead Sea inhabited in biblical times by the descendants of Esau, Jacob's brother.

Emir Muslim ruler or prince of an area known as an emirate.

Eschatology Literally, "study of last things"; the branch of theology dealing with such things as death, immortality, resurrection, judgment, and the end of the world.

Ethnocentrism A built-in bias according to one's ethnic group, nation, or culture that colors one's perceptions, often resulting in judgmental attitudes, racial and ethnic stereotypes, and double standards.

Exodus Latin form of a Greek term for "exit" or "departure," for which the second book of the Old Testament is named.

Fatah Literally, "to liberate"; one of the oldest Palestinian terror groups, founded in 1958 by Yasser Arafat, and a cornerstone of the PLO.

Fatwa Islamic religious edict having the force of law for Muslims; the declaration of jihad against a people or a death warrant for an individual, such as the famous Iranian writer Salman Rushdie, would be a fatwa.

Frankincense A costly, fragrant gum resin obtained from Arabian and African trees, among the royal gifts to the Christ child; some see this as evidence that the magi might have come from Arabia rather than Persia or Babylon.

Fundamentalist One who believes in all the fundamentals of religious faith, whether Christian, Jewish, or Muslim. This is based on a literal interpretation of Scripture.

Geopolitics Political relations among nations, especially as they involve claims and disputes pertaining to borders and territories; the Iran and Iraq dispute over the Shatt al-Arab waterway would be geopolitical.

Great Tribulation A seven-year period of great violence and affliction in the last days during which the Antichrist will rule; according to some interpretations, it will be climaxed by the battle of Armageddon and the return of Christ.

Hadith Traditions and oral teachings of Muhammad, revered just behind the Quran.

Hajj Pilgrimage; one of the five pillars of Islam.

Hamas Anti-Israel group favoring creation of an Islamic state, the destruction of Israel, and the use of terrorism, including suicide bombing, as a legitimate tactic.

Hamite Descendant of Noah's son Ham, especially the peoples of North Africa.

Hasidic A subset of Orthodox Judaism with an even stricter legalism and a more mystical view, including fervent anticipation for the imminent coming of a Jewish Messiah.

Hezbollah An Iranian-backed Palestinian terrorist organization headquartered in the Bekaa Valley of southern Lebanon.

Hijra Muhammad's flight to Medina after the Arabs of Mecca initially rejected the teachings of Islam in 622 A.D., which initiates the Muslim calendar; also known as *hegira*.

Holocaust The systematic, genocidal destruction of more than six million Jews by the Nazis before and during World War II. Originally, a religious term for a whole burnt offering. There have been some attempts by anti-Semitic people to deny that the Holocaust actually occurred.

Iblis The devil in Islam, in charge of the demons.

Indo-European People identified by a family of related languages, including European and some Asian groups, as distinct from other groups, such as Afro-Asiatic.

Infidel A non-believer; in Islam it originally applied to polytheists and pagans, not Christians and Jews.

Intifada Literally, shaking off, uprising; specifically, the Palestinian Arab revolt against Israeli rule in Palestinian areas, beginning in 1987 A.D. and resuming in September 2000.

Ishmael Abraham's elder son by Sarah's Egyptian maid, Hagar, and the ancestor of the Arab peoples.

Islam The monotheistic religion whose god is Allah, whose prophet is Muhammad, and whose truth is revealed in the Quran.

Jew Name used for a Hebrew resident of Judea and descendant of Judah, one of the twelve tribes of Jacob.

Jihad Struggle, holy war; any form of struggle, including simple personal disciplines of self-improvement, but always the ultimate end of submission to Allah and usually with the connotation of the use of force.

Jinn In Muslim theology, a race of supernatural beings created 2,000 years before Adam, equal to the angels but turned into demons after they rebelled against Adam; equivalent to the English word *genie*; also related, *genius* originally meant a guardian spirit attached to an individual.

Judaism The oldest of the major monotheistic religions and its people, descended from the first Jew, Abraham.

Judah The southern kingdom after the unified kingdom of Israel split under Solomon's son, Rehoboam; it was conquered in 586 B.C. by Nebuchadezzar of Babylon.

Judea The name given to the land of Judah after it was captured in 63 B.C. by the Roman general Pompey.

Ka'aba A 50-foot cube in Mecca that enshrines a large black stone venerated as holy and believed to have been sent by astral deities; also the object of pilgrimage for every Muslim once in his or her lifetime.

Kach An extremist anti-Arab political party in Israel that was eventually banned.

Kharijites Literally, "seceders"; Islamic extremists who believed only in God's law and the use of violence to advance their political agenda; they assassinated the fourth caliph, Ali, after he accepted human arbitration in a dispute.

Kleptocracy   Rule by thieves; sarcastic term for corrupt regimes in the Middle East.

Knesset   Israeli parliament.

Kosher   Clean or fit to eat according to Jewish dietary laws, originally based on Leviticus 11.

Kurds   The world's largest ethnic group—25 million people—without a country, mostly Muslim; they are scattered across Iran, Iraq, Syria, and Turkey, are ethnically distinct from Arabs, Turks, and Persians, and are believed descended from the ancient Medes.

Last Day   Or Judgment Day in Islam, when every person's good deeds will be weighed against his or her bad deeds to determine who goes to paradise.

Maghreb   Arabic name for North African nations west of Egypt and Libya—Tunisia, Algeria, and Morocco.

Mahdi   An Islamic (Shi'ite) messiah figure predicted to come to earth at Judgment Day to punish the wicked and reward the righteous.

Mamluk   Turkish military dynasty that ruled portions of the Islamic Empire after the Mongol invasion, 1250–1517 A.D., and drove out the last Crusaders.

Manna   Literally, "what is it?"; food miraculously provided for the Israelites in the wilderness, appearing on the ground each morning during their stay in the desert; Jesus called himself "the true bread of heaven." (John 6:32)

Maronite   A Christian sect in communion with the Roman Catholic Church, most prevalent in northern Lebanon and Cyprus.

Matrilineal   Tracing family descent according to the mother's family line.

Mawali   A non-Arab convert to Islam.

Mecca   Birthplace of the prophet Muhammad in Arabia; a major center of commerce on the ancient trade routes, today the holiest place of Islam with the Great Mosque and the Ka'aba; site of the annual pilgrimage called the hajj.

Mesopotamia   Literally, the land "between rivers," meaning the Tigris and Euphrates; the ancient birthplace of civilization; modern Iraq.

Messiah   Literally, "anointed" one; the promised and expected deliverer of the Jews, who will bring an era of peace and justice; equivalent to the Greek Christos, from which the English "Christ" is derived.

Middle East   Countries of the Fertile Crescent, Arabian peninsula, and North Africa.

Monogenesis   The idea that all language families have a singular common origin, something not likely if already widely scattered tribes had gradually evolved their different languages separately.

Monophysites   Literally, "single nature"; Christians in the fourth and fifth centuries, particularly Egyptians and Syrians, who opposed the idea that Christ had both a human and a divine nature; their view was condemned by the Church in 451 A.D. as heretical. This sect is still found in the Middle East.

Monotheism   Belief in one god, as opposed to polytheism, belief in multiple gods; Judaism, Christianity, and Islam are monotheistic religions.

Mosque   Place of communal worship for Muslims.

Mossad   Israeli foreign intelligence service; it has been involved in many successful counter-terrorism operations, as well as assassinations, the invasion of Lebanon, and the Iran-Contra scandal in the United States; perhaps its greatest failure has been its unsuccessful attempts to eliminate Saddam Hussein.

Muezzin   A crier who calls other Muslims to prayer from a mosque roof or minaret.

Mufti   Chief interpreter of Islamic law for a region, a religious leader who issues fatwas, much like a judge.

Muhammad   The founder and prophet of Islam who lived in Medina and Mecca, Arabia, from 570 to 632 A.D.

Mujaheddin   Literally, "holy warriors"; Muslim guerrillas claiming divine authority for their activities, especially anti-Soviet freedom fighters in Afghanistan.

Muntazar   An Islamic (Sunni) messiah figure predicted to come to earth at Judgment Day to punish the wicked and reward the righteous.

Muslim   A follower of Islam, one who has submitted to the will of Allah.

Nebuchadnezzar   The Babylonian king who conquered Judah, destroyed the Temple of Jerusalem in 586 B.C., and took the Jews into captivity to Babylon.

Nominalism   Identification with a faith in name only, as opposed to being a practicing member.

Occupied Territories   Disputed Arab territories within Israel, especially those held by Israel since the 1967 Six Day War—the West Bank, Gaza Strip, Golan Heights. Israel also held the Sinai Peninsula for a few years until a peace treaty with Egypt in 1979 A.D.

OPEC   Organization of Petroleum Exporting Countries, formed in 1960–1961 A.D. to regulate the price of oil by controlling its supply; originally composed of some Gulf states plus Venezuela, it eventually expanded to include other members from Latin America, Africa, and Asia.

Orthodox   The branch of Judaism following more traditional religious practices and rituals, including regular reading of the Torah, observance of Kosher dietary laws and Sabbath restrictions, and separation of men and women in the congregation. Not to be confused with various branches of Eastern Christian churches, originally centered in Constantinople, or modern Istanbul, in Turkey.

Ottomans   Turkish empire that succeeded the Islamic Empire and conquered the Byzantines, capturing Constantinople, 1300–1922 A.D.

Palestine   The name replacing Judea after the Romans crushed a revolt and threw the Jews out of Jerusalem in 135 A.D.; in order to eradicate its Jewish identity, the Romans renamed it "Aelia Capitalina" or "Syria Palestina"—or, simply, Palestine; today a politicized term implying the illegitimacy of the state of Israel.

Palestine Liberation Organization   Formed in 1964 as an umbrella organization for various Palestinian groups, named official representative of Palestinian people in 1974; generally associated with terrorism, the PLO formally disavowed political violence in 1988.

Pan-Arabism   The belief that Arabs everywhere belong to one community; some adherents have literally sought to create a single Arab state, reminiscent of the caliphate that ruled during the old Islamic Empire.

Passover   The incident described in Exodus 12 when all the firstborn males of Egypt died but those of Israel were "passed over" where their doorposts and lintels were smeared with the blood of a lamb.

Patrilineal   Tracing family descent according to the father's family line.

Pax Romana   Roman law and order.

Peripheries   Arab North Africa, including Egypt, Libya, Tunisia, Algeria, Morocco, Sudan.

Persia   Ancient or biblical name for modern Iran.

Petro-Islam   A linking of foreign policy to religion with the goal of achieving Islamic dominance through shrewd financial strategies and economic dominance; a strategy of buying power.

Petroleum   From Latin and Greek *petra* (rock) + *oleum* (oil); an oily, flammable liquid solution of hydrocarbons, yellowish-green to black in color, occurring naturally in the rock strata of certain geological formations; useful for fuel and other purposes when distilled.

Philistines   A sea people who migrated to the Mediterranean coast of Canaan and became major adversaries of the Israelites; Palestine derives its name from this people.

Phoenicia   Ancient or biblical name for modern Lebanon.

Pogrom   Organized persecution and massacre of a minority group, especially applied to Jews in czarist Russia.

Polygamy   Taking multiple wives; restricted by Muhammad to no more than four.

Polytheism   Belief in multiple gods, as opposed to monotheism, belief in one god.

Propaganda   Derived from Roman Catholic committee for Propagation of the Faith or missions; systematic, widespread dissemination of ideas or doctrines to further one's own cause or to damage another, now often involving deception.

Qadisiyah   Site of a battle in 637 A.D. in which the Arabs defeated the Sassanian Persians and drove them from central Iraq; this victory has been emphasized in Saddam Hussein's Iraq because of hatred toward the Iranians.

Al-Qaeda Literally, "the base"; a terrorist organization founded by Osama bin Laden and committed to the destruction of the United States and Israel and the creation of a worldwide caliphate under Islamic law.

Quartet A collaboration of the United States, Russia, the United Nations, and the European Union to try to revive the Middle East peace process.

Quran Literally, "recitation"; collection of revelations in 114 chapters that Muslims believe God delivered to Muhammad through Gabriel, about the size of the Christian New Testament; source of Islamic law, literature, and culture; also known as the Koran.

Ramadan The ninth month of the Islamic calendar, during which Muslims are required to fast during the day, from sun up to sun down.

Reform The branch of Judaism most concerned with adapting traditional religion to modern life, typically with more secular, humanistic, and liberal outlooks and world-views than Conservative or Orthodox. Not to be confused with churches emanating from the Protestant Reformation in Christendom.

Replacement Theology A doctrine holding that the Jews had lost their position with God as his chosen people and all of the covenant promises to Israel had transferred over to the Church.

Resolution 242 A United Nations resolution in 1967 A.D. calling for Israel to return occupied territories and guaranteeing its right to exist within secure borders; an approach called "land for peace."

Saladin Leader of the Muslim armies that liberated Jerusalem from the Crusaders in the twelfth century.

Salat Ritual prayer; one of the five pillars of Islam.

Samaria The northern kingdom after the unified kingdom of Israel split under Solomon's son, Rehoboam; it was conquered by the Assyrians in 722 B.C.

Sassanian Persian ruling family from 227 to 651 A.D.

Sawm Fasting; one of the five pillars of Islam.

Semite A descendant of Noah's son Shem, particularly Jews and Arabs.

Sephardic Primarily African and Asian Jews.

Seven Sisters Seven Western oil companies, mostly American, that for years controlled about 80 percent of Middle East oil production.

Shahadah Confession of the creed; one of the five pillars of Islam; also, martyrdom; a *shahid* is one who sacrifices his life for Allah; most commonly practiced by use of an explosives belt, allowing the shahid to inflict maximum damage with careful timing and proximity to his target.

Sharia Totality of Islamic law, especially as applied to life in an Islamic state or theocracy; Sharia calls for murderers to be beheaded by the sword, thieves to have their right hands cut off, adulterers to be stoned to death, and drunkards to be flogged.

Shatt al-Arab   The confluence of the Tigris and Euphrates rivers before it empties into the Persian Gulf; it separates Iran and Iraq and has been the source of much conflict between the two countries.

Sheikh   Literally, "elder"; Arab tribal leader, ruler, or learned Muslim.

Shi'ite   Breakaway sect of Islam, which believes that the descendants of Ali—Muhammad's cousin and son-in-law—should be the rightful successors to Muhammad; it confers greater authority on spiritual leaders—*imams* and *ayatollahs*—for the interpretation of Islam.

Shuttle diplomacy   Negotiations between hostile countries or groups conducted by a mediator who travels back and forth between the parties involved; made famous by Henry Kissinger, secretary of state under President Richard Nixon.

Sufi   Mystical Muslims who worship through religious music, poetry, and dance (for example, the whirling dervish).

Sultan   Title of ruler in certain Muslim lands, especially in the Seljuk and Ottoman Empires.

Sunni   The majority branch of Islam, which accepts the legitimacy of all the first caliphs after Muhammad and bases all authority on the Quran and the Hadith.

Synagogue   Literally, "assembly"; the local congregation of Jews after the destruction the Temple in Jerusalem and the scattering of the Jews; forerunner of the Christian church.

Taliban   Literally, "students"; the ruling party of Afghanistan, composed of former radical students and teachers in Islamic schools, until they were defeated by U.S. coalition and Northern Alliance forces for harboring Osama bin Laden and al-Qaeda.

Talmud   The collection of writings constituting the Jewish civil and religious law, including the *Mishna* (text) and *Gemara* (commentary).

Temple Mount   The elevated platform atop Mount Moriah in Jerusalem where the Jewish Temple once stood; now the site of the Muslim Dome of the Rock and al-Aqsa Mosque.

Terrorism   Premeditated, politically motivated violence aimed at intimidating and demoralizing civilians by clandestine agents or subnational groups; that is, not an army belonging to an officially recognized state or government.

Theocracy   Literally, "God rule"; government rule by religious clergy.

Torah   The law or the *Pentateuch*, the first five books of the Old Testament containing early Jewish history and God's covenants with them.

Totalitarianism   Rule by a government or state in which one party or group maintains complete control under a dictatorship and bans all others.

Transjordan   Earlier name for the kingdom to the east of the Jordan River, now simply Jordan.

Twelver Shi'as   The majority faction of Shi'ites who believe in the line of twelve imams through Ali and expect the twelfth and last imam (the Madhi) to return someday; Iran's Khomeini asserted that the faithful meanwhile should be led by a supreme religious figure.

Ulama   Experts in Islamic law and theology; in some Sunni countries they are government employees.

Umayyad   The first dynasty of the Islamic Empire in Damascus, 661–750 A.D., from the Quraysh tribe of Arabia.

UNMOVIC   The United Nations Monitoring, Inspection, and Verification Commission formed to replace UNSCOM (UN Special Commission) to inspect Iraq for weapons of mass destruction.

Ur   Ancient Sumerian city on the Euphrates River in what is now southern Iraq; the home of Abraham's ancestors and worshipers of the moon god.

Wahhabism   A puritanical form of Islam that banned music, dancing, and poetry and prohibited the use of silk, gold ornaments, and jewelry; the state religion of Saudi Arabia, but also has followers in Central Asia, Afghanistan, Pakistan, and India.

Waqf   Muslim religious trust, usually an endowment of property and often the name also for the trustees; in Jerusalem, it is the Muslim supreme religious council responsible for the Temple Mount.

Zakat   Giving of alms; one of the five pillars of Islam.

Ziggurat   A high tower in Mesopotamia, usually dedicated to the worship of the moon god.

Zionism   The historic movement to reestablish and support a national Jewish homeland in the land of Israel, named after Mount Zion at Jerusalem.

Zoroastrian   Religion of the Persians before their conversion to Islam; belief in the existence of a universal spirit involved in a cosmic struggle between good and evil.

Appendix B

Bibliography

Al-Masih, Abd. *Islam from a Biblical Perspective*. Light of Life, 1997.

Arabian Peninsula. Time-Life Books, 1985.

Archbold, Norma P. *The Mountains of Israel: The Bible and the West Bank*. Phoebe's Song, Fourth Edition, 1996.

Bennis, Phyllis, and Michel Moushabeck, ed. *Beyond the Storm: A Gulf Crisis Reader*. Olive Branch Press, 1991.

Bondansky, Yossef. *Bin Laden: The Man Who Declared War on America*. Forum/Prima Publishing, 2001.

Brown, Anthony Cave. *Oil, God, and Gold: The Story of Aramco and the Saudi Kings*. Houghton Mifflin, 1999.

Budd, Jack. *Studies on Islam: A Simple Outline of the Islamic Faith*. Stanley L. Hunt, 1978.

Chapman, Colin. *Whose Promised Land?* Lion Publishing, 1983.

———. *The Cross and the Crescent*. Intervarsity Press, 2002.

Emerson, Steven. *American Jihad*. The Free Press, 2002.

Fregosi, Paul. *Jihad in the West: Muslim Conquests from the 7th to the 21st Centuries*. Prometheus Books, 1998.

Goldschmidt Jr., Arthur. *A Concise History of the Middle East*. Westview Press, Sixth Edition, 1999.

Hiro, Dilip. *Dictionary of the Middle East*. St. Martin's Press, 1996.

Mackey, Sandra. *The Reckoning: Iraq and the Legacy of Saddam Hussein*. W.W. Norton & Co., 2002.

———. *The Saudis: Inside the Desert Kingdom*. Houghton Mifflin, 1987.

Miller, Judith. *God Has Ninety-Nine Names*. Simon & Schuster, 1996.

Netanyahu, Benjamin. *A Place Among the Nations*. Bantam Books, 1993.

Peretz, Don. *The Arab-Israel Dispute*. Facts On File, 1996.

Peters, Joan. *From Time Immemorial: The Origins of the Arab-Jewish Conflict over Palestine*. JKAP Publications, 1984.

Pimlott, John. *The Middle East Conflicts*. Bedford Press, 1983.

Price, Randall. *Unholy War*. Harvest House, 2001.

Pryce-Jones, David. *The Closed Circle*. Harper & Row, 1989.

Reeve, Simon. *One Day in September*. Arcade Publishing, 2000.

———. *The New Jackals: Ramzi Yousef, Osama bin Laden and the Future of Terrorism*. Northeastern University Press, 1999.

Reston, James Jr. *Warriors of God: Richard the Lionheart and Saladin in the Third Crusade*. Anchor Books, 2001.

Rossel, Seymour. *Israel: Covenant People, Covenant Land*. Union of American Hebrew Congregations, 1985.

Shanks, Hershel, ed. *Ancient Israel*. Biblical Archaeology Society, 1988.

Stewart, Desmond. *Early Islam*. Time-Life Books, 1967.

Vos, Howard F. *Exploring Church History*. Thomas Nelson, 1994.

Wright, Robin. *Sacred Rage*. Simon & Schuster, 1986.

Yahya, Dr. Adel, ed. *PACE Tour Guide of the West Bank & Gaza Strip: "Palestine" Historical & Archaeological Guide*. Palestinian Association for Cultural Exchange, 1999.

Index

W–X–Y–Z